May you be blessed
as you read these
devotions each day!
Debbie
2 Peter 3:18

DAILY DEVOTIONS

with Debbie Debbie

*"Many waters cannot
quench love, nor can
rivers drown it."*

Debbie Clendenen

Daily Devotions with Debbie Debbie
by Debbie Clendenen

First Print Edition, February 2023
ISBN 9798372743281 (pbk)

Unless otherwise indicated, all Scripture quotations are from the KING JAMES VERSION of the Bible.

I also used scripture quotations from:
English Standard Version
New King James Version
New Living Translation
Living Bible
New Life Version
Amplified Bible

Cover art "Forest Lake" by Chakkree Chantakad, Pixabay
Cover and interior design by Suzanne Fyhrie Parrott

Order additional copies of this book and other resources by Rick Clendenen online at: www.AFruitfulLife.org

Or contact Debbie Clendenen at:

Rick Clendenen Ministries
PO Box 287
Benton, KY 42025
Office: (385) 434-0475

Please provide feedback
Printed in U.S.A.

ACKNOWLEDGMENTS

This was a huge undertaking for me to complete this devotional. I realize that it could not have been accomplished without the help of a lot of people.

First, I want to give all praise to Jesus Christ. Without Him, there would have been nothing to write about. I owe everything to Him, and I love Him with my whole heart! Thank you, Jesus, for giving me the strength, grace, inspiration, and wisdom that was needed to make this project possible. I couldn't make it a single day without You. Thank You for putting this on my heart and for being with me every step of the way.

Secondly, thank you to all of those that reviewed these devotions as I finished them a month at a time. Your encouragement meant the world to me and gave me the incentive I needed to continue writing. I love each of you.

I want to give a big thank you to my special friend, Renee Driskoll, who volunteered to be my content editor. You made each devotion sound so much better. I love you and appreciate all the time you put into this for me.

As always, there is no way to fully express my thanks to Suzanne Fyhrie Parrott. The work you put into the cover and the formatting of this book was invaluable, even in the midst of your own trial. Thank you so much, Suz. You're a jewel!

A special thank you to my family. Even though my husband, Rick, is no longer with us, I know he would have been a support to me as I was writing this devotional. My love for him remains strong, even now, and I thank him for helping me to be who I am today. To my children and their spouses: Richie and Jenny, Renee and Landon. You inspire me more than you know; I love each of you! My three grandchildren, Trey, Kyndal, and Liam are the joy of my life. What a precious gift each of you are to me. No matter what, always keep Jesus first in your lives. That's the only way to survive in this world!

Finally, thank you, my readers, for purchasing this book. I pray that each of these devotions will be an inspiration, encouragement, and help to you as you face life head-on. May you be blessed as you always look to Jesus!

TABLE OF CONTENTS

April

May

June

July

August

September

October

November

December

INTRODUCTION

Jireh, You are Enough

As I thought on writing this devotional, I was not sure that I could do it. But I felt strongly that God was leading me in this direction. As a matter of fact, He had been talking to me about this for quite a while.

I have never felt like I was a writer, but when God calls you to a task, He qualifies you for the job. I was at church when I finally made the decision to accept the assignment that He was giving me. The worship team was singing the song, "Jireh, You are Enough" and I felt God say that He would be enough to help me accomplish this task. I totally trusted that God would give me the thoughts and words to write for each day, and He has done just that.

I have titled this devotional, "Daily Devotions with Debbie Debbie." My grandson, Trey, has called me Debbie Debbie since he's been able to talk. And when my husband, Rick, and I began a millennial class, that is the name that most of them call me as well. My granddaughter, Kyndal, suggested it and so I decided to go with that name.

As you get into this devotional, you will see pages throughout titled NOTES. Use these to record your own personal thoughts about what you have been reading. Also, I have desired for Rick and I to write a daily devotional together. Since we were not able to make that happen, I have included several devotions that were taken from various messages and Facebook posts from my husband, Rick.

It was not my choice to be a widow, but there are things that God has taught me, and continues to do so, during my journey of grief that I have intertwined in this devotional. Since I don't want to constantly dwell on the grief, I've included other areas of life as well. One of the main things I have learned is that in whatever circumstances that you and I face, Jesus is enough to help us through them.

Jireh is one of the Hebrew names of God. When coupled with Jehovah, it means "God will provide." Not only will He provide for our physical needs, but He will also provide comfort, peace, understanding, love, joy, strength... Whatever we need, in whatever situation we find ourselves, Jireh is enough!

Each day brings new challenges that we must face, but it also brings God's mercy because, as we are told in Lamentations 3:22-23, they are new every morning. It is my desire for you to be blessed as you read this each day, and you can truly feel in your heart and be able to say, "Jireh, You are enough."

JANUARY 1

A New Year...
A New Perspective

"But in your hearts honor Christ the Lord as holy, always being prepared to make a defense to anyone who asks you for a reason for the hope that is in you; yet do it with gentleness and respect." ESV

1 Peter 3:15

Do you make New Year's resolutions every year and intend on following through with them? Then, after a few weeks, you realize that those resolutions have gone out the window!

Wikipedia's definition of a New Year's resolution is "a tradition in which a person resolves to continue good practices, change an undesired trait or behavior, accomplish a personal goal, or otherwise improve their life at the start of a new year."

Personally, I don't make them. Because I know that I cannot keep them in my own strength. But therein lies the key..."in my own strength." I am not strong enough in myself to accomplish much, but with God, I can do all things.

So, with that in mind, I don't have a New Year's resolution, but I choose to honor Him in all I do and to live my life so that others may see more of Jesus and less of me. In that is where our success lies.

JANUARY 2

Out of the Ashes

"...to bestow on them a crown of beauty instead of ashes, the oil of joy instead of mourning, and a garment of praise instead of a spirit of despair." NIV

Isaiah 61:3b

My son made a very good statement in his sermon today. He said, "God's story never ends in ashes." It stirred my heart when I heard him make that powerful statement!

We all have our own life story, each one different than the other. We may think that because of circumstances in our lives or of things that we may have done that our story is done. But, God says that it's not over!

The truth of the matter is...your story gets much better when you pick yourself up and choose to follow Jesus. The ashes that you thought had ended your story will only add to it and give you a greater testimony.

Never believe that God's story of you will end in ashes! As in the above scripture, He will give you beauty for ashes, joy instead of mourning, and praise to replace despair. I promise you that it will be a help to others as you share your story.

JANUARY 3

Trusting God

"[5]Trust in the Lord with all your heart and lean not on your own understanding; [6]in all your ways submit to him, and he will make your paths straight." NIV

Proverbs 3:5-6

Today was the birthday of a powerful Christian lady that now resides in her heavenly home. Her name is Jean Barger, and she was my sister-in-law.

Jean was such a very sweet and caring person. Anyone that knew her could see that she was full of Jesus. I love her and miss her greatly.

My husband, Rick, was her baby brother and it was because of her prayers that he moved to Murray, KY and lived with her for a time. It was also because of her and her family that we met. You see, Jean fasted and prayed for Rick for three weeks and God answered her prayer. There's a lot more to that story but there's not room to write it here.

We don't know what's up ahead on this road of life, but we can be confident on this one thing: It's all in His hands and in His great plan. Our part is to trust Him with it all. It's not always easy, especially if you are a person, like me, that wants to know before I go what's on the road ahead. But when we get to the point of trusting Him, it will be a rewarding journey. Allow God to be your roadmap!

JANUARY 4

Call On the Name of Jesus

"And everyone who calls on the name of the Lord will be saved." NIV

Acts 2:21

Did you know that there is nothing you must do to prepare yourself to receive Jesus? You don't have to clean yourself up before coming to Him. You don't have to "give up" this or that before coming to Him—Jesus will take care of that later.

All you have to do is this:

◊ BELIEVE that Jesus came in the flesh, died, and rose again.

◊ REPENT of your sins and admit that you are a sinner.

◊ ACCEPT Jesus as your Lord and Savior.

It's that simple! Just a pure act of faith is all it takes. If you have not invited Jesus into your heart, do it today! It will be the greatest decision you will ever make!

JANUARY 5

Be Faithful

"I have fought a good fight, I have finished my course, I have kept the faith."

2 Timothy 4:7

At the end of his life Paul said, "I have fought a good fight, I have finished my course, I have kept the faith." I wonder how much of that statement I will be able to say at the end of my life.

Have I fought a good fight? How many times have I fought for the wrong team? Things I have said when I should have kept silent. Or even the opposite—the times that I should have said words that God gave me to speak to someone and for whatever reason, I remained quiet.

Can I say that I finished my course when my last days come? I believe that God has a path (course) for us all to walk, designed especially for us in particular.

Will I be able to say that I have kept the faith? This is one area that I am sure I am doing. I trust God with everything in my life. I have kept my faith in Him. Life is not always easy. But God never promised that after becoming His child things would be easy; but He did promise that He would go with us through all things.

All I know to do is to examine all of these areas in my life, ask God for forgiveness in the areas that I have failed, and set my mind to do these things that God has called me to do with excellence and faithfulness. One thing I know is that God is good, and He is faithful. Thank you God for your love.

JANUARY 6

Daily Exercises

"Physical training is good, but training for godliness is much better, promising benefits in this life and in the life to come." NLT

I Timothy 4:8

There are many resolutions made at the beginning of each year. One of the most popular is to start an exercise program. I would venture to say that in a lot of cases it doesn't last very long.

Taking care of our bodies (our physical man) is very important. As a matter of fact, the Bible tells us in 1 Corinthians 6:19 NLT, "Don't you realize that your body is the temple of the Holy Spirit, who lives in you and was given to you by God? You do not belong to yourself." So we should take care of our bodies.

But more importantly, we need to take care of our spirit man. Jude 1:20-21 NIV tells us, "[20] But you, dear friends, by building yourselves up in your most holy faith and praying in the Holy Spirit, [21] keep yourselves in God's love as you wait for the mercy of our Lord Jesus Christ to bring you to eternal life."

How do we build ourselves up? By getting into the Word of God daily. There are several daily Bibles out there that divide the Scriptures into daily readings. My favorite is a daily Chronological Bible. Also, develop a daily prayer life. You may want to develop a prayer list that you pray over. Or you may want to allow the Holy Spirit to bring needs to your mind when you come to Him in prayer.

Make the choice today to exercise your mind and build up your faith by doing these things. You will be amazed at what a difference it will make each day in your life.

JANUARY 7

The Goodness of God

"O give thanks unto the Lord; for he is good; for his mercy endureth for ever."

I Chronicles 16:34

There is simply no way to describe the goodness of God! I have felt it, I have seen it, and I have experienced it. But, unless you have known it yourself, I cannot describe it to you

It is hard to imagine how people live without having God in their lives. How can they face difficult times in their lives without having Him to lean on? I have faced quite a few, what I would call, hard times in my life, but nothing as hard as when my husband, Rick, passed away. He was my companion, my soulmate, my sweetheart, my confidante, my best friend.... There's just not enough words to describe what he meant to me.

I never wanted to face life without him in it, but that's where I am. I don't blame God for taking Him. He is with the One that Rick taught about, that he loved with all his heart, that he desired to be with. I knew all along that I was second place in His life—that God was first! And that's ok; that's the way it should be.

God has been so gracious and good to me and my family. He has never left our side as we have gone through the grieving process. I knew we could depend on that fact as the song says, "All my life He has been faithful; all my life He has been so, so good." And because of that, I can say, "With every breathe that I am able; I will sing of the goodness of God."

If you are going through a difficult time right now, take the time to think about all God has done for you. Write them down and rehearse them in your mind. Keep them as Mary did and ponder on them often in your heart. Always remember that God is with you and will never leave you nor forsake you. We serve a good and faithful God.

NOTES

JANUARY 8

Living in the Here and Now

"In peace I will lie down and sleep, for you alone, LORD, make me dwell in safety.." NIV

Psalm 4:8

A lot of people have regrets about things they have done. They often wish they could go back and change some things in their lives to erase those regrets.

But you know what? That is impossible to do! You cannot live in the past and neither can you change it. If you live your life looking in the rearview mirror, you are destined to crash. All you can do is pray for God's forgiveness and then forgive yourself. You can now move on with your life in Jesus. There's much more living for you to do and you can't do that with a regretful mindset.

Jesus is waiting and willing for you to come to Him. And when you do, you will feel a sweet peace that will saturate your mind and heart. You will be able to look ahead with expectation, instead of looking back with regret.

Make it a priority to enjoy your life; only you can make that choice. Stop staring into the rearview mirror and start living in the here and now. Allow Jesus to lead you in all you do. He will give you His peace!

JANUARY 9

Train Your Children to Love God

"We will not hide them from their children, shewing to the generation to come the praises of the Lord, and his strength, and his wonderful works that he hath done."

Psalm 78:4

I hate to start something and not finish it. I cannot count the number of times that I have stayed late at work to finish what I was doing before I went home. As I write this, I think about those times and how I put my family on the "back burner" while trying to be a faithful employee and get my work done.

God Himself established the home when he formed Adam and Eve. So it is a very important institution. It is also important that you spend time building that home and spending time with the precious people that God gave you.

Family should be high on your priority list, second only to your personal relationship with God. Too many times, families are torn apart because ministry, friends, hobbies, jobs, just to name a few, are placed above the family.

We are taught in God's Word to train our children in the ways of the Lord. What an awesome and heavy responsibility on us as parents. We must provide them with a Godly example; otherwise, their example will come from the world around them. And that world is getting farther and farther from God.

So be that example and train them to follow God for all their days. God gave us the promise in Proverbs 22:6 that if we would do this, they would not depart from it.

JANUARY 10

Our Purpose in Life

"The Lord will fulfill his purpose for me;
your steadfast love, O Lord, endures forever.
Do not forsake the work of your hands." ESV

Psalm 138:8

Back several years ago, I went through a time in my life trying to discover my purpose. I wanted to find out the reason God put me on this earth, questioning in my mind if I was accomplishing all that I was meant to do. I did a lot of soul searching and never really came up with a definite answer, but I did feel that I was in the right spot at the right time doing the right thing.

As I was pondering on that, I began to think about where I was then in my life, and where I am now. My job at the time was the office assistant for the mission organization where I was employed. I had a lot of responsibilities, but one was taking care of the finances of the organization. I knew very little when I started this job and knew nothing about the computer program that I used. It was something that I "learned as I went". Now, working as secretary of our own ministry, I am using that same computer program and doing the same work as I did before.

That's the way it is with life. A lot of times, we have no clue why we are doing what we do at the present time; but God knows the road ahead. If we will just listen to Him, and follow His instructions, He will lead us to places that we are unaware of and will use our previous experiences to help us along the way. All we have to do is to trust Him and know that He has our future in His hands.

JANUARY 11

What is Jesus to You?

"The Lord is good, a strong hold in the day of trouble; and he knoweth them that trust in him."

Nahum 1:7

Life always has and always will have its challenges. And they are all different for every person. The challenges we face in our individual lives are difficult for all of us. But our answer lies in Jesus Christ.

Sometimes, when we face those rough times in our lives, we feel like there's nowhere to turn, and no answer to our dilemma. But those are the times that we find our solace in Jesus! He tells us in His Word that He would never leave us, nor forsake us.

He is and always will be our shoulder to lean on, our advocate before our Heavenly Father, our peace in the storm, our rest in times of turmoil, our substitute for our sins, our ________ ___ ____ ____... *(You fill in the blanks.)*

What is Jesus to you? Allow Him to speak to your heart in your troubling times. Those times won't necessarily go away, but He will never let go of your hand as He goes through them with you. It is in them that we find our greatest growth in Him.

JANUARY 12

Draw Close to God

"Come close to God, and God will come close to you." NLT

James 4:8a

Another New Year's resolution for many Christians is to draw closer to God than they have ever been. That, in itself, is a very good thing to do. But it shouldn't be something that you do at the beginning of a new year; it should be a way of life.

Leaning on God for every answer for your life is a life well lived. People who live without God have a miserable life. They don't know that they can be happy in their souls even through the dark times of their lives. They don't know that they can totally depend on Him to help them overcome whatever is in their lives that doesn't need to be there. They don't know just how much He loves them and that they don't have to change before coming to Him.

How many of us take the time to tell them about God and what He can do in their lives? We come across people every day that need to hear what He can do for them. Are you willing to be led by the Holy Spirit and show these people the answers they are looking for? He will lead you if you are willing to obey Him! And every time you tell someone about God, you will draw closer to Him yourself.

JANUARY 13

Live Peaceably with All Men

"Do all that you can to live in peace with everyone." NLT

Romans 12:18

This verse is not an easy thing to do. There are some people that just rub us the wrong way. But the verse does not say to live in peace with those that you like and enjoy being with. It says to live in peace with EVERYONE!

There was a time in our ministry that some people disagreed with Rick so much so that they spent hours on the phone with some of our supporters, trying to convince them to stop sending donations to our ministry. We lost quite a bit of monthly support because of that.

We could have turned against them and become bitter toward them. But we chose to forgive and pray for them. For one thing, there were other people watching us just to see what our response would be. We chose to represent Jesus in the situation.

Once, as we were eating at a restaurant with a spiritual son and daughter, that couple passed by our table. Rick and I stood and hugged them, as if nothing had happened. And that is just how we both felt. We truly still loved them.

Not only did it touch those people that had been a part of the attack on us and our ministry, but it was a lesson in action for our spiritual son and daughter. They knew the background of what had happened, and they silently sat and observed that it is possible to live in peace with everyone. The issues were not even mentioned to them but, with God's help, we were able to show them His love.

JANUARY 14

What Are You Doing with Your Time?

"Redeeming the time, because the days are evil."

Ephesians 5:16

God gives everybody the same amount of time in each day. Are you using your time wisely? Are you representing Jesus is all that you do?

Years ago, my husband, Rick used to sing a song entitled, "It's My Desire". The lyrics talk about having that desire to live for Jesus and to show others the way to Him. That was truly Rick's testimony. He lived for Jesus and led many others to the saving knowledge of Him.

He spent a lot of time with Jesus through prayer, Bible study, mentoring others, and preaching God's Word. He often called his car, his prayer closet. Most of the time, I would ride with him for a couple of hours each day, while he prayed over his list of over 400 people. It was truly his deepest desire to represent Jesus in all he did.

What about you? Can you say that you spend your time living your life so that others can see Jesus living in you? We all have 24 hours in every day. How much time are you giving to Jesus? It's time for us to take inventory of our lives and make it our desire to be more like Him.

NOTES

JANUARY 15

Let Benjamin Go

"But Jacob replied, "My son shall not go down with you, for his brother Joseph is dead and he alone is left of his mother's children. If anything should happen to him, I would die." TLB

Genesis 42:38

We are all familiar with this story. Joseph was born to Jacob and Rachel. He loved Rachel more than his other wives and he felt the same about Joseph, which made the other brothers jealous of him. They eventually concocted a plan to kill Joseph but sold him into slavery instead.

Many years later, Joseph was made second to Pharaoh in Egypt and was placed over distribution of grain during the famine. Jacob sent his sons, all but Benjamin, to buy food there. Joseph knew his brothers, but they did not recognize him. After asking about their family, he told them they would be considered spies, and dealt with as such, unless they brought their younger brother to him.

Upon arriving home and giving their father the admonition from Joseph, he would not consent to let Benjamin go to Egypt with them. Benjamin was the only other son of Rachel, and he didn't want to lose him too. Finally, he consented since that was the only way to buy more grain. Only then did Jacob receive not only his Benjamin back, but he also received what he thought was dead, Joseph.

What is your Benjamin? What do you need to release from your hands in order to receive what God has for you? It's there for you, but you cannot receive it with your hands clenched, holding onto "stuff". Just choose to let your Benjamin go and see what God will do!

JANUARY 16

Stand on Your Promises

"God is not a man, so he does not lie.
He is not human, so he does not change his mind.
Has he ever spoken and failed to act?
Has he ever promised and not carried it through?" NLT

Numbers 23:19

The Bible is full of promises. You can be assured of the fact that if God said it, then it will come to pass. As the saying goes, you can take that to the bank! It may take many years to see them come to fruition, but it will happen.

Abram was given a promise from God that he would be the father of many. His name actually meant "exalted father." Can you imagine what people thought when he would tell them his name? "My name is Daddy, but I'm not a father….yet!" And then God Himself changed his name to Abraham, which means "father of a multitude!" He had to carry this name for many years without any visible evidence.

Abraham was 86 years old when he became a father for the first time, yet this was not the promised seed. He had to wait 14 more years before Isaac was born!

Has God given you a promise and are you still waiting for it come to pass? Remember this: God does not lie, and He does not change His mind. Believe and trust that He will do what He says He will do!

JANUARY 17

20/20 Vision

"Call unto me, and I will answer thee, and show thee great and mighty things, which thou knowest not."

Jeremiah 33:3

As we grow older, our body naturally goes through a lot of changes. We realize that we are not able to do some things as well as we used to. One area that changes is our eyes. What was once 20/20 vision is now far from it and we will most likely have to wear glasses to see correctly.

It should be different with our Christian life though. As we grow in God, our "spiritual" vision should improve instead of decrease. We should see things more clearly as we learn more and more about Him.

We can improve that vision by allowing God to speak to us through prayer, reading and studying the Word of God, worshipping with other believers, telling others about Jesus, etc.

Simply put, make God your number one priority and you will see more clearly what it means to follow Jesus as you draw closer and closer to Him.

JANUARY 18

God Gives Us Mercy

"Let us therefore come boldly unto the throne of grace, that we may obtain mercy, and find grace to help in time of need."

Hebrews 4:16

The definition of mercy is "compassion or forgiveness shown toward someone whom it is within one's power to punish or harm."

John Claypool, an Episcopal priest, was attributed with this quote: "The real meaning of mercy is that it can look on failure and still see a future." This statement is so true. Even though we feel that we have failed in certain areas of our lives, God will show us His mercy each and every time because of His faithfulness to us!

Another quote comes from Timothy Keller, a Presbyterian pastor and author, "Mercy and forgiveness must be free and unmerited to the wrongdoer. If the wrongdoer has to do something to merit it, then it isn't mercy." God's mercy is unfailing. We cannot do anything that would deserve us receiving it.

Isn't it a wonderful and freeing thing to know that we can come to Jesus in all of our failures, and He will respond back with His mercy and grace? Every single time!

JANUARY 19

The Grace of God

"For the grace of God that bringeth salvation hath appeared to all men."

Titus 2:11

Although they are closely related, there is a difference between mercy and grace. Mercy is God's forgiveness in spite of what we deserve, grace is even though we don't deserve it, God still blesses us.

We receive God's grace because of His great love for us. It is nothing that we did, or that we can ever do, to deserve His grace toward us. Jesus died on the cross as payment for our sins so that we can receive that grace. A familiar acronym for grace is:

God's

Riches

At

Christ's

Expense

So, when you sing those familiar songs about God's grace, realize that it's not just words. God did give all of us a chance to experience His grace, not because we deserve it, but because of His great love for us.

JANUARY 20

Worship...It Does a Body Good

"Let my mouth be filled with thy praise and with thy honour all the day."

Psalm 71:8

In the 1980's, in an attempt to convince kids (and adults) to drink more milk, someone came up with the slogan, "Milk...it does a body good!"

I'd like to "borrow" the slogan and say, "Worship...it does a body good." It not only does your body good, but it does your mind and spirit good as well.

Since losing my husband in May of 2020, I have spent a lot of time in worship to my Saviour during my grieving times. I have found that even though my heart is hurting, my worship to the Lord remains in my spirit. And the result is that as I begin to worship, I can feel that healing in my heart and an uplifting in my spirit.

But we don't have to wait for trying times to come. We should worship at all times. We should have a spirit of praise in our heart in whatever situations we find ourselves. It will lift us above our circumstances in rough times, as well as take our spirit higher in the good times.

So, in whatever place you find yourself today, take a little time, turn on some worship music, and sing praises to your Lord. You will find that your day will go better, and you can face whatever comes your way with a smile.

JANUARY 21

Be A Worshipper

"....if any man be a worshipper of God, and doeth His will, him He heareth."

John 9:31b

David is a prime example of one who worshipped God. Do you realize that David was able to face Goliath because of his relationship with God? He did not stop and "get his heart right" beforehand—He was already at that place; it was his lifestyle.

All those months out in the fields alone tending his father's sheep, David spent a lot of time conversing with God. He worshipped Him in his alone times so therefore, he could worship when he was with the crowd. I could just imagine him playing his harp and even dancing before the Lord while he was alone.

Have you ever done that? There have been times that I have been at home just me and the Lord, and I have danced around the house, worshipping Him. I felt such an awesome peace come in my soul that lasted all day long.

Being in His presence is wonderful. It may not change your circumstances, but it'll give you assurance and peace that you will be able to face whatever "giant" comes your way because you'll feel His nearness throughout your day!

NOTES

JANUARY 22

Looking in the Rearview Mirror

"No, dear brothers and sisters, I have not achieved it, but I focus on this one thing: Forgetting the past and looking forward to what lies ahead." NLT

Philippians 3:13

A rearview mirror is a good thing when it is used as it is supposed to be. But we should not live the rest of our lives looking at it.

In driving a car, if we need to see what's behind us, or if we need to back up for some reason, a rearview mirror is a necessity. Drivers should check it often as they are driving. But if we drive with our eyes continually on the rearview mirror, instead of on the road ahead, we will end up in a wreck!

The same is true with life. It is good, sometimes, to look back and see how God has been with us throughout our lives. But we can't live there. We must look straight ahead and follow the path that the Lord has laid before us. If not, then our lives will turn into a wreck.

Look back to see where God has brought you from, but then, look at where you are today. Then, continue on this road of life, looking to Jesus to be your guide and navigator.

JANUARY 23

Don't Answer the Door

"Guard your heart above all else, for it determines the course of your life." NLT

Proverbs 4:23

We've all heard the saying, "If Satan knocks on your door, send Jesus to answer it." We need to take notice of what tries to enter the doors of our minds and hearts.

Satan is sly and will come to us disguised as something completely different. For example, he will come to the door as abortion, which means to scrub a mission. In reality, it is murder. Or as luxury, which in excess is uncleanness, which can turn into idolatry.

We read about the works of the flesh in Galatians 5:19-21. Satan will give all of these another name so we will accept them. In 2 Corinthians 11:14 NLT we read, "But I am not surprised! Even Satan disguises himself as an angel of light."

So, let's be very careful when Satan comes to our door; allow Jesus to answer his knock. For truly this will determine the course of our lives.

JANUARY 24

White as Snow

"Come now, and let us reason together, saith the Lord: though your sins be as scarlet, they shall be as white as snow; though they be red like crimson, they shall be as wool."

Isaiah 1:18

As I write this devotion, I can look out my window and see a skiff of snow that fell during the night. I think fresh fallen snow is beautiful, covering the imperfections of the ground: the brown dead grass, the leaves that have fallen from the trees, the unlevel areas of the yard. But it will soon melt away as the temperature rises in the 40's and above.

That's the way it is when we come to Jesus. Our lives are a mess and in need of a Savior. Before surrendering to Jesus, we become as the grass and leaves in the winter, ugly and dead. Sometimes we spiral out of control as our lives encounter the dips and potholes that are in our path.

Then, as we turn to Jesus and accept Him as Lord and Savior, His red blood will turn our black hearts as white as snow. And, as the old song says, He makes something beautiful of our lives.

But here's the difference; that will never melt away as the snow does. Jesus said in Hebrews 13:5b, "for he hath said, I will never leave thee, nor forsake thee." That is a promise that will last throughout eternity!

JANUARY 25

Learning to Lean

"Trust in the Lord with all thine heart;
and lean not unto thine own understanding."
Proverbs 3:5

Life can hit us hard sometimes, especially when we're not expecting it. Sickness, financial stress, abuse, discouragement, betrayal of friends, loss of business, death of loved ones…the list goes on and on. To whom can we turn when these difficult situations come at us like a hurricane?

There's only one answer to that question and that is Jesus! He knows and understands it all. He will be our healer, our provider, our peace, our encouragement, our comfort...whatever we need, that is what He will be to us.

The song by John Stallings, "Learning to Lean", has meant so much to me during my times of grief. These words have ministered to me so many times. Here are the words to the chorus.

Learning to lean; learning to lean
I'm learning to lean on Jesus
Finding more power than I'd ever dreamed
I'm learning to lean on Jesus

Not only in grief, but in every other situation you find yourself, lean on and trust in Him. You, too, will feel the power from Jesus that you didn't even realize you had.

JANUARY 26

What's Between the Dashes

"In the same way, let your good deeds shine out for all to see, so that everyone will praise your heavenly Father." NLT

Matthew 5:16

Whenever you read a biography of someone, or read the epitaph on a tombstone, you will see the date of their birth, then a dash, and finally, the date of their death. My husband, Rick's would read, December 1, 1954-May 19, 2020.

He did a lot of living in the dash. When he died, the family made the remark that he would be totally surprised when he reached Heaven and found out just what an influence he had and the mark that he made on the world around him.

What will people say about you when you pass away. Are you doing anything significant for Jesus with your life? Have you made a difference in someone else? Will Jesus say, "Well done, thou good and faithful servant"?

If you answered "No" to these questions, it's time to make a change before the dash is ended and your death date is applied. You can start now to truly look at yourself and ask Jesus how to help you to be a positive influence in other people's lives. Don't let the God opportunities pass you by—let others see Jesus in you during your dash!

JANUARY 27

What Voices Are You Listening To?

"[4]And when he putteth forth his own sheep, he goeth before them, and the sheep follow him: for they know his voice. [5]And a stranger will they not follow, but will flee from him: for they know not the voice of strangers."

John 10:4-5

Jesus is teaching us that not all voices are the same, nor should all voices have the same impact in our lives! In other words, when all voices carry equal weight in your life, it produces chaos. But when you're able to elevate the right voices, it brings comfort!

Every voice we choose to listen to should be trusted, proven, Biblically sound, and Holy Spirit confirmed. Don't let your ears become garbage cans for so-called experts that have come out of the woodworks to lead through difficult times in our lives.

Everyone is not sent by God; some were sent, others just went! Learn to hear the voice of God and then choose to listen to those that carry His heart for the world! Be sure to choose wisely.

~ Rick Clendenen

JANUARY 28

Does Your Passion Agree with God's Desire for You?

"Take delight in the Lord,
and he will give you your heart's desires." NLT
Psalm 37:4

According to Webster's Dictionary, the definition of passion is "a strong feeling of enthusiasm or excitement for something or about doing something." It also means "strong liking or desire." Notice the word, strong, in both definitions. Passion is not a simple desire; it is a strong feeling, being enthusiastic, excited!

For what do you have a passion? What do you do or what do you have that gets you enthused or very excited? Is it a certain object or a special person in your life?

There is a requirement that we must do in order for the Lord to give us the desires of our hearts. That is to take delight in the Lord. What exactly does that mean?

To me, it means to make sure our passion or desire is pleasing to the Lord. When we do that, our desires will change from our own view to God's view. And then, our desire and passion will come in line with what God has in store for us as we seek to please Him in all we do.

JANUARY 29

As For Me and My House

"And if it seem evil unto you to serve the Lord, choose you this day whom ye will serve; whether the gods which your fathers served that were on the other side of the flood, or the gods of the Amorites, in whose land ye dwell: but as for me and my house, we will serve the Lord."

Joshua 24:15

In the above verse, Joshua was talking to the children of Israel, telling them to choose who they were going to serve. He made the bold statement that he and his house were going to serve the Lord.

My husband and I were firm believers that in order to train our children, it was our responsibility to live a Godly life in front of them. That is what training is all about! They see what we do and then follow suit.

Although this is not an exhaustive list, this is how we chose to train them…

As for me and my house, we will serve the Lord.
As for me and my house, we will go to church.
As for me and my house, we will pay tithe to our church.
As for me and my house, we will read God's Word.
As for me and my house, we will pray.
As for me and my house, we will believe He hears our prayers.

I've only named a few in the above list. Make your own list and decide today that you are going to train your kids in those areas. I guarantee you that by watching you, they will fall in love with Jesus on their own. And what a blessing that will be!

JANUARY 30

Submitting to God's Will

"[9]For this cause we also, since the day we heard it, do not cease to pray for you, and to desire that ye might be filled with the knowledge of his will in all wisdom and spiritual understanding;
[10]That ye might walk worthy of the Lord
unto all pleasing, being fruitful in every good work, and increasing in the knowledge of God;"

Colossians 1:9-10

Paul is telling the people that he is continually praying for God to give them complete knowledge of His will and that He will give them spiritual wisdom and understanding. What a peace and joy comes in knowing that someone is continually praying that over you!

Vs. 10 goes on to say that as they receive that, the way they live will always honor and please the Lord. And their lives will produce every kind of good fruit. In doing so, they will grow as they learn to know God more fully.

Do we really want to submit to God's will, or do we want Him to adjust His will to fit our own agenda? I must confess that I have been there...many times. But the tragedy is that in keeping this as our mindset, we miss the opportunity to know God better.

Let's make a conscious decision to totally submit to His will, to spend more time in His Word and learn more truths about Him, to decrease and allow God to increase more in our lives. If we do these things, then people will see Jesus in and through us! And they will desire the same thing for their own lives.

JANUARY 31

God Uses Ordinary People

"I will praise thee;
for I am fearfully and wonderfully made:
marvellous are thy works;
and that my soul knoweth right well."

Psalm 139:14

God uses ordinary people to do extraordinary things! David was an ordinary guy. Actually, in His time, he was less than ordinary. His father, Jesse, thought so low of David that when Samuel came to anoint one of his sons as king, he didn't even line him up with his brothers! Jesse was obviously ashamed of David, as were his brothers! But God didn't see David as everyone else did. While others saw shame and embarrassment, God saw great potential.

The same is true with many others in the Bible, such as Gideon. Even though Gideon felt he was the lowest of the low, God called him a mighty man of valor! And what about Mary, the mother of Jesus? She was just a teenager when the angel appeared to her and told her that she was highly favored and blessed among women.

What about you? Do you have a low self-esteem, thinking that God can't use you? No matter your age, your occupation, or your own opinion of yourself, God's idea of you is much different than what you or others think. Keep that in mind the next time an angel appears to you or when you feel God calling you in a certain direction. You are important to Him!

NOTES

FEBRUARY 1

The Love of Jesus

*"The Lord hath appeared of old unto me, saying,
Yea, I have loved thee with an everlasting love:
therefore with lovingkindness have I drawn thee."*

Jeremiah 31:3

"Jesus Loves Me" is a song we all learned when we were children. These simple words are so true and touches the hearts of young and old.

Jesus loves me this I know, For the Bible tells me so
Little ones to Him belong, They are weak, but He is strong
Yes, Jesus loves me, Yes, Jesus loves me
Yes, Jesus loves me, the Bible tells me so.

This is a fact that will last throughout eternity and will never change. Jesus loves us! Not because of anything we have done nor anything that we will ever do. Did you know that we can never do anything to make Jesus love us more than He does right now? Nor can we ever do anything to make Him love us any less?

I am so thankful that He loves me. Because of that, I want to show love to others so that they, too, can experience His love for them. How about you? Are you loving the way Jesus loves? If not, then start today and love like Jesus!

FEBRUARY 2

No Greater Love Than This

"Greater love hath no man than this, that a man lay down his life for his friends."

John 15:13

The greatest love for mankind was shown by Jesus Christ when He took our place on the cross for each and every one of us.

He felt every pain that went through his body when He was crucified. He was whipped with a cat of nine tails, a whip with nine thongs, embedded with bits of metal or bone, meant to tear flesh from a person's body.

A crown of thorns had been plaited so that multiple long, sharp thorns would protrude from it. It was not only placed on his head but was pushed down so the thorns would puncture and embed into Jesus' skin, causing blood to run down His face.

He was nailed by His hands and feet to a cross as a substitute for our sins. The roughness of the wood on His back made the tears from the whips even worse as He tried to push Himself up just to get a breath.

But do you realize that Jesus Himself made the very things that would become what would one day cause Him excruciating pain? But He made them anyway and endured it all because He loves us so much! My friend, there is no love greater than that! He loves you and me!

FEBRUARY 3

We Are So Loved

"[14a]When I think of the wisdom and scope of God's plan, I fall to my knees and pray to the Father…. [18]And may you have the power to understand, as all God's people should, how wide, how long, how high, and how deep His love really is." NLT

Ephesians 3:14a, 18

As I was reading this morning, I came across the above scripture, and it hit me deep in my spirit. How often do we consider the extent of what God did to accomplish his plan for us?

As most of you know, we have a son and I know that it would be extremely difficult and most likely impossible for me to give my son's life for someone else; especially for those that have been vicious and mean to him or to me. But that is exactly what God did even though He knew the torture Jesus would have to endure. He knew the mean and hurtful things people would say about Him and to Him, the anguish He would have to go through just to see His plan come to fruition.

God knew from the beginning of time what would occur years later for the salvation of man. Imagine just how much He loves us! It is overwhelming to me the extent of His love. Even though I fail Him time and time again, He is ready and willing for me to fall on my knees (or a better way of putting it is to crawl in His lap), asking forgiveness for my failures, and continue on my spiritual journey with Him. I love Him-don't you??

FEBRUARY 4

Oh How He Loves Us

"But God commendeth His love toward us, in that, while we were yet sinners, Christ died for us."

Romans 5:8

I heard an old hymn the other day that I had never heard before. The name of the song was "Before the Throne of God Above" and a couple of lines really touched my heart. It was a beautiful song, but these two lines spoke to me:

My name is graven in His hands
My name is written on His heart

I realized that my name is on the spikes that went through His hands and feet, on the spear that went through His side, on every thorn in the crown on His head, and on every stripe He bore on His back. With all the pain He knew was coming, He went to the cross anyway—for me!

And the good news is that He did it for you, too. He loves us so much! He doesn't want us to endure what sin would do to us, so He bore our sins and gave us a way of escape.

Won't you give your life to Him? He has a plan for you—all you have to do is surrender to Him and trust your all with Him.

FEBRUARY 5

Love Each Other

"My command is this:
Love each other
as I have loved you." NIV

John 15:12

Are there people that just get on your nerves or that rubs you the wrong way? I'm sure we all have some like that in our lives. I must admit that I do!

As I think about those people, I often wonder what is going on in their lives that make them respond to things the way they do. I have even made statements such as, "If I were them, I would… or I wouldn't…!" The truth of the matter is I don't know their specific situation and I don't know how I would respond if I were in their place.

It's time we realize that we are not called to tell everyone else how to run their own lives. But we are called to love one another, just as Jesus loves us. Let us all look past our feelings against those people that irritate us and strive to give them Christ's love that dwells within us. You'll be amazed at the change that takes place, not so much in them, but in you.

FEBRUARY 6

God is Love

"Whoever claims to love God
yet hates a brother or sister is a liar.
For whoever does not love their brother and sister,
whom they have seen,
cannot love God,
whom they have not seen." NIV

I John 4:20

I have heard people say, "I hate them!" This phrase even comes out of the mouth of some Christians. Is this something that needs to be said by a follower of Christ? Is this showing the God of love?

It really doesn't matter why you are feeling the way you do against someone. You may have been extremely hurt either physically or mentally. But, according to the verse above, you cannot love God if you hate a brother or sister.

Hate should never be in the vocabulary of a Christian in speaking of another person. Jesus was brutally whipped, lied about, spat upon, ridiculed, and so much more. But while He was on that cruel cross, He asked God to forgive them—He showed His love for even those that did those things to Him.

If you feel genuine hate toward anyone, seek wisdom from God and He will show you how to begin to feel God's love toward them. I can promise you that your love for God will return and it will make you a much happier person.

FEBRUARY 7

Do You Really Love Your Spouse?

"A new command I give you: Love one another. As I have loved you, so you must love one another." NIV

John 13:34

The definition for love, given by Dictionary.com, is "a profoundly tender, passionate affection for another person." To go even further, LiveInTheMoment.org tells us that there are 3 qualities of love:

- ◊ ***Love is complete acceptance***: Accepting someone just the way they are and not trying to change them.
- ◊ ***Love is completely unconditional***: We can't stop loving someone, no matter what they say or do.
- ◊ ***Love is selfless***: Putting the person you love above your own wishes and desires.

I truly believe that God puts people in our lives so that we can experience that kind of love. My husband, Rick and I possessed that kind of love for each other, and I thank God for it.

Can you say that about your spouse? Do you completely accept and love them for who they are? Do you love them unconditionally and selflessly? If not, ask God to fill you with that kind of love. You'll find that you will be much more content with your life if you do this!

NOTES

FEBRUARY 8

Being Christ's Disciple By Your Love

"By this shall all men know that ye are my disciples, if ye have love one to another."

John 13:35

This verse is one that should really make us look deep within our hearts. Can the world tell that we are Christ's disciples? Do we have love one for another?

If you come from a naturally loving family, it is easy to love them…most of the time. I have that kind of family. We may have disagreements among ourselves, but we would fight a saber-tooth tiger if anyone else would try to hurt any of them. We love each other that much!

But what kind of love do you and I show to the alcoholic on skid row? How do we feel about the prostitute on the streets? Do we love the drug addict that even sells his drugs to innocent young ones? Did you know that Jesus loves them just as much as He loves us?

According to John 13:35, we must have love for everyone, including those mentioned above. That is how they know that we are true followers of Christ, if we have love for them.

God, help us to realize that to be like Jesus, we must love everyone, so that they will experience God's love themselves. Help us to show Your love to others, even to the unlovable.

FEBRUARY 9

God Kind of Love

*"Keep yourselves in the love of God,
looking for the mercy of
our Lord Jesus Christ unto eternal life."*

Jude 1:21

Our English language only has one word to describe our deep feelings toward a person or thing, which we call love. We may say, "I love my car," "I love my pet," "I love hot dogs," "I love my husband," "I love God." I would hope that your love would not be in this order!

We use the word "love" for so many things with so many meanings. But in the Greek, there are four different words for love.

◊ ***Eros***: This is romantic love, reserved for marriage.

◊ ***Storge***: The second type is love for family.

◊ ***Philia***: This is the love Christians have toward each other.

◊ ***Agape***: This is the divine love that comes from God.

These four words describe the different types of love, and their meanings are very specific. The highest form of love is agape, and it only comes from God. The reason for this type of love is because God's very nature is to love.

Have you experienced that love from Him lately? I can assure you, there is nothing like it. To know that God loves us with such an everlasting love is a feeling like no other. And to know that we can experience it every day is an incredible feeling. Allow God to show you His love today.

FEBRUARY 10

Why We Should Love Others

"Dear friends, since God so loved us, we also ought to love one another." NIV

I John 4:11

It is such a simple answer to the question, "why should I love others?" We find it in the verse above. It is because God so loved us!

I know there may be people in the world, or maybe I should say, in your world, that just seems so hard to love. But God doesn't tell us to only love the ones that we like to be around or to only love our family. The Bible tells us over and over again to love one another.

Do you think that Jesus ever had the thought that He just couldn't love this one or that someone else has too much sin in his/her life for Him to love them? The answer is a resounding NO. Jesus loves everybody! He doesn't just love, He IS love. He embodies love and will never turn anyone away.

If it is our desire to be like Jesus, we must love everyone too. No matter what they may have said to you or even done against you. Because God loved us, then we must love others. Ask Him to give you that kind of love today.

FEBRUARY 11

The Evidence of Loving God

"If you love me, you will keep my commandments." ESV

John 14:15

Do you love God? Do you really love God? If you do, then are you keeping His commandments?

This is not referring solely to the Ten Commandments, but to the life that we are living and doing what God has told us in His Word to do. Here are some examples and the scripture references where they are found:

◊ **Matthew 3:2**-"And saying, Repent ye: for the kingdom of heaven is at hand."

◊ **Mark 11:22**-"And Jesus answering saith unto them, Have faith in God."

◊ **Luke 6:36**-"Be ye therefore merciful, as your Father also is merciful."

◊ **John 14:1**-"Let not your heart be troubled: ye believe in God, believe also in me."

◊ **1 Corinthians 4:16**-"Wherefore I beseech you, be ye followers of me."

These are only a very few commands that Jesus gives us, but there are many, many more. Take the time to research these; it will take some time! And then examine your heart and see if you are following them. As John wrote, "If you love me, you will keep my commandments." Are you showing your love for Him by following His commands?

FEBRUARY 12

The Faithfulness of God's Love

"For the mountains may move and the hills disappear,
but even then my faithful love for you will remain.
My covenant of blessing will never be broken, says the Lord,
who has mercy on you." NLT

Isaiah 54:10

It is a settled fact that God is faithful with His love for us. And it will never go away or ever change!

I was raised in a Christian home, and I grew up knowing that God loved me. I didn't know just how much until I became an adult and began facing difficult times in my life.

One such situation happened right after my future husband, Rick, and I became engaged. He was preaching at a small church that we had never been to before. I knew at the time that I loved Rick, but I was struggling a bit to know that it was truly God's will for us to get married. That night, the pastor called Rick and I to the front and prayed for us. I had told no one about my concerns, but God knew. The pastor proceeded to tell me specifically that it was God that had brought us together and it was indeed His will for us to be married.

God didn't have to do that for me, but I truly believe that He calmed my mind and spirit that night about this most important decision we were making because of His love for me. He will do the same for you if You'll just ask Him. He loves you that much!

FEBRUARY 13

Love Your Neighbor

"And the second is like unto it,
Thou shalt love thy neighbour as thyself."

Matthew 22:39

Relationships with neighbors are nowhere close to what it used to be. And that is sad. But what is sadder is that most people do not even know who their neighbors are!

When we moved into the house when I currently reside, we did not know anything about our neighbors; we just barely knew their names. But God had a plan to change that.

We had learned that one of them had recently lost his wife. God spoke to Rick that he not only lost his wife, but he had also lost his cook. He specifically told him to have me to bake him a German Chocolate Cake, which I did. Rick and our daughter, Renee crossed the street and took it to him. He cried and told them that it was his favorite cake. God knew that fact, but we didn't.

We learned a valuable lesson. Even though we really didn't know our neighbors, God still used us to bless this one that day. We began to love them and speak to them when we saw them.

Do you know your neighbors? Do you make yourself available to them when they have a need? God tells us to love them; the first step is to get to know them.

FEBRUARY 14

Show Your Love

"I love them that love me;
and those that seek me early
shall find me."

Proverbs 8:17

Today is Valentine's Day. It is a day set aside to show your love to those that are closest to you. It may be giving of flowers, candy, cards, or it could be giving of your time to that special someone.

My husband, Rick, was very good at showing his love for me. One thing he did was to buy me roses on this day every year, as well as my favorite candy and a beautiful card with a handwritten note. He loved to lavish me with gifts.

He didn't have to do this to prove his love because I knew he loved me. He told me every day, just as I told him. I loved hearing him say, "I love you!"

Do you realize that God loves to hear us tell Him of our love for Him? Sometimes, we just need to come to God, not asking for anything, but lavish our love on Him. That is actually something we need to say to our loving Father every day. Have you told Him today how much you love Him?

NOTES

FEBRUARY 15

Is There a Limit to God's Love?

"[38]For I am sure that neither death nor life,
nor angels nor rulers, nor things present nor things to come,
nor powers, [39]nor height nor depth, nor anything else
in all creation, will be able to separate us
from the love of God in Christ Jesus our Lord." ESV

Romans 8:38-39

Have you heard a sinner say, "I've gone too far for God to love me?" or maybe they have even said, "God can't love me because of all the bad things I have done."

Maybe it is you that is having these thoughts about yourself! Do you really think that you are able to go too far away from God for Him to not love you anymore or that He wouldn't accept you if you tried to come back?

Do you not realize that there is no limit to the love of God! He loves you and me with an everlasting love. That means we can't go far enough away from Him that He will stop loving us!

If you've been struggling with that and maybe even have said those statements above, stop, turn your life over to Jesus, and feel His love surround you every day! He's waiting on you!

FEBRUARY 16

The Greatest Love

"For God so loved the world, that he gave his only begotten Son, that whosoever believeth in him should not perish, but have everlasting life."

John 3:16

The verse above is the greatest verse in the entire Bible. It tells us that God loved us so much that He gave His only Son to be crucified so that we could have everlasting life with Him. Why did Jesus pay the ultimate price? Because of His great love for us.

There is an older worship song that has been one of my all-time favorites since I first heard it. It is "Oh How He Loves You and Me." It has simple lyrics, but they are so powerful and so true.

Oh how He loves you and me
Oh how He loves you and me
He gave His life—what more could He give
Oh how He loves you—oh how he loves me
Oh how He loves you and me

He freely gave His life because He loved us so much. He was the substitute for our sins so that we may have life and have it more abundantly. As the song says, Oh how He loves you and me!

This is a love that is greater than any other that we could possibly have. Thank you, Jesus, for loving us that much. Because of Your love, we are able to have everlasting life with You. My heart and my love belong to You!

FEBRUARY 17

Love in Action

"Let all that you do be done in love." ESV

1 Corinthians 16:14

Oscar Hammerstein supposedly wrote the following in a note and gave it to his leading lady. It is a powerful message!

A bell is not a bell until you ring it
A song is not a song until you sing it
Love in your heart isn't put there to stay
Love isn't love until you give it away

That's such a true analogy! How in the world can people know that you love them if you don't show them? This talks of love in action, not just idle words.

A bell is just a brass object until someone rings it and we hear the beautiful sound it makes. If you write a poem, intending it to be a song, it won't be until you sing it. And when you have love for someone hidden in your heart, it was not meant to stay there. It turns into love when you "give it away."

Buy that special someone the gift that they've been wanting. Or give them your time: take them out for dinner, go to a movie, go shopping, do something with them that they want to do. That is how you give love away. Don't keep it hidden in your heart because it's not love until you do something with it!

FEBRUARY 18

Love and Trust

"Let the morning bring me word of your unfailing love, for I have put my trust in you. Show me the way I should go, for to you I entrust my life." NIV

Psalm 143:8

Love and trust go together like a hand in a glove. In talking about relationships, I don't believe you can have one without the other.

The same is true with your relationship with God. A large part of loving Him is to trust Him. If you love Him with your whole heart, then trusting Him just comes naturally.

Even though I have been through the worst time of my life in losing my husband, I love God more today than I ever have. I choose not to blame God, but to trust that He knew what was best for Rick and for me.

Are you going through a difficult time right now? Do you feel at a loss on what to do? Put your trust in your Heavenly Father and love Him with everything in you. Your situation may not immediately change, but you can feel the indescribable peace that only comes from above. I can promise you that He is waiting for you to make that step and He will show you just what to do!

FEBRUARY 19

Keep Love in Your Heart

"And above all these put on love, which binds everything together in perfect harmony." ESV

Colossians 3:14

Oscar Wilde, an Irish poet and playwright, made this statement about love, "Keep love in your heart. A life without it is like a sunless garden when the flowers are dead."

To keep love in your heart is something at which you have to work. You may not always agree with what is going on in your world, even with your loved ones. It is in those times that you must determine in your mind that your love is not based on circumstances, but rather on what lies deep in your heart.

As Mr. Wilde said, if you don't have love in your heart, it will be like a garden of dead flowers because there was no sunshine. By keeping that love alive will cause life to be much brighter, no matter where you find yourself.

So, strive every day to love those around you and you'll see a difference in how you view things. Love can change your perspective!

FEBRUARY 20

Love Your Enemies

"But I tell you, love your enemies
and pray for those who persecute you." NIV

Matthew 5:44

This command from Jesus is sometimes a very hard thing to do. You may be thinking, just as I did, "I just don't know if I can do this or not!"

It really doesn't matter what you think; you are letting your mind think on the wrong things. Jesus can and will help you overcome the reason why you even have enemies. And He will help you be able to love and pray for them.

It may be a situation like my mother-in-law faced when my husband and his siblings were small children. Whenever they would go outside to play, a neighbor would begin to throw rocks at them. God impressed my mother-in-law to bake her a cake and take it to her. After some arguing with God, that's just what she did! There was never another rock thrown and they became good friends.

In situations like this, it would seem a crazy idea to do something nice for the person that is persecuting you, or in this situation, persecuting your children. But God knew the woman's heart and knew she needed some Godly love shown to her. Determine in your heart to love and pray for your enemies and watch what God will do!

FEBRUARY 21

God Loves Us Anyway

"But God commendeth his love toward us, in that, while we were yet sinners, Christ died for us."

Romans 5:8

The love that our loving Father had, and continues to have, is just amazing. He sent His Son, Jesus, from Heaven to endure indescribable pain because of His love for us, even while we were sinners! We did not deserve that kind of love, but He exhibited it anyway.

The word for commendeth used in this scripture verse, from Strong's Concordance means to demonstrate. So God demonstrated His love for us by sending Jesus to be our sacrifice so that we could become His children. And it was all done even while we were sinners!

That is the true definition of love. How can we not come to Him, knowing that we are loved that much, and freely accept His gift of love and salvation? It's a puzzling thought to me that there are still so many out in the world that have not made that step toward salvation. Is it because we don't love them enough to tell them that God loves them that much too? That they are included in those to whom God demonstrated His love?

Maybe we should examine our own hearts and see if we truly do have a love toward mankind, just as God does. I don't want to have the attitude of "my four and no more" when it comes to seeing sinners come to the saving knowledge of Jesus. If we love God, we must love LIKE Him and seek out the lost, showing them the way to Him. No matter how far in sin they may have gone, we should love them anyway just like God does!

NOTES

FEBRUARY 22

Love That Lasts

"Many waters cannot quench love, nor can rivers drown it. If a man tried to buy love with all his wealth, his offer would be utterly scorned." NLT

Song of Solomon 8:7

Love is a very powerful thing. It can make the strongest man be brought to his knees. It can turn the hardest heart of stone into one full of gentleness and kindness. The verse above tells us that love cannot be quenched by an abundance of water, nor can it be drowned by rivers. Love is invincible.

On the website, ThoughtCatalog.com, are several statements that describe love. Here are a few:

◊ It creates an inner warmth and willingness to be loving and kind to others.

◊ It makes every one of life's hardships and tragedies seem worth it.

◊ It provides a sense of purpose.

◊ It compels so deeply you'd risk or give your life.

◊ It closes personal distance.

◊ It takes down otherwise unbreakable walls.

◊ It is unwavering with compassion and forgiveness.

The best thing about love is that it comes from God. The love that we feel for other people does not compare in the least to how God feels about us. And this kind of love will last forever.

Thank you, God, for giving us such a wonderful trait to experience in our lives. And thank you for giving us Your love as an example of how to love others.

FEBRUARY 23

The Importance of Love

"I speak in the tongues of men or of angels, but do not have love, I am only a resounding gong or a clanging cymbal.
2 If I have the gift of prophecy and can fathom all mysteries and all knowledge, and if I have a faith that can move mountains, but do not have love, I am nothing.
3 If I give all I possess to the poor and give over my body to hardship that I may boast but do not have love, I gain nothing." NIV

I Corinthians 13:1-3

Paul tells us in these first three verses of 1 Corinthians 13 that if we don't have love, then we have nothing, we are nothing. Even if we have an eloquent speaking ability that people enjoy listening to and we don't possess love, our words will mean nothing to the listeners.

How many of you enjoy listening to someone clanging a cymbal? That's how it is to hear someone speak that we know does not have love in their hearts.

Paul continues to say that whatever spiritual gift we may possess or even if we give all that we have to the poor, it does no good for us if we do what we do with the absence of love.

Over the next few days, we are going to delve into the importance of love, according to 1 Corinthians 13. As we all know, this is called the love chapter. We will see what God has to say about love through the pen of Paul.

FEBRUARY 24

Love is Patient Love is Kind

"Love is patient, love is kind.
It does not envy, it does not boast, it is not proud." NIV
I Corinthians 13:4

Being patient has not been a virtue that comes easy for me. I want what I want when I want it. I sometimes struggle with that attitude with people. I often become annoyed because they are not acting as I think they should.

But that is not how God tells us to handle, or to love, people. We are to be patient with our love toward them. The definition for patient from Bing.com is, being able to accept or tolerate delays, problems, or suffering without becoming annoyed or anxious. Ouch! I've been guilty of having those attitudes against some people!

Not only is love patient, it's also kind. To be kind means, having or showing a friendly, generous, sympathetic, or warm-hearted nature. (*Wikipedia*) In other words, having God's nature with those we love.

This verse goes on to say that love doesn't boast because it isn't proud. Being boastful and proud is a quick turn-off to those around you. Jesus certainly did not have this attitude toward people.

Let us all check our hearts and make sure that the love that we show to others is patient and kind and is not boastful and proud. That's what we must do if we want others to see Jesus in us.

FEBRUARY 25

Love is Not Self-Seeking

"It does not dishonor others, it is not self-seeking, it is not easily angered, it keeps no record of wrongs." NIV

I Corinthians 13:5

In this verse, we see some things that love does not do. It's an amazing thing for me to hear some people say that they love someone, but yet they have no regard to the feelings of the other person.

In the above verse, it tells us that when you love others, you will not dishonor them. How many times have we talked down about our loved one to others and in the next breath, say that we love them? What about the times that we are selfish, wanting our own way, not even considering the ones we say we love? God tells us not to be self-seeking.

What about getting angry with our loved ones or keeping a record of the wrong that we think has been done to us, whether it is written down or by making a mental note of them?

If we find ourselves doing these things, we should turn them over to God, asking Him to forgive us and help us to change. Make an intentional effort to display His kind of love to others.

FEBRUARY 26

Love Doesn't Delight in Evil

"Love does not delight in evil but rejoices with the truth." NIV

I Corinthians 13:6

I have heard some Christians say, "I'm so glad that happened to them because of what they did to me!" My friend, this is not the attitude that God desires us to have. We have already established that Jesus told us to love our neighbor, and even called it a great commandment, second only to loving God with all your heart, soul, and mind.

I know you may be thinking that no one knows what this particular person did to you. But Jesus didn't say for us only to love those that do good to us; He said to love your neighbor! So we mustn't be glad when something bad befalls those people that have wronged us. The secret is to love them anyway and let God deal with the consequences of what was done.

We are also told in the above verse to rejoice with the truth. What does this mean? I think that one thing it means is turn it over to God, rejoice when this person comes to the knowledge of what Jesus did for them, and gives their life to Him. For the truth is that Jesus loves them and desires to live within them so that they, too, can show the love of Christ to others.

So, let's not rejoice when evil befalls these people but pray for them and love them into the Kingdom. That's what showing the love of Jesus is about!

FEBRUARY 27

Love Will Always...

"[7]It always protects, always trusts, always hopes, always perseveres. [8a]Love never fails..." NIV

I Corinthians 13:7-8a

What a comforting thought to know that love always protects, trusts, hopes, perseveres...and so much more! We can not only know that God's love toward us does these things, but also, that it is possible for us to love others in the same manner because He lives within us.

While my husband, Rick, was alive, I knew that he would always make sure I was protected because of his love for me. And because of our love for each other, we both knew that we could and would always trust each other, share our dreams and hopes with each other, and know that our love would persevere and last forever. We believed that because we knew that our love came from God above.

If we always display the God kind of love, then we can know with a surety that it will never fail. We must let the love of Jesus that is in our hearts be our guide to how we love others.

FEBRUARY 28

The Greatest of These is Love

"And now these three remain: faith, hope and love. But the greatest of these is love." NIV

I Corinthians 13:13

The definition of faith is found in Hebrews 11:1 NIV, "Now faith is confidence in what we hope for and assurance about what we do not see." We obtain salvation through faith in Jesus. By faith, we believe that God formed the earth. We can read in Hebrews 11 about how patriarchs and matriarchs lived their lives by faith.

I like the definition of hope found in Holman Bible Dictionary. It says, "the anticipation of a favorable outcome under God's guidance." We are told in God's Word to rest in hope, have hope in God, wait for hope of righteousness, look for the blessed hope of the coming of Jesus...

We learned in an earlier devotion that the definition of love, given by www.dictionary.com, is "a profoundly tender, passionate affection for another person." In God's Word, we see that we are to love God first and foremost. We are to love our neighbor, love our enemies, love one another, just to name a few.

Faith and hope are human graces; love is a divine grace. It exists, has always existed, and will exist evermore. We can see how important love should be in our lives. For us to represent God, we must love as He loves. It must not be something that we do, it must be something that we are! Represent Him well and be a person of love.

FEBRUARY 29 (LEAP YEAR)

God's Love According to John

"As the Father hath loved me,
so have I loved you:
continue ye in my love."

John 15:9

Webster defines love as a feeling. In fact, he uses 47 descriptions, trying to explain it. But the problem with those descriptions is that love is more than a feeling.

We can learn several things about love in John 15:10-17.

- ◊ Verse 10 tells us that love fully expressed requires obedience to the Word of God.
- ◊ Verse 11 says that love is the only avenue to continual joy.
- ◊ In Verse 12, we learn that Jesus Himself is the standard by which love is to be measured.
- ◊ Verse 13 speaks of what Jesus did because of His love.
- ◊ Verse 16 tells us that love is a choice that fully incorporates the intellect, the will, and the emotions. It requires the full use of your faculties.
- ◊ And verse 17 gives us the command to love.

Love is a choice that we all make. And if you do what you know to do, feelings will follow.

~ Rick Clendenen

NOTES

MARCH 1

Not One Hoof

*"Our cattle also shall go with us;
there shall not a hoof be left behind..."*

Exodus 10:26a

In Exodus, we read about the account of Moses and Aaron going before Pharaoh and telling him to let their people go. Moses wanted him to know that when they left, they would leave nothing behind!

Pharaoh told them they could go and worship their God but to not go very far in the wilderness. Several times he told them just who they could take with them: For instance, only the men; then the men, women, and the children, but leave the animals, etc. Moses was getting frustrated with Pharaoh because he kept changing the rules, and he proclaimed to him, "Not one hoof will be left behind when we go!"

We need that kind of tenacity when we pray for our lost loved ones. We need to take that stand with the devil and tell him that he can't have any of them! Don't give up! Be like Moses and Aaron, be persistent with your prayers, and watch what God will do!

MARCH 2

Some Water, Some Plant

"I have planted, Apollos watered; but God gave the increase. So then neither is he that planteth anything, neither he that watereth; but God that giveth the increase."

I Corinthians 3:6, 7

Have you ever taken the time to think about those that have planted and watered in your life?

Our family has had a lot of people that have planted the Word of God in our hearts. But there is one couple that has watered that Word, and that is JT Parish, and his precious wife, Noretta. I love and appreciate these two so much. They have been by our sides during our difficulties and have urged us to continue with God when we were discouraged. Most of all, their love for us has never waned and their prayers have never stopped.

The Greek word for watered used in this verse is potidzo, meaning to irrigate. When farmers irrigate their fields, they are saturating them with water.

Who has taken time to saturate the Word of God that has already been planted in your heart? Take time out of your day to send them your heartfelt thanks. And while you're at it, thank the ones that first planted that Word in you. It's because of them that you are where you're at today!

MARCH 3

How's Your Training Going?

"Train up a child in the way he should go,
And when he is old he will not depart from it."

Proverbs 22:6

I sat behind a couple and their young boy at church this morning. He was around nine or ten years old. During worship and with no apprehension, I noticed that he had both of his hands raised to God in worship to Him. That blessed my socks off!

Do you know why he did that? It's because his parents chose to bring him to church and train him to love God and worship Him.

What are you teaching your children? Do they see you worshipping God? Do they know that they will be going to church when Sunday comes?

Train them in the way they should go, and they will love God with all their hearts. Train them in the way they should go, and they will love going to church. Train them in the way they should go, and they will turn to God throughout their life. That, my friend, is successful parenting!

MARCH 4

Nevertheless Moments

"There are many devices in a man's heart; nevertheless the counsel of the Lord, that shall stand."

Proverbs 19:21

While researching the Bible for "nevertheless moments", I discovered that there are quite a few of them throughout the scriptures. It takes a committed heart toward God to say, "Nevertheless…" in those moments in life when it's not always convenient to follow what God is telling us. Some examples are:

- ◊ **2 Kings 2:10**-When it came time for Elijah to leave this earth, Elisha asked for a double portion to be upon him. Elijah told him that he had asked a hard thing but **nevertheless**, if he saw him taken away, then he would receive it.
- ◊ **Nehemiah 4:9**-There were those that came against Nehemiah as they rebuilt the walls of Jerusalem, **nevertheless**, they kept watch against them as they continued their work.
- ◊ **2 Timothy 1:12**-Even though Paul was called to the ministry, he suffered many things because of it. In this verse, he says, "…**nevertheless**, I am not ashamed…" He believed that God would take care of him.
- ◊ **Matthew 26:39**-Jesus spoke a "nevertheless moment." He knew of the horrible things that would be done to Him in the next few days, and He asked the Father if it were possible, "let this cup pass from me." He continued to say, "**nevertheless** not as I will, but as thou wilt."

How many "nevertheless moments" have you had in your life? It's not easy to make that statement, but it is so worth it. True happiness comes when you submit your will to your Heavenly Father, just as Jesus did.

MARCH 5

A Good Thing or a God Thing?

"And we know that in all things God works for the good of those who love him, who have been called according to his purpose." NIV

Romans 8:28

We already know that everything we do should be for the glory of God. We are told this in 1 Corinthians 10:31, "So whether you eat or drink, or whatever you do, do it all for the glory of God."

Have you ever thought about all the things that you are doing...are you doing them for the glory of God or for your own glory? Has God called you to do them or are you doing them in your own power and strength?

Let's say that you are busy, from sunup to sundown, doing what you think is the work of the Lord. But that leaves no time for your spouse or your children. Those things you are doing may be good things, but it is certainly not a God thing if you are not taking care of the blessings that God has given you.

Or perhaps you are giving financially to every cause that comes across your path. It is good to give to the needy, but if your family does without because of it, it's not a God thing.

I'm not saying these are bad things to do, because God does call us to do them at times. But my husband and I learned a valuable lesson in this area and God spoke to him these words, "I cannot reward what I did not command."

Yes, work for God. Yes, God does call you to do certain things. But make sure what you do is not only a good thing, but it is also a God thing.

MARCH 6

What Does Your Future Look Like?

"Boast not thyself of tomorrow; for thou knowest not what a day may bring forth."

Proverbs 27:1

I read a Facebook post from a dear lady announcing the death of her husband to their friends. What she wrote touched me and got me to thinking. She said, "My husband has begun his future!"

I've never heard it put that way before, but it is so true. Sure, we have a future here on earth, but our ultimate desire is to spend our future in Heaven!

We all begin our Heavenly future at different periods in our lives. My mom began hers on Nov. 4, 2012—she was 83 years old; my husband, on May 19, 2020, being 65 years old; my dad on March 11, 2021, one month from 96 years old. You can see all different dates on tombstones and figure out the different ages in which these people died. Some were very young, some very old, and all ages in between.

None of us are even promised tomorrow. But we don't need to worry how long we have left in our lives. We just need to live for Christ every day and look forward to the future He has in store for us.

MARCH 7

He'll Do It Again

"His disciples replied, How are we supposed to find enough food to feed them out here in the wilderness?" NLT

Mark 8:4

The above scripture is the disciples' response when Jesus told them that the crowd of 4,000 men (not including women and children) needed something to eat. The disciples asked Jesus how they were supposed to find food for that many people.

What were they thinking? Or were they not even thinking at all? Did they not remember what happened with the earlier feeding of the 5,000? Did they forget that Jesus multiplied the loaves and fishes then with quite a bit left over?

There is a song that was popular about 20 years ago, but the message it contains is relevant today just as much as it was then. Here are some of the lyrics:

He'll do it again; He'll do it again.
If you'll just take a look at where you are now
And where you've been.
Hasn't He always come through for you
He's the same now as then.
You may not know how, you may not know when
But He'll do it again

We don't know how God will work out our situations. And you know what? We don't have to know. All we need to realize and believe is that He will take care of any problem that comes our way, every single time! He'll do it again and again and again!

NOTES

MARCH 8

The "Almost" Times

"Then Agrippa said unto Paul,
Almost thou persuadest me to be a Christian."
Acts 26:28

How many "almost" times have you encountered? How many of these times are recorded in the Bible? I'm sure there are many, but I will only list a few.

Let's start with Cain. He was upset at God because He didn't accept his offering. The thought is that it was because it wasn't a blood sacrifice. Genesis 4:3 says, "In the process of time…" Do you think that maybe God didn't accept it because it was as if it was an afterthought, not the first thing he did? Abel gave of the "firstlings" as we're told in verse four. Cain did not show the proper honor because it wasn't important to him. He "almost" did the right thing but fell short!

The next one I thought about was Orpah. When Naomi's husband and sons died, she decided to return to her homeland. Orpah and Ruth chose to go with her, but Orpah soon changed her mind and turned around. I wonder what would have happened with Orpah if she had carried through with her "almost" decision to follow Naomi and Ruth.

Another is a familiar story found in Acts 26. Paul was telling King Agrippa about Jesus. He comes close to accepting Him, but he tells Paul that he almost persuaded him to be a Christian. Almost!

I don't want to live in the land of "almost." I want to go further in my relationship with God and go past the "almost" moments to receive all He has for me. How about you?

MARCH 9

Church Attendance is Important

"Not neglecting to meet together, as is the habit of some, but encouraging one another, and all the more as you see the Day drawing near." ESV

Hebrews 10:25

Growing up, my brother and I were never given the choice of whether or not we went to church. It was a settled fact that we were going and that's how we both raised our kids and they, in turn, are training their kids the same. There are many excuses that people give for not going to church; here are just a few.

"That's the only day I can rest. After all, Sunday is supposed to be a day of rest." Although that may be true, what better way to get rest for your soul than to come to church and worship together with other believers. As your soul is refreshed, then your body will receive rest as well.

"The kids need time to rest before starting school again on Monday." What do you think they are thinking when they see you sporadically attend church? If it's not important to you, it won't be important to them. And they won't turn to God when problems arise. "Train up a child in the way he should go: and when he is old, he will not depart from it." Proverbs 22:6.

"I can watch church on TV." The Covid pandemic has not helped with this point. I am thankful that we were able to view our church services online during that unprecedented time, but there is just no comparison to being with your brothers and sisters in Christ, fellowshipping and worshipping together. My husband always said that fellowship is two fellows in one ship! You can't fellowship by yourself.

Make it a habit to be faithful in your church attendance. There's just nothing like being in the presence of God, being in one mind and one accord, worshipping together!

MARCH 10

My Version of Psalm 23

"The Lord is my Shepherd; I shall not want."

Psalm 23:1

God is my shepherd and because of that, there's nothing else that I want to fulfill that place. At various times in my life, during trials that I face, He gives me rest and refreshing. By doing that, my soul is restored. As He leads me in paths He has prepared for me, I will go in His Name.

Even though death may be at my door for me or my family, I will send God to answer the door because He IS with me. I will not fear what evil unsuccessfully tries to do to me because You, God, are an encourager to me. Even though I have enemies, You will lift me above all they try to do to me and will bless me in spite of it.

From the depths of my heart, I know that Your goodness and Your mercy will be with me forever because I choose to live with You and for You all the rest of my days!

This is an exercise that you should try. Choose a chapter from the Bible and write down, verse by verse, just what it means to you. It will bless you!

MARCH 11

He's Always Close

"...for he hath said, I will never leave thee, nor forsake thee."

Hebrews 13:5b

This morning, I was looking for my iPhone. I pinged it on my watch and heard it dinging but could not locate it. Even though I pinged it several more times, I still couldn't find it. Everywhere I would go, it was somewhere close. I then realized that it was in my pocket! I felt a little dumb. Let's be honest, I felt a "whole lot dumb"! But it got me to thinking.

I am so thankful that we don't have to go looking for Jesus because He's always near. Just the mere mention of His name and we can feel His presence. He's always ready to commune with us. He's always there to hear our cry. He's always available to listen to our praise to Him.

Jesus can be our dearest Friend if we allow Him to be. All it takes is an open heart to Him. He patiently waits for us to give our lives totally to Him and experience that nearness that will be with us throughout our lives.

We don't have to "ping" Him to try and find Him. He is with us because He lives in our hearts and goes with us everywhere we go. No need for us to fear losing Him, He will never leave us! What a great comfort!

MARCH 12

Don't Let Your Heart Be Troubled

"Let not your heart be troubled: ye believe in God, believe also in me."

John 14:1

Jesus Himself told us to not let our hearts be troubled. What great advice He has given us with that one statement! It can be said about so many different things in our lives.

If you are sick or are having pain in your body, let not your hearts be troubled because "But he was wounded for our transgressions, he was bruised for our iniquities: the chastisement of our peace was upon him; and with his stripes we are healed." Isaiah 53:5

If you are facing financial pressures, let not your hearts be troubled because "But my God shall supply all your need according to his riches in glory by Christ Jesus." Philippians 4:19

If you feel alone, let not your hearts be troubled because "Blessed be God, even the Father of our Lord Jesus Christ, the Father of mercies, and the God of all comfort;" 2 Corinthians 1:3

If you are discouraged, let not your hearts be troubled because "But you, O Lord, are a shield around me; you are my glory, the one who holds my head high." NLT Psalm 3:3

If you ________________ *(fill in your own blank)*, let not your hearts be troubled because __________________ *(there's a scripture for that!)*

Whatever need you have, be assured that Jesus is the answer. He will calm your hearts and bring peace to your difficult situation.

MARCH 13

Find Your Way to The Mountain

"And he removed from thence unto a mountain...."

Genesis 12:8a

This passage of scripture occurs after God spoke to Abram asking him to leave his country, his kindred, and his father's house. He didn't know where he was going—only that God would show him the way. Abram did leave and arrived at Shechem. This is the point that the above scripture comes: He removed from THENCE.

I once heard my husband, Rick, preach on this passage and my mind began thinking about this thought: What is my THENCE?

I thought about times when I had felt hurt from people that I thought were close to me, times when sickness and pain wracked my body, times of discouragement, fear, and frustration. All these low times were THENCE moments in my life. But as I turned to God, I found that I could remove myself to the mountain, away from thence, and find my answers there.

God is the answer to all the troublesome times in your life, but you must remove yourself from thence and find your way to the mountain.

MARCH 14

What Kind of Label Do You Carry?

"One who is righteous is a guide to his neighbor, but the way of the wicked leads them astray." ESV

Proverbs 12:26

This may seem like an odd title but let me ask the question in another way. How would people describe you in a few words? Let me give a few examples.

Would people say you are "arrogant?" An arrogant person is one that has a strong opinion and believes that theirs is the only correct one. They give it freely and don't care if they offend anyone or not.

What about this one—"that person has a temper!" Do people see this adverse reaction in you when things don't go your way? This type of person could even be called a hot head.

Do people look at you and say that you are always "angry" about something? Nothing seems to go like you think it should and you're always looking for someone to blame. This type of person just seems to be angry at the world and is very seldom seen as happy.

We can name many others, but I don't want to carry any of these labels in my life. Do you? It should be the desire of all of us that Jesus shines through us and we represent Him in all that we do.

NOTES

MARCH 15

Let Them See Jesus in You

"Therefore be imitators of God, as beloved children." ESV

Ephesians 5:1

In the devotion yesterday, I listed a few negative traits that some people possess. Today, let's look at some positive ones.

The number one trait of a Christian is "love." We should always portray love if we want to look like Jesus. You know why? Because God not only loves, He IS love. If Jesus, the Son of God, lives in us, then we should also be known for our love.

Another trait is "compassion." We should have compassion on those around us and seek to show them Jesus, by word and by deed. Jesus showed compassion to those around Him and sought to deliver them from their sins. We should do the same.

"Forgiveness" is another character trait of a Christian. In this life, there will be many situations and times that we don't want to forgive others for what they may have done to us or against us. But, to follow Jesus, we must forgive. None of us will ever go through what Jesus did, and He readily forgave. We should do the same.

As in yesterday's devotion, this is only a small list. Take time to study it out and make your own list. Then, search your heart, find out if you possess these traits so that others may see Jesus living in you and desire the same for their lives.

MARCH 16

Who's Watching You?

"Be ye followers of me,
even as I also am of Christ."

I Corinthians 11:1

I'm sure you've all heard the phrase, "You may be the only Bible some people read." It may be a cliché, but it is so true!

Think about it—how much of your lives would you want someone to actually read and pattern their lives after? Has your life always honored God in everything you have done?

Sadly, when I think of myself, I have to answer, "No! I haven't always been a person I would want others to follow." But, as I have gotten older and hopefully wiser, I pray that has changed. I want my life to be one that others can see Jesus in me.

What about you? Do you have the same desire for your own life? If so, start today to pay more attention to what you say, what you do, and even where you go. Represent Jesus in all things so that, as Paul stated in the above verse, others may want to follow you as you follow Christ!

MARCH 17

Your Resume

"[20]And so he that had received five talents came and brought other five talents, saying, lord, thou deliverest unto me five talents: behold I have gained beside them five talents more. [21]His lord said unto him, Well done, thou good and faith servant: thou hast been faithful over a few things, I will make thee ruler over many things: enter thou into the joy of thy lord."

Matthew 25:20-21

If you had to present a resume to Jesus, how would yours read? A resume begins with simple information, such as name, address, phone number, etc. That would be easy for anyone to answer. It's the sections that follow that may be more difficult.

Where did you receive your training and at what level did you stop? The receiving of your training is not as important as the last part of the question. You need to make sure that your church is Biblically based and that your leader is teaching the Word of God. But is there a level at which you've stopped your training? There should never be a time in your life when you stop learning. Always be a learner.

What kind of talents do you possess that would be useful to you in the position to which you are applying? Remember that the talents you possess come from God. God is not impressed by those talents that He has given you but by your faithfulness in using them.

Could you list at least three references that could speak positively about your character? Are you the kind of person that is the same no matter where you are or who you are with?

As in life, you not only represent the organization for which you work, but the leaders as well. As Christians, we must represent Jesus Christ to the extent that others can see Him in us. No matter where you are or what job you are doing in the Kingdom, remember to be faithful—someone is watching you!

MARCH 18

Repentance vs Remorse

"I tell you, no; but unless you repent [change your old way of thinking, turn from your sinful ways and live changed lives], you will all likewise perish." AMP

Luke 13:5

Have you ever thought about the difference between repentance and remorse? Or maybe a better question would be do you think they are the same thing? I can tell you that they are not! Although you will feel remorse on your way to repentance, they are definitely not the same thing.

Mr. Webster defines remorse as, "a gnawing distress arising from a sense of guilt for past wrongs." On the other hand, his definition of repentance is, "to turn from sin and dedicate oneself to the amendment of one's life."

The key phrase is "to turn from sin." It's not enough to just feel the remorse of your sin, you must turn from it and live a totally different life than you did before. Otherwise, it's not repentance.

My husband's grandfather used to say, "If someone comes to the altar for salvation and you don't see a change, it's because there hasn't been one!" That's a true statement, my friend. True repentance will bring true change!

MARCH 19

God Uses Our Brokenness

"The Lord is close to the brokenhearted; he rescues those whose spirits are crushed."

Psalm 34:18

Some people would say that it is not a good thing to be broken. But I beg to differ. Being broken is a prerequisite for being used by God. That simply means that you are no longer trusting in yourself, but you are trusting in God.

Remember that an egg cannot be used until it is broken. The same is true with us. Being at this point, we are now pliable, and God is able to mold us into what He has called us to be.

As I was pondering on this, I began to think about various ways in which eggs are used in our cooking. Some use them to make deviled eggs, egg salad, or omelets, among many other things. Eggs are one of the ingredients in a cake, in cornbread, in pudding, etc. There are many uses for the egg.

We are all different, and God uses people in different manners. Some are apostles, prophets, evangelists, pastors, and teachers, as we are told in Ephesians 4:11. There are also many other gifts each of us possess to be used in His service.

It all comes about as we experience brokenness in our lives and allow God to change us into what He sees that we can be. So, don't fear when you find yourself broken; it's just the beginning of finding greater trust in God.

MARCH 20

Who is God?

"Who is like unto thee, O Lord, among the gods? who is like thee, glorious in holiness, fearful in praises, doing wonders?"

Exodus 15:11

If you ask different people to describe God, you will receive a variety of answers. My question to you is, who is He to you? Let's make it personal.

Do you see Him with a big stick just waiting for you to mess up, so He can hit you with it and punish you for your wrongdoing? Do you see Him as God but yet He is far, far away? Do you think that He is too busy with other people to even see what you are going through and just doesn't have the time to meet your needs? I'm here to tell you that those are not attributes of God! Every one of them are lies from Satan.

Here are some things about God that are absolutely true. We can rely on Him for what we need:

◊ He is love. 1 John 4:8
◊ He is patient. 2 Peter 3:9 NIV
◊ He is always near. Psalm 145:18
◊ He unchanging. James 1:17 NIV
◊ He is trustworthy. Isaiah 41:10
◊ He is forgiving. 1 John 1:9
◊ He is all of these and so much more!

Remember these when Satan comes to distract your mind away from God. Look up these scriptures and keep them close to your heart so that you can dispute what He tries to tell you about your Heavenly Father. God is good all the time!

MARCH 21

For Such a Time as This

"....and who knoweth whether thou art come to the kingdom for such a time as this?"

Esther 4:14b

In the above text, Esther had been taken to the palace to participate in a sort of beauty pageant to choose a new queen. The king was very happy with Esther, and she was eventually chosen. She was a beautiful woman and had a lot of wonderful characteristics, but that is not the reason she was chosen. This process was orchestrated by God Almighty to save His chosen people.

Here are a few thoughts to remember in "such a time as this" moments.

- ◊ Previous experiences are for "such a time as this."
- ◊ "Such a time as this" is many times a crisis time.
- ◊ "Such a time as this" is a prayer time.
- ◊ "Such a time as this" is a time for obedience and boldness.
- ◊ "Such a time as this" is pivotal for future influences.

We don't always see a reason for things that occur in our lives, and we may never know why they happen. But I have found that I cannot effectively minister to someone unless I have gone through a similar experience.

We must put our total trust in God, believe that He knows what's ahead of us, and knows who He will bring across our paths that will need our counseling and wisdom. Then, we can be in the right place and have the right attitude for our "such a time as this" moments.

NOTES

MARCH 22

He Was with Them—He Is with Us

"Remember the days of old,
consider the years of many generations:
ask thy father, and he will shew thee;
thy elders, and they will tell thee."

Deuteronomy 32:7

What a comfort to know that God is with us in every situation we face, just as He was to those we read about in the Bible. Let's look at Moses and Joshua.

When God called Moses to deliver His people from bondage in Egypt, He told him to remove his shoes because he was standing on holy ground. Did you know that God told Joshua the same thing before the fall of Jericho?

We all know how God parted the Red Sea for Moses and the children of Israel. Did you know that God did the same thing when Joshua was their leader as they approached the Jordan River?

Joshua remembered those times and knew that he could trust God too, just as Moses had done. It would do us good to listen to stories of our elders as they tell their own experiences of God's goodness in their lives. It would build our faith to know that what God did for them, He will do for us!

MARCH 23

Faith vs Fear

*"For God hath not given us the spirit of fear;
but of power, and of love, and of a sound mind."*

2 Timothy 1:7

As I was traveling down the road today, I began to think of all the people that I would encounter. I wondered what would be on all of their minds as they went about their day.

There are many things going on in the world today that are very scary and worrisome. If you're not careful, these things can keep you up at night and make you fearful of tomorrow. But you don't have to fear if you are a child of God.

I love the lyrics of the song, "No Longer Slaves." The song talks about not being a slave to fear because of being a child of God. That is so true—we don't have to fear because we have placed our lives in the hands of the Almighty God. We know that no matter what the world around us may look like we don't have to fear.

Fear is the opposite of faith. We know that faith comes from God, so guess where fear comes from? We can choose to give over to those fears or we can replace it with faith in God. Make the better choice!

MARCH 24

Microwave or Crockpot?

"Beloved, think it not strange concerning the fiery trial which is to try you, as though some strange thing happened unto you."

I Peter 4:12

Are you a person that wants results and you want it right now? We're addicted to quick results—I've heard it called "microwave living." What we need is "crockpot living".

When you cook a meal in a crockpot, it takes a while before it's done. For example, in making beef stew, you must cut up the meat (if you didn't already buy it that way), coat it, and brown it, before ever adding any vegetables; then you add the necessary spices. Now, you can walk off and leave it for several hours. It really starts smelling so good!

It is that way with our Christian life. God prepares us to become what He sees we can be. He allows things to be added that alone seem to us to be very hard and unnecessary, but together, the result makes us a much better person. And this process takes time, as cooking stew in a crockpot. But oh, the things we learn along the way! There will be times that we must spend in the fire but what happens in those times is very important to our development.

One promise we have is that God will go with us through it all. We can make it and we'll come out better for it. We will become a sweet savor to the nostrils of God.

MARCH 25

Representing Jesus

"And whatever you do, in word or deed, do everything in the name of the Lord Jesus, giving thanks to God the Father through him."

Colossians 3:17

How much does your life represent Jesus, especially to your children? Do they see Jesus in you as they watch you go through life?

Today is my mother's birthday. As of this writing, she would have been 93 years old. She went to her Heavenly home in 2012. She was an amazing woman and experienced a lot of things. But never in my life did I see her want to give up on God, hear her curse Him, or blame Him for anything she went through.

I saw how she supported her husband, whether it was in ministry or in daily life. "Nevertheless let every one of you in particular so love his wife even as himself; and the wife see that she reverence her husband." Ephesians 5:33

I experienced first-hand how she loved and stood behind my brother and me, making sure that we were taught the Word of God. "Train up a child in the way he should go: and when he is old, he will not depart from it." Proverbs 22:6

I watched as she cared for her parents; many times, when she was so tired and needed rest, she continued to honor them. "[2]Honour thy father and mother; which is the first commandment with promise; [3]That it may be well with thee, and thou mayest live long on the earth." Ephesians 6:2-3

And I saw much more from her life that is with me still today. You know why she did all of that? Because Jesus was number one in her life, and it was her desire to follow what He had called her to do. Can you say that about your own life? Let's represent Jesus in all we do!

MARCH 26

Give To Be a Blessing

"Remember this—a farmer who plants only a few seeds will get a small crop. But the one who plants generously will get a generous crop." NLT

2 Corinthians 9:6

Do you realize that God gives to us so that we can bless others? It is a joy and privilege to be used by God to help those in need. God meets our needs, as well as gives us seeds to sow in others.

I heard the story of a missionary from India that came to the states to raise support for his ministry. There was a woman in the service that only had a quarter, and she was ashamed that it was such a small amount. But God spoke to her and said to give it, and she did.

The following year, the missionary came back, thanked the people for their financial giving, and told the people that they had needed one specific screw to fix a door on one of their orphanages. They needed to close the doors before nightfall each night to keep the cobras from entering and biting the children there. Without knowing that the woman had given the quarter the previous year, he told the church that it took a quarter to buy the screw! God was so good to let the woman know that her giving was indeed a blessing.

Sometimes we don't know the true need of the person to whom God asks us to give. Our responsibility is to obey what God tells us to do. Being obedient in our giving will not only bless others, but we will be blessed as well. Remember that a seed cannot grow if it is not sown. Be a giver and see what God will do in your life!

MARCH 27

Spring has Sprung.... Or Has It?

"God is our refuge and strength, a very present help in trouble."
Psalm 46:1

This morning as I looked out the window, I had this thought—Spring has sprung! But when I stepped outside, the cold wind let me know that may not be the case. This is not particularly my favorite season; the time when winter is losing its grip and spring is trying to come forth. We just don't know what the weather is going to be at this time of year. One day it may be in the 70's and you think, 'Yes! Springtime is here!' But then the next day could be very cold, even having temperatures below freezing!

We go through times like these in our lives. Everything seems to be going perfect and then, suddenly, a tragedy occurs, or severe sickness hits, or any number of things that are unexpected happens. And it seems that we are in the midst of a winter season. But don't lose hope; our answer lies in Jesus!

That's the time for us to draw closer to Him. Because in the valley of our lives is when we learn to lean on Him in every situation that we encounter. And the good thing is not only is He with us on the mountaintop, He is also with us in every valley experience as well. He is always present, always available, and always ready to encourage us as we turn to Him. As the old song says, "Turn your eyes upon Jesus. Look full in His wonderful face. And the things of earth will grow strangely dim. In the light of His glory and grace!"

MARCH 28

Prepare For the Change of Seasons

*"While the earth remaineth,
seedtime and harvest, and cold and heat,
and summer and winter, and day and night
shall not cease."*

Genesis 8:22

Are you prepared for the changing of the seasons? What does that require of you? It simply requires you to also change! The struggle we face in life is that we have forgotten that life also is seasonal, and we struggle to adjust to the next season God has for us.

In preparation for a new season, it will require changing our clothes, converting from heat to air conditioning, schedules must change according to the weather etc. I think you get my point! But why do we believe that a new season in our lives can occur without also bringing drastic change?

Maybe it's time for us to examine what season we are in now and what areas that God is desiring to change in us to prepare us for the next season of our lives. The only thing that is here to stay is change!

~ Rick Clendenen

MARCH 29

Can You Just Wait a Minute?

"Wait on the Lord: be of good courage, and he shall strengthen thine heart: wait, I say, on the Lord."

Psalm 27:14

Have you ever said this to your kids, "Can you just wait a minute"? Children are naturally impatient. It's very hard for them to learn how to wait. That is also true for a lot of adults as well.

Waiting can be very frustrating, especially if you have been waiting for a long time. During those times, you may just want to give up. You may even doubt the word of the Lord that you have been standing on for so long.

But the Bible tells us in a very familiar verse found in Isaiah 40:31, "But they that wait upon the Lord shall renew their strength; they shall mount up with wings as eagles; they shall run, and not be weary; and they shall walk, and not faint."

There is where we find our answer. If we wait on the Lord, our strength will be renewed, and we will be able to continue to stand in faith and know that His strength will become our strength. What a blessed hope we can have if we simply learn the benefits of waiting.

MARCH 30

Jesus is All You Need

"The blessing of the Lord brings [true] riches,
And He adds no sorrow to it
[for it comes as a blessing from God]."AMP

Proverbs 10:22

Do you really feel that Jesus is all you need? Can you face any situation that may come your way and know you can make it because Jesus resides in your heart and life?

My first mission trip was made to India over twenty years ago. I still carry in my heart what I experienced on that trip. I was with my husband, Rick, along with several others. One place we visited was an orphanage. They were waiting for us when we got there and were assembled in rows, sitting on the floor. After we were seated, the missionary introduced several of the children to us. One at a time, he brought them up and he would tell us their heartbreaking stories. When he finished with each one, the missionary would ask them if they were poor, and their response was, "We're not poor, we have Jesus!"

That touched my heart and made me realize that I was not grateful for what I had in America. You must realize that these children came from extreme poverty, but they did not consider that at all. All they needed was Jesus and that made them rich!

Oh, that we could see what we have when we receive Jesus as Lord and Savior! When we make that choice, we become the richest people on earth. He is certainly all we need!

MARCH 31

Your Testimony Matters to Someone

"He comforts us in all our troubles so that we can comfort others. When they are troubled, we will be able to give them the same comfort God has given us." NLT

2 Corinthians 1:4

I have often heard my husband, Rick, say, "You can't have a testimony without a test; you can't have a message without a mess!" It is in those times that our testimony and message are born.

Too many times, we want a testimony, but we don't want to go through the test to achieve it. At least that is the way it is with me. I also don't want others to see and know that I have made a mess of things in my life. But what kind of testimony or message could I give to others if I don't go through those troubled times and see victory in the end?

Jesus wants us to know that whatever we go through in this life, we will one day be able to use it to help someone else. The things we face and the victories we acquire become our testimony and our message. We will be able to share with others that are going through similar situations and report victory to them.

God will send those people across our paths so they can know that, just like us, they can make it through difficult times, too. Look for opportunities to share those experiences. There's nothing to share until you make it through the test; your testimony matters to someone!

NOTES

APRIL 1

Be Friendly

"And as ye would that men should do to you, do ye also to them likewise."

Luke 6:31

Hello! Isn't it a great feeling to hear someone greet us with that word when we encounter people, our neighbor, someone we meet at Wal-Mart, at the gas station, at the ballpark, anywhere we may go? It will bring a smile to our faces and uplift our spirits.

Language doesn't matter; it's the same all over the world. It could be Spanish (*Hola*), French (*Bonjour*), Italian (*Ciao*), Mandarin Chinese (*Nǐ hǎo*), or any of the other over 7,000 languages. It is also different words from region to region within the United States, yet it all means hello! Examples would be: Howdy!, Hey!, Mornin'!, What's up?, How's it going?, etc. It just makes us feel good to know that someone took the time to speak to us as we go about our day.

Jesus wants us to do the same with Him. He loves to hear from us, not just once, but many times each day. We can talk to Him as if He is in the room with us because…He is!

As you wake up every morning, greet Jesus. I once read that we need to say, "Good morning, Lord" instead of "Good Lord, it's morning!" When you start practicing that each day, you will notice that it will bring a smile to your face and cause your day to go better! Mornin' Jesus…thank You for this day!

APRIL 2

He Will Bring it To Your Remembrance

*"But the Comforter, which is the Holy Ghost,
whom the Father will send in my name,
he shall teach you all things, and bring all things to your
remembrance, whatsoever I have said unto you."*

John 14:26

Have you ever been in a discussion with someone about the Bible and you felt the Lord bring a scripture to your mind at just the moment you need it? The Bible tells us that He will do that very thing.

But there's something that we must do before He can do that. We must read the Word of God. That is where we learn what Jesus has said to us. How can the Holy Spirit bring it to our remembrance if we haven't read it in the first place?

I have read a Chronological Daily Bible for several years. It is divided into daily readings and to be quite honest, all of it is not enjoyable reading and sometimes I get quite distracted. I was complaining to my son one day about it and I made the statement, "I ***have*** to read the boring parts of the Bible today!" His response to that statement floored me. It was five simple words, "You ***get*** to read it!" That changed my outlook tremendously on the Word of God.

So, I say to you, look forward to reading God's Word. If it's in your heart, then God can bring it to your remembrance when it is needed. You'll be glad you did!

APRIL 3

God Has Been Good to Me

"O taste and see that the Lord is good: blessed is the man that trusteth in him."

Psalm 34:8

I woke up early this morning and was thinking of how good God has been to me. There is not enough room in this book nor in many other books to tell of experiences and times that He has been there for me. I love Him with all my heart and want to live for Him the rest of my days.

I thank God that I was born in a Christian family that taught my brother and me about Jesus and what He did for us on the cross. It was an easy choice when I came to the age of accountability and gave my life to Him at twelve years of age.

I thank Him for being with me throughout my younger years. I never had a desire to give up on God after I accepted Him as Lord and Savior. I'm so grateful to Him for causing Rick and my paths to meet; it was all in His great plan for our lives. I thank God for the two children He gave us, their awesome spouses, and our wonderful grandchildren.

I give Him praise for the life Rick and I made together, the travels we made, the times we had worshipping God in various places of the world. Volumes could be written about those times.

There is so much more for which I thank Him. He is all I have ever needed and all I will ever need. He desires to be the same for you. Take time today to write down what He has done for you. It will bless you more than you know. He is good all the time; all the time He is good!

APRIL 4

Putting on the Armor of God

"Finally, my brethren, be strong in the Lord, and in the power of his might."

Ephesians 6:10

For the next few days, I want to look into the armor of God that we are to "put on" each day. But before we begin examining each piece of armor, let's look at verse 10.

Paul wrote the book of Ephesians to the church at Ephesus while he was in prison. In it, he gave instructions on how to be a mature Christian. These first few verses will help us grow in our relationship with others and with God.

He advises us to be strong in the Lord but instructs us to also be strong in the power of His might. If we are a child of God, we have His strength and the power of His might that we can depend on in every circumstance that we face. It's up to us to decide to grasp it and "wear it" in our lives.

It should be a great encouragement to know that the Lord can and will give us His strength and His power as we face each day. With God on my side, I can make it through anything…and so can you!

APRIL 5

The Belt of Truth

"Stand therefore, having your loins girt about with truth..."
Ephesians 6:14a

Before we get ready to face each day, we must physically put on our clothes. Some people may wear suits or dresses to work, while others put on uniforms when they go to their jobs. Others may go to the gym each day and that requires different clothing. The point is, we must put on our clothes before we go out into the world.

The belt, as the Roman soldier would wear, was worn around the body and contained long, metals pieces that would normally reach to the knees. It would protect the vital organs of the lower torso, so it was a very important part of the armor.

Paul tells us in Ephesians 6:14 that we should gird our loins with truth. Several other versions call it the belt of truth. Of course, we know that this is referring to the truth of God's Word. Without this truth, the rest of the armor is of no use to us.

So, the first thing is to get the truth in our hearts. We all need to read the Bible daily and ask God to sear it in our minds. For within its pages is the truth of God.

APRIL 6

The Breastplate of Righteousness

"...and having on the breastplate of righteousness;"
Ephesians 6:14b

The next piece of the armor that we should put on is the breastplate of righteousness. Let's look at it.

The breastplate was a metal plate worn as a defensive armor for the breast and was part of the Roman soldier's armor. Its purpose was to protect the vital organs of the upper body, including the heart and other life-sustaining organs.

According to Strong's Concordance, to be righteous is to be "upright, just, innocent, true, sincere." The Biblical definition for righteousness is "right standing with God."

As the breastplate protected the warrior from swords and spears, so is the Christian protected if he/she puts on the breastplate of righteousness. To do this, we need to regularly spend time with God through prayer, reading and studying the Word, and worship. Then we can be victorious when Satan tries to come after us.

Let's put on this important piece of the armor of God so when the enemy tries to attack the most vulnerable part of our spirit man, our heart, he will never succeed.

APRIL 7

Feet Carrying the Gospel of Peace

"And your feet shod with the preparation of the gospel of peace;"

Ephesians 6:15

Have you ever seen pictures of Roman soldiers fully clothed for battle that are barefoot? Or, for that matter, any people of the military that have no shoes on? I can answer that for you—No, you haven't.

This part of the armor for the feet is very needful, having to do with your walk, or how you walk out your life from day-to-day. You never know who God will bring across your path with which you can share the Gospel of peace.

The Christian soldier must be prepared to present it at any given moment. This means to be ready to take the Gospel of peace to others, wherever He may lead you. This brings to mind the verse found in Isaiah 52:7, "How beautiful on the mountains are the feet of the messenger who brings good news, the good news of peace and salvation, the news that the God of Israel reigns!" NLT

You cannot go without the proper preparation. Prepare yourself to be the kind of person that can give the answer that people are seeking, the Gospel of peace that only comes from above.

NOTES

APRIL 8

Taking Up the Shield of Faith

"Above all, taking the shield of faith, wherewith ye shall be able to quench all the fiery darts of the wicked."

Ephesians 6:16

The shield is a very important part of the armor of the Roman soldier. It was used for protection to ward off the arrows or spears from the opposing side. It also identified for whom you were fighting. Oftentimes, the shield bore marks of the army for which the soldier belonged.

The same is true of a Christian that wears the full armor of God. He is identifying to the enemy that he is a child of God, and that he is fully protected by Him.

When we take up the shield of faith, we are declaring our belief that God is going to protect us against anything the devil may throw at us, whether it be fear, doubt, condemnation, or whatever he uses that is in his arsenal. When we fully lean on God and His Word, thereby taking up the shield of faith, then the lies of enemy lose their power as we become overcomers.

So, allow the shield of faith be a large part of your armor so that, as Ephesians 5:16 tells us, we will be able to quench all the fiery darts of the wicked. God does not lie but Satan is the father of them; believe what God says!

APRIL 9

The Helmet of Salvation

"And take the helmet of salvation..."
Ephesians 6:17a

The helmet is the last piece of armor that the Roman soldier puts on. It protects the head from enemy attack that could possibly cause death. It actually protects what is inside the head and that is the brain. The brain is where you store the Word of God that you use against the attacks of Satan.

As we put on this helmet of salvation, we can be assured that God's Word will be protected in our minds. The mind can be compared to a file cabinet. As we read and study the Word of God, it is placed in the files of our mind and will be brought to our memory when we need it. And that Word that we have stored there will be protected from the attacks of the enemy.

We also use our mind (or our brain) when we realize that we are sinners in need of a Savior. The devil certainly doesn't want us to experience salvation and will do everything in his power to turn us away from God. That is the reason we need the helmet of salvation- to protect our minds from Satan's evil plans.

In order to combat the plans of Satan, we must get into the Word of God so we can use the holy scriptures to defeat him, just as Jesus did. This will happen when we put on the helmet of salvation and be assured that we are a child of God and Satan cannot talk us out of having that experience.

APRIL 10

The Sword of the Spirit

"...and the sword of the Spirit, which is the word of God:"

Ephesians 6:17b

In the above verse, we see that the Word of God is the sword of the Spirit. A Roman soldier never went to battle without his sword, which was his defense weapon. It was strapped to his side, within easy reach. We should consider the Word of God as our defense against the enemy!

When we get the Word down deep in our hearts and our minds, it becomes a part of us and a part of our arsenal. There's no doubt that Satan's attacks will come, but we can be prepared to fight him if our arsenal is full of the Word of God.

As we found out in yesterday's devotion, the Word is protected by the helmet of salvation. So then, we can pull the Word from the file cabinet in our mind and use it as our defense against the temptations from Satan, just as Jesus did.

What a comforting thought to know that as we put on the whole armor of God as we are told in Ephesians 6:11, we can be the victor over our enemy every time he comes at us. Are you fully clothed as a soldier in God's army?

APRIL 11

Don't Worry—Be Happy

"Who of you by worrying can add a single hour to your life?" NIV

Luke 12:25

There are times in our lives that we want to worry about different things that are happening. But it is our decision whether we worry or whether we choose to be happy by giving it to God. Jesus tells us not to worry. And we don't have to if we know and understand that He has everything under control.

As a widow, I can sit and mull over things that I will never do again. Rick and I had many adventures in our lives, visited many places, and saw many things, and we did them together. I will never be able to do those kinds of things with him again.

I could choose to live with unrealized dreams and feel that I was somewhat shortchanged because of the things we wanted to do, but now that chance is gone or I could decide to be happy about what we were able to do and appreciate the times that we did spend together.

Our lives very seldom turn out the way we think they are going to. But we can choose not to worry but be happy in all circumstances. Worry will not add anything to our lives but stress and anxiety. In 1 Peter 5:7, we see what we need to do with our worries, "Casting all your care upon him; for he careth for you." What a relaxing thought!

APRIL 12

Recipe for a Happy Life

"If ye know these things, happy are ye if ye do them."

John 13:17

In Psalm 37:3-7 is found four words that gives us the recipe for a happy life. Let's look into the instructions found in these verses.

The first thing we must do as found in verse 3 is to **trust** in the Lord. It's not always an easy thing to do, but it is always worth it.

In verse 4, we discover that we should **delight** ourselves in the Lord. It goes on to say that if we do that, He will give us the desires of our heart. The secret is when we delight ourselves in Him our desires will change!

Verse 5 says to **commit** our ways to the Lord (along with trusting in Him) and He shall bring it to pass. Unless we commit our ways to Him, it will not happen!

Finally, as we're told in verse 7, we should **rest** in the Lord and wait patiently. We can rest if we trust, commit, and delight in the Lord.

What a peace comes when we can follow these four steps in every situation we encounter in our lives. As the old TV commercial said, "try it—you'll like it!"

APRIL 13

Find Your Peace in Him

"Now may the Lord of peace himself give you peace at all times and in every way. The Lord be with all of you." ESV

2 Thessalonians 3:16

I'm really enjoying my time with the Lord lately and I've been surprised at how the Eternal Word of God is relevant to every situation we face!

There's always been a struggle for power and there always will be! We can so easily get caught up in it. If we're not careful, we will find ourselves trying to prove a point that won't be received or fighting a battle that can't be won! That's why we need the Word of God!

Jesus didn't allow Himself to get caught up in the fray of political struggles or in the arguments of religious scholars because He had nothing to prove! He learned the secret to living in peace. Walking in victory was found not in fighting battles, but rather in complete surrender to the will of The Father!

He offers that peace to you today as soon as you lay down your cause, pick up your cross, and follow Him! The peace you can win through personal victories pale in comparison to the peace you can find in Him!

~ Rick Clendenen

APRIL 14

Are You Out of Control?

"Many are the plans in the mind of a man, but it is the purpose of the Lord that will stand." ESV

Proverbs 19:21

I am the kind of person that wants to be in control of every area of my life. I have found that this will not always work! As a matter of fact, none of us needs to be in control when we are a child of God. When we become a Christian, we must choose to give God complete control of our lives. The greatest thing we can do is to be out of control!

I have compared this to a parade. We are standing on the sidewalk watching as each float, each band, each antique car, etc. passes by. We don't know what is coming next. We simply watch as each one moves past us. But it's as if God is on top of a building watching the same parade. The difference is He can see the first float, the last antique car, and everything in between. He knows what is next in the parade.

It is the same with our lives. We don't know what is going to happen in our future, but God does. We can only see what we are facing at the present time, but He knows the beginning and the end of it all. If we can just totally turn over the control of every area of our lives to God that would put us right where we need to be.

I want to be out of control and have God in the driver's seat. Don't you?

NOTES

APRIL 15

On The Journey

"For I know the plans I have for you, declares the Lord, plans to prosper you and not to harm you, plans to give you hope and a future." NIV

Jeremiah 29:11

Are you like me? Do you want important information ahead of time? For example, when we go on vacation, I want to know where we are going, how long we're going to be there, what we're doing each day while we are there, etc. Some people call this obnoxious—I call it planning!

One thing I've learned on my life journey is that I can't plan my own way with God. He has his own plans for me as the above scripture says. And they are plans that will not harm me but will prosper me.

The children of Israel learned that God would give them what they needed on the journey, not beforehand, but ON the journey. They learned that He would give them what they needed WHEN they needed it. Even though they grumbled and complained most of the way, He still supplied their needs.

I think of the many times that I have complained to God about situations in my life. Things would have gone so much better if I would just have remembered this truth--God will provide for me what I need, when I need it. And that He doesn't have to OK it with me ahead of time, or even let me in on what He is about to do. Help me, Lord, to trust You and know that You are on this journey with me and will be with me till the end.

APRIL 16

Don't Believe What the Devil Says

"...for who is this uncircumcised Philistine, that he should defy the armies of the living God?"

I Samuel 17:26b

Everybody knows the story of David and Goliath from 1 Samuel 17. We've heard it since we've been young children. But every time I read this story, there is something that riles up within me.

I can just imagine David putting it this way, "How dare he defy the name of the living God in whom we trust! He does not know who he is dealing with!" We need to have the same tenacity when the devil come knocking at our door with his accusations against us and our God.

- ◊ When he says that God is not interested in your problems, remind him of 1 Peter 5:7-"Casting all your care upon him; for he careth for you."
- ◊ When he says God will not help you win your battles, remind him of Romans 8:31-"What shall we then say to these things? If God be for us, who can be against us?"
- ◊ When he says that you are too weak to follow God, remind him of Exodus 15:2a-"The Lord is my strength and song, and he is become my salvation..."
- ◊ When he says you are a failure, remind him of Romans 8:37-"Nay, in all these things we are more than conquerors through him that loved us."

◊ When he says you can't be forgiven, remind him of Psalm 86:5-"For thou, Lord, art good, and ready to forgive; and plenteous in mercy unto all them that call upon thee."

All the accusations and condemnations that you hear are from Satan. He will try to tell you that God is not who He says He is, but there is always scripture to combat what the devil says. Don't believe him! Be bold and believe what God says about you!

APRIL 17

What Does Easter Mean to You?

"And they shall scourge Him, and put Him to death: and the third day He shall rise again."

Luke 18:33

Easter! This means different things to different people. I was flipping through the channels the other day and I passed by Jay Leno on The Tonight Show interviewing people on the streets, asking them different questions about Easter. It was amazing to me that many of them didn't know the real reason for Easter.

To some, it is a time for new clothes to wear on Sunday. It is a time to attend church, a once-a-year event for a few people! For others, it is a time to decorate eggs and have an egg hunt for the children. It may be a time for the beginning of Spring Break and the feeling that the winter is finally over. What does it mean to you?

For the Christian world, Easter is the time we celebrate the resurrection of our Lord. What He had suffered the Friday before is indescribable. "The Passion of Christ" was extremely hard to watch but the actual event was much worse than was shown on that movie. But we know that after being buried, He arose on the third day and is alive forevermore!

Easter is a time of new beginnings; spring will soon follow Easter (if it hasn't already arrived) and a time of new life comes. Let's remember as we are enjoying the warm spring after the cold, hard winter, that Jesus gave His life for us, and that He gives us new life in Him. Let's live for Him, not just on Easter, but throughout each day of the year.

APRIL 18

The Only Thing That Will Last

"Whereas ye know not what shall be on the morrow. For what is your life? It is even a vapour, that appeareth for a little time, and then vanisheth away."

James 4:14

On April 18, 1975, I changed my last name to Clendenen when I married my husband. This year (2022) would have been our 47th wedding anniversary. Since Rick is in Heaven, and I am still here on earth, I won't be pampered by him as he was always prone to do. No flowers, no gifts, no eating a steak dinner together…

But this time of year is a time to celebrate a greater event that took place over 2000 years ago. It was the day our precious Lord and Savior completed his work on earth by resurrecting from the dead so that we can have life and have it more abundantly!

Life here is but a vapor and will be gone one day. Today I choose not to grieve over my husband no longer being with me on this special day; I choose to celebrate that my Lord and Savior loved me so much that He gave His very life for me!

Whatever you may be facing today, put things in perspective and remember what Jesus did for us with His death and resurrection! That, my friend, is the only thing that will last!

APRIL 19

What Does Your Face Say?

"I pray that our faith together will help you know all the good things you have through Christ Jesus." NLV

Philemon 1:6

There are some people that when you see them, you don't even have to ask how they are doing—you can tell it on their face!

You may ask, "We're having beautiful weather today, aren't we?" And they will answer, "It's supposed to rain on Thursday!" Or you might simply say, "How are you today?" Their answer would go something like this: "I have so many aches and pains, I'm depressed, nobody cares about me," and on and on it goes.

But you know what? No matter what you are going through or what you are facing today, you can still glory in the fact that you are a child of God. He said He would never leave you nor forsake you. You are the apple of His eye. He has you in the palm of His hand. He's there to carry your every burden.

He has promised to be your strength, your comforter, your guide, your rest, your hope, your peace, your refuge, your victor, your healer, your advocate, your supplier...whatever you need, He will be.

Does your face show to others just what God is to you? Take a moment to think on those things and then, as the kid's song says, "If you're happy and you know it, then your face will surely show it." Reflect Him to others!

APRIL 20

God's Promises

"The son of the slave-wife was born in a human attempt to bring about the fulfillment of God's promise. But the son of the freeborn wife was born as God's own fulfillment of His promise." NLT

Galatians 4:23

In this text, Paul is talking about how Abraham and Sarah tried to make the promise of God come about with their own doing. God had promised him over twenty years earlier that he would be the father of many nations. So after all the waiting, they thought they would take matters into their own hands and try to make it happen. Abraham indeed did have a son with Sarah's servant, Hagar, but this was not the seed that God had promised.

Too many times we try to do the same thing with the promises that God gives us. We just don't want to wait for it to develop and we want to give Him a little help. Waiting is so hard for us to do. If you have a promise from God, hang onto that promise and believe that it will come in God's timing, not yours.

Have you ever baked a cake and it was smelling so good that you decided you would take it out of the oven before the time was up? I have! I even thought that my oven cooked faster than what the recipe called for and I wanted to have a piece! What a disappointment it was when I cut it and the middle was still runny. It looked so good on the outside and the smell had my taste buds expecting great things. But it turned out to be a flop. It just doesn't work that way.

Neither does it work that way with God. What He promises, He will deliver but in His own time. You can hold onto the promise and when it comes there will be resounding peace and unspeakable joy for you, knowing that you not only believed that it was coming, but that you waited until God said it was time.

APRIL 21

The Real You

"[16]All scripture is given by inspiration of God, and is profitable for doctrine, for reproof, for correction, for instruction in righteousness: [17]That the man of God may be perfect, thoroughly furnished unto all good works."

2 Timothy 3:16-17

Several years ago, at the beginning of the year, God impressed on me to do a personal Bible study, so I made a trip to the Christian Book Store and found a book entitled ***Women Overcoming Fear***. This is a 30-day Bible study, and it is very good. The author is Leighann McCoy.

It was quite a journey, and it wasn't always easy. There were sleepless nights and times of soul searching. Going through this study, I felt that God was bringing out fears in me that I had hidden from years before. God was being gentle with me—bringing out a few fears at a time, allowing me to deal with those before bringing up more that I needed to deal with. At times, I had even laid the study book aside for a while until I was ready to deal with more in my life that needed God's change.

God sees us different than we see ourselves. He sees potential in us that we never thought was there. He knows everything about us because He's the One who made us! We just need to start believing in who He says we can be and allow Him to help us change into that person.

If you decide to delve into a personal study, be prepared for God to speak to you. Allow Him to lead you to the right book, along with the Bible, and be determined to do what He asks you to do. It will take some soul searching and you, too, may have some sleepless nights. But you will be better as the real you comes forth.

NOTES

APRIL 22

Someone's Watching

".....God had richly blessed Obed-edom." NLT

I Chronicles 26:5b

In the above scripture, God had richly blessed Obed-edom. His children had surely seen the life that their father had lived before them as well as the blessings their household had received because the Ark of the Lord (or the presence of the Lord) had previously stayed at their house. (2 Samuel 6:11) And they had been a part of that blessing.

It's apparent that because of what they had seen in their father they became gatekeepers at the house of God themselves. How very important it is for us to live Godly lives, especially in our homes in front of our impressionable children.

Years ago, our son, Richie, preached at our church and as always, allowed time for him to pray for those who had a need at the end of the service. His young son, Trey, (almost 5 years old at the time) was sitting with me. Even though it didn't appear that he was paying attention to what his dad was doing, I soon realized that he was. He told me that he wanted to go up and let his dad pray for his stomach because it was hurting. Then several minutes later, he was finding people that he could pray for himself. It blessed my heart to see that not just because he was my grandson, but that his dad had made such a good impression on him, he wanted to do what Richie was doing.

Lord, let me always be impressionable for You and don't let my actions hinder my family, or others, from serving you.

APRIL 23

Greater is He

"Ye are of God, little children, and have overcome them: because greater is he that is in you, than he that is in the world."

I John 4:4

What a great encouraging verse! This is one of those verses that we need to quote to ourselves several times a day, especially when we are going through trials and tribulations.

When we face the difficult times, we just need to realize that God is greater than anything that we go through in our lives. And He is waiting for us to turn it over to Him, knowing that He is and will continue to be with us through it all.

◊ Greater is He that is in me (when I fail Him) than he that is in the world (who tells me that God is done with me).

◊ Greater is He that is in me (when I disobey Him) than he that is in the world (who tells me that God won't forgive me).

◊ Greater is He that is in me (when I struggle financially) than he that is in the world (who tells me that God will not meet my needs).

◊ Greater is He that is in me (when I am discouraged) than he that is in the world (who tells me that God doesn't care what I'm going through).

Anytime we struggle, we can be sure that the devil will be there to tempt us to turn against God and believe that He is not going to help us this time. But he is a liar as he always will be. God is greater than anything the devil tells us. Praise God!

APRIL 24

What Can I Do?

"Rejoice in our confident hope. Be patient in trouble, and keep on praying." NLT

Romans 12:12

Today would have been my father's 97th birthday. His residence was moved to heaven in March of 2021. That move was his life-long desire. That was what he lived for!

He was the patriarch of our family and we depended on his prayers. For years, he would get up between 3:00 and 4:00 AM and would pray for a minimum of six hours each day. That is dedication! When he would finish, he would spend several hours reading the Word of God. He told me on many occasions that every time he would read it, he would learn something new!

When we get older, we tend to think that we are no longer useful to the Kingdom of God. But that is simply not true! Just as my father did, you can pray, and you can read God's Word every day. Your family and those who you pray for need those prayers. And they need the counsel that you can give them from what you have learned from the Word of God.

Don't ever think that you are not important because you are! You still have purpose, that is why you are still here. Make prayer a priority and Bible reading a necessity in your life. No matter your age, you can, at the least, do these two things and be a blessing to others.

APRIL 25

Let Me See Through Your Eyes

"...for the Lord seeth not as man seeth; for man looketh on the outward appearance, but the Lord looketh on the heart."

I Samuel 16:7b

I read a quote this morning that is advice we all should follow. It said, "Don't look down on anyone unless you are admiring their shoes!" Too many times we are prone to think more highly of ourselves than we should, and we tend to look down on others, sometimes without even realizing that is what we are doing.

Take, for example, the clothes that some people wear to church that we "don't approve of." It may be the only "presentable" clothes that they have. We need to be thankful that they are there and can hear the Word of God.

Perhaps it's the homeless person on the street holding the cardboard sign asking for money. I know there are some that are trying to beat the system that could be working at a job instead of begging for food and/or money. But there are some that this is their only means of support.

Think about your own examples. Are you looking down on people because you feel you are better than they are? That is not how God wants us to think of them. We need to all realize that we could be in their situation had it not been for us turning to God. That's what they need to do themselves and we need to show them His love, not our pity and contempt. Lord, help us see them through Your eyes!

APRIL 26

The Link Between History and Destiny

"[5]He established a testimony in Jacob and appointed a law in Israel, which he commanded our fathers to teach to their children, [6]that the next generation might know them, the children yet unborn, and arise and tell them to their children." ESV

Psalm 78:5-6

A few months before my husband passed away in 2020, he gave a gift and a card to our son. The gift was his grandfather's Bible along with one that belonged to his father and one of his own. The card read in part "Always remember that you are the link between our history and our destiny."

That was quite a statement! In this case these were all great men of God, as is Richie. And he is the link to carry on the Christian heritage, to teach his sons to love God and live their lives for him so that they, too, can take it to the next generation.

What kind of legacy are you leaving for your children? Can they say that God is number one in your life? Do they see you lean on Him in times of trial? Do they know that they can trust Him too in every situation that comes up in their own lives? Do they hear you sing praises to God in the good and not so good times? Have you told them about how the former generations trusted God with everything? If not, it's time to start training them to understand that God wants that kind of relationship with them.

If you don't have a Godly heritage, you can start it yourself. Teach your children about how good God is and how much He loves them. When they get it down deep in their hearts then they can, in turn, teach it to the next generation and it will be carried to many more. Be that link, whether it's the first link or somewhere in the middle of the chain. It's our responsibility to teach them. Let's not let the chain be broken!

APRIL 27

I Can't!.....Or Can I?

"For nothing will be impossible with God." ESV

Luke 1:37

How many times have we given the excuse, "I can't", when God has asked us to do something? I hate to admit this, but I know I have been guilty multiple times.

Moses gave five excuses when God called him to be the one to lead the children of Israel out of Egypt. They are:

- ◊ Who am I that You'd call me to this task?
- ◊ What am I supposed to say?
- ◊ They won't believe me!
- ◊ I am not good at speaking; I have a speech impediment!
- ◊ Please send someone besides me!

God had an answer for every excuse that Moses gave. (I encourage you to read the third and fourth chapters of Exodus.) But He knew who Moses was and He knew that Moses was the man for the job! God feels the same about us. He's not looking for ability; He's looking for availability. If we are depending on our own strength to accomplish what God has called us to do, then we are not trusting in Him. This is the recipe for failure!

So, stop saying, "I can't" and start saying, "With God by my side, I can!" He will never fail you if you put your total trust in Him.

APRIL 28

Loose Him and Let Him Go

"And he that was dead came forth, bound hand and foot with graveclothes: and his face was bound about with a napkin. Jesus saith unto them, Loose him and let him go."

John 11:44

We all know the story in the above scripture text. Although Lazarus had already died and been buried, Jesus said that he was only sleeping and that he was going to awake him out of sleep.

As I pondered on this event, I began to relate Lazarus to people in the Christian world. God has placed spiritual gifts within each of us. But how many of us have bound and buried those talents and gifts that we possess, thinking that they are dead?

I have good news for you. You can speak to those things buried deep within you in Jesus' name; those things that God Himself has given you. Those talents are not dead; they are only sleeping.

Even though they may be bound, and you can't see or understand how God can use you through them because of the "napkin" covering your eyes, speak the same words that Jesus spoke concerning Lazarus, "Loose him (them) and let him (them) go." Ask God to awaken and loose those things bound in your heart so that you can use those talents to the fullest to glorify God!

APRIL 29

How Big is God in Your Eyes?

Jesus Christ the same yesterday, and to day, and for ever."

Hebrews 13:8

Are there times in your life when you see God different than you did the day before? I'm sure all of us have had those times! But we should remember what God has done and then realize that if He met our need yesterday, He will meet it today, tomorrow, and every other day!

Let's take, for example, that you had an extremely large bill due within the next few days. After doing all you could, you still had more month left than you did money. God then impresses on someone to give you the exact amount that you need without even knowing that you had a need. The next time you have a financial need do you remember the last time He supplied that need or do you worry and fret and forget that He's the same yesterday, today, and forever?

I can tell you this: God is not wringing His hands, and saying, "The 15th is coming, and we don't have the money to pay the light bill here in Heaven! What are we going to do?" I know that may be a silly analogy, but God does not worry, and neither should we!

It's true, you know! God is a big, big God and He is willing to meet our every need if we just come to Him and ask. Don't let the circumstances you may be facing become bigger in your eyes than the God that you serve. When you've done all you can, then stand on His Word and see what He will do!

APRIL 30

Be Still and Know

"Be still and know that I am God...."

Psalm 46:10a

Be still and know! The first two words are very important–BE STILL. That is a difficult thing for us to do in our world. There are so many times that our minds are just not at rest, and we can't even hear God through all the interruptions that we face. But God's peace will come if we take the time to listen to Him. The first step is to BE STILL!

- ◊ ***Be still and know*** that God will supply all your needs according to His riches in glory. Philippians 4:19
- ◊ ***Be still and know*** that you are more than conquerors through Him that loves you. Romans 8:37
- ◊ ***Be still and know*** that what God has promised, He is able to perform. Romans 4:21
- ◊ ***Be still and know*** that weeping may endure for a night, but joy comes in the morning. Psalm 30:5

In all the busyness and hustle-bustle of life, it is imperative to be still and listen to what God wants to tell you. You can't hear Him if your mind is too full of the things around you. Choose to give God some time every day and He will speak divine truths to you.

NOTES

MAY 1

A Tribute to Godly Mothers

"Charm is deceptive, and beauty is fleeting; but a woman who fears the Lord is to be praised." NIV

Proverbs 31:30

Since May is the month that we celebrate Mother's Day, we are going to be talking about mothers. I have included devotions honoring my own mother, daughter, and daughter-in-law, some Biblical mothers, and mothers in general. This first one was written by my husband, Rick.

Mother's Day is set aside to celebrate some very special ladies. In Proverbs 31, we can see ten characteristics of a Godly mother.

◊ ***She is virtuous.*** The conduct of a Godly mother sets the moral standard for the entire family.

◊ ***She is valuable.*** There is no higher position for a woman to fill than that of a loving wife and a Godly mother.

◊ ***She is trustworthy.*** A Godly mother is a symbol of trust in the home. She is trusted by her husband and her children.

◊ ***She is genuinely good.*** A Godly mother's actions are based on her love for her family.

◊ ***She is willing to labor for her family.*** A Godly mother doesn't consider her labors a chore but rather a privilege.

◊ ***She possesses endurance.*** Godly mothers are not governed by clocks, but by love and the needs of her family.

◊ ***She is compassionate.*** Godly mothers are always the first in extending a helping hand.

◊ ***She is supportive.*** A Godly mother carries on with her own work and supports the entire family in their ventures.

◊ ***She is strong.*** Godly mothers may never be able to lift 100 pounds, but she carries the world on her shoulders.

◊ ***She is a witness.*** The witness of Godly mothers is passed from generation to generation; her labor is not soon forgotten.

~ Rick Clendenen

MAY 2

Rubena Peal, the Training Mother

"Consequently, faith comes from hearing the message, and the message is heard through the word about Christ." NIV

Romans 10:17

I cannot talk about mothers without mentioning my own mama. She is no longer with us, but she left us with quite a legacy. Though there were many things that she taught me and my brother, I will tell you of one that still dwells with us today.

We were trained in the ways of the Lord all of our lives. It is because of our mother and father's Christian example that we are both living for God today, along with all the members of our families.

We were taken to church every Sunday morning, Sunday night, and Wednesday night, as well as any special services that our church had. We had no say in the matter; if there was a service, we went! But it was there that we met Jesus and chose to follow Him.

Giving us the love for attending church is just one thing that our mother (and father) did for us. How well are you doing in that area? Are you training your children to love the church, or do you allow them to make the decision of whether or not they attend service? Be that example and they will make church a priority in their lives.

MAY 3

Renee Owen, the Involved Mother

"For everything there is a season, a time for every activity under heaven." NLT

Ecclesiastes 3:1

This is my daughter, but she's more than that. She is the mother of my granddaughter, Kyndal. She is also a nurse, sings on the worship team at church, co-owns a business with her husband, Landon. You can see that she is a busy person!

But she takes time from her busy schedule to spend with Kyndal. There are things that only the two of them do together and that makes it a special time for them.

Kyndal is involved in a lot of different sports. Renee is at her games as much as she can be, cheering her on. Sometimes she must work, but she always wants updates of how the games are going either from me or from Landon. It is her desire to be involved in what Kyndal is doing.

The most important thing you can give your children, along with your love, is your time. They need to know that you will be right by their side if they need you, no matter what you are doing at the time.

Can you say that you are involved in your children's lives? Do they know that they are a priority to you? Make it a habit to spend time with each one of them and let them know just how important they are.

MAY 4

Jenny Clendenen, the Managing Mother

"For where your treasure is, there will your heart be also."
Luke 12:34

Jenny is my daughter-in-law and the mother of my grandsons, Trey and Liam. She is one of the most hospitable women that I know and loves to serve others, especially her family. I am amazed by how she can manage her time to take care of her family, and still work (she's a teacher) and be a full-time pastor's wife.

Even though she has other responsibilities that take up a lot of her time, she always puts her family first. Trey and Liam's needs are high on her priority list. I've seen her spend hours helping Trey with his homework, knowing that she will have to get up early to go to work the next morning. I know that she has gotten up in the middle of the night many times with Liam, with no complaints.

She reminds me of the Mary, the mother of Jesus, when the shepherds came to visit after Jesus was born. The Bible tells us that she kept all those things and pondered them in her heart. I'm sure Jenny has many moments like that, where she would ponder in her heart the many precious times with her sons.

Jenny is a very loving mother and manages to make time for both of her children. How are you doing at making sure you give time to yours? They are a gift from God; enjoy having them and taking time with them. They will love it and so will you!

MAY 5

Eve, the First Mother

"And Adam said, This is now bone of my bones, and flesh of my flesh: she shall be called Woman, because she was taken out of Man."

Genesis 2:23

The Bible does not give us much detail about Eve. What we do know is that she is the first woman, the first wife, and the first mother. The most memorable thing we know is that she was deceived by the serpent.

We just have to try and imagine what she was like. One website says that "she was an independent and strong-minded woman who, like all humans, was both creative and destructive, clever, and short-sighted." But this is just one person's supposition. We simply don't know how she was.

She did not have a mother to train her in the ways of a wife. This was uncharted territory for her. Neither did she have anyone to advise her on how to raise her children. No other woman with whom to share her fears and her joys.

In the third chapter of Genesis, she and Adam were banned from the Garden of Eden because of their disobedience and for believing in what the deceiver, Satan, had told them. It was after this occurred that Adam gave her the name, Eve, instead of Woman. Even though they gave in to the temptation, God was still with them and still provided for them.

We can be assured of the fact that God is always with us. We often feel like we are failing as mothers. But God is ever present, no matter what circumstances we are facing or situations in which we find ourselves. Just remember that His love for us far outweighs our self-proclaimed failures. He sees us much different than we see ourselves! Don't allow the deceiver to convince you otherwise.

MAY 6

Noah's Wife, the Supportive Mother

"Hear, my son, your father's instruction, and forsake not your mother's teaching," ESV

Proverbs 1:8

This woman was the wife of Noah, the famous builder of the Ark. She was also the mother of their three sons, Ham, Shem, and Japheth. We are not told very much at all about her. As a matter of fact, their entire story is told in only four chapters of Genesis.

If you will give me some room for supposition, these are a few of my thoughts on the wife of Noah.

◊ ***I believe*** that she was a strong supporter of her husband and that God found grace in her just as He did in Noah.

◊ ***I believe*** she was a Godly mother and that she helped Noah raise their boys to love and respect God.

◊ ***I believe*** she taught them to also respect their father and to be a help to him.

◊ ***I believe*** it was because of the example that she set in front of them that they believed that their father had heard from God, and they helped him build the ark.

◊ ***I believe*** that as she took her part in taking care of the animals inside the ark, and that her daughters-in-law followed her lead and did their part as well.

None of these may be true. But then, again, they could be! How many of these can you say that you do with your husband and children? Do you teach your children to love and respect God, as well as their father? Do you set a good example for them to follow? Can God say that He finds grace with you?

These are important questions that we must all consider. If we don't train our children in the way they should go, as we read in Proverbs 22:6, somebody else will. Will it be you or will it be the world? Take your God-given responsibility very serious!

MAY 7

Sarah, the Waiting Mother

"It was by faith that even Sarah was able to have a child, though she was barren and was too old. She believed that God would keep his promise." NLT

Hebrews 11:11

Sarah was the wife of the Patriarch, Abraham. They had been married for many, many years and she had been unable to conceive children. God had promised Abraham that he would be the father of many nations, but they had to wait 25 years before that promise was fulfilled.

In that time period, if a woman was past child-bearing age, she could give her consent for another woman to bear children from her husband and then, she would raise the child as her own. Since she was at that point in her life, this is what was on Sarah's mind when she offered her servant, Hagar, to Abraham. She did indeed give Abraham a son and named him Ishmael. But this was not God's promised seed.

Eventually, God did fulfill His promise and gave Sarah and Abraham a baby boy. He was named Isaac. But Ishmael began to make fun of him. This did not sit well with Sarah, and she demanded that Hagar and her son leave.

Have you had a time in your life that you tried to make God's promise come to pass before its time? As I'm sure you found out, that never works. God's time is different from ours and we must trust that God will bring it to pass in His perfect time.

NOTES

MAY 8

Rebekah, the Scheming Mother

"And Rebekah took goodly raiment of her eldest son Esau, which were with her in the house, and put them upon Jacob her younger son:"

Genesis 27:15

Rebekah was the wife of Isaac. She was barren for a while, but God heard their prayers, and she gave birth to twins, the first recorded in the Bible. Even before they were born, Jacob and Esau struggled in the womb, which continued at different times throughout their lives.

The meaning of Jacob's name is deceiver. Through a series of events, he was true to his name, even down to buying Esau's blessing, as the eldest son, with a bowl of pottage.

It was the custom in those days for the father to bless his sons when his death was near, with the eldest son receiving a double portion. It was no different with Isaac. But to prevent Esau from receiving the eldest son's blessing, Rebekah devised a scheme that it would go to Jacob instead of to Esau. So in this case, she, as well as her son, Jacob, were deceivers.

I certainly don't want to be known as a deceiver, especially in the ways of God. We must remember that our children are watching what we do and will often times, come to be just like us. Let's remember this very important point as we are raising our children. Pray for yourself to become everything that God wants you to be and then they will have a Godly example to follow.

MAY 9

Leah, the Unloved Mother

"How precious is your steadfast love, O God! The children of mankind take refuge in the shadow of your wings." ESV

Psalm 36:7

Scripture tells us that Jacob had fallen in love with Leah's sister, Rachel and thought that he was marrying her. He had worked seven years for their father, Laban, as payment for taking her as his wife. But Laban deceived Jacob and gave him Leah instead, under the guise of her being the older sister. We know that Jacob confronted his new father-in-law about this. He did give Rachel to him a week later, but Joseph worked another seven years for her.

Even though Leah was married to Jacob, she knew that he loved Rachel more than herself. Because of this, according to Genesis 29:31, God opened Leah's womb and she birthed six sons to Jacob. She made statements when they were born, such as, "Surely the Lord hath looked upon my affliction; now therefore my husband will love me," "Because the Lord hath heard I was hated, he hath therefore given me this son also," and "Now this time will my husband be joined unto me, because I have born him three sons."

Leah made the mistake of trying to make Jacob love her through her children, and that never works. She was trying to find her identity through them; she had to learn that it comes from God alone. She finally realized that when she had her fourth son when she said, "Now will I praise the Lord."

We, too, must learn to find our identity in God. He loves us more than we can even imagine and sees us as much more than we see ourselves. Believe that the God of the universe thinks you are something special… because you are!

MAY 10

Rachel, the Questioning Mother

"If you need wisdom, ask our generous God, and he will give it to you. He will not rebuke you for asking." NLT

James 1:5

Even though Rachel was the wife of Jacob, a patriarch of the Bible, we are not given a lot of information about her as a mother. I wonder how much she questioned God throughout her life.

After hearing the dreams of Joseph (Genesis 37), did she ask God if these were truly from Him? Did she really believe that God would exalt him above all his brothers? Did she see the reaction that the brothers had toward Joseph's dreams?

Did she question God about the jealously of the brothers toward Joseph because he was the favorite son? Was she concerned that this would eventually cause problems between them?

She must have been heartbroken when she saw Joseph's coat covered in blood. (The incident itself is also recorded in Genesis 37. Her reaction is not recorded in the Bible.) Did she question God about taking her son after she had waited so many years to be a mother?

Did you know that there is nothing wrong with asking God questions? He may not answer us in the way we want to hear but the secret is to completely trust Him, no matter the result. He really does know what's best!

MAY 11

Jochebed, the Believing Mother

"When I am afraid, I put my trust in you." ESV

Psalm 56:3

Jochebed was the mother of Miriam, Aaron, and Moses. She gave birth to Moses during the time that Pharaoh feared that the Israelites would become too powerful, so he decreed that all baby boys be thrown into the river.

After hiding Moses for three months, Jochebed, not wanting her baby boy to be killed, made a waterproof basket, and put Moses in it, placing it among the reeds in the river. While bathing close by, Pharaoh's daughter heard his cries and ordered that the basket be brought to her. When she saw him, she chose to keep him as her own. Upon this discovery, Miriam was watching nearby and asked her if she needed an Israelite woman to care for him, which she agreed to.

Not only was Jochebed able to nurse and care for her own son for a period of time, but Pharaoh's daughter also paid her wages to do it! Jochebed was simply trying to save her son from imminent death, but God had bigger plans for Moses.

God also has big plans for each of our lives. We don't know how He will work them out, our job is to believe that He will! Find peace and strength in knowing that He will bring those plans to fruition if we only believe in Him.

MAY 12

Hannah, the Prayerful Mother

"For therein is the righteousness of God revealed from faith to faith: as it is written, The just shall live by faith."

Romans 1:17

Hannah was one of two wives of Elkanah, but she was barren. The other wife, Peninnah, had several children and made fun of Hannah because she had none. Not being able to bear children was quite the reproach and could be a cause of divorce in that time.

Each year, Elkanah would travel to Shiloh with his family to worship the Lord and to offer sacrifices. On one particular year, Hannah chose to go to the tabernacle and with great anguish, pray for God to give her a son. She made a vow to Him that if He would answer her prayer, she would give him back to God to be His servant.

As we all know, God did answer her prayer. And, after weaning her son, Samuel, she did give him to the priest, Eli, to serve him. This was her response to God, found in 1 Samuel 1:27-28: "[27]For this child I prayed; and the Lord hath given me my petition which I asked of him: [28]Therefore also I have lent him to the Lord; as long as he liveth he shall be lent to the Lord. And he worshipped the Lord there."

Hannah had faith that God would hear her prayer. How is your faith level? Do you truly believe that He will hear you when you pray? I can tell you that He will! He cares about our every need, and He wants us to bring them to Him.

MAY 13

Naomi, the Grieving Mother

"Blessed are those who mourn, for they will be comforted." ESV

Matthew 5:4

The next mother I want to talk about is Naomi. She lived in Bethlehem with her husband, Elimelech, and their two sons, Mahlon and Kilion.

When a famine came to their area they moved to Moab; the sons were married while they lived there. But tragedy hit as Naomi's husband, as well as both of their sons, died. This left her and the two daughters-in-law, Orpah and Ruth, as widows.

Naomi heard that the famine was over at home, and she decided to return there. Orpah chose to stay in Moab, but Ruth went with her mother-in-law. Even though Naomi was grieving, she found it in her heart to advise Ruth concerning Boaz. She chose to not dwell in her grief; she realized that she still had breath, so she still had purpose.

What about you? Have you lost your purpose because of tragedy that has come near your door? Jesus desires for you to find your God-given purpose and to fulfill it to the fullest.

MAY 14

Bathsheba, the Forgiven Mother

"If we confess our sins, he is faithful and just to forgive us our sins, and to cleanse us from all unrighteousness."

I John 1:9

Bathsheba and King David committed a terrible sin which resulted in the death of her husband, Uriah. I'll give the main points here of her story.

The eleventh chapter of 2 Samuel tells us that David sent Joab and his army to battle, but he chose to stay home. In verses 2-4, he goes out to his roof and sees Bathsheba bathing. He thought she was very beautiful and had his servant to summon her to come to see him. He and Bathsheba lay together and she became pregnant. David decided to have Uriah killed so he could marry Bathsheba and cover up their sin.

The plan worked and Uriah died in battle, making it possible for David to have Bathsheba as his wife. But that's not the end of the story. She delivered the baby boy, but he became very ill and eventually died.

We can only assume that Bathsheba agreed with David in the plan to kill Uriah. So she and David were both participants in the sin of adultery and of murder. The Bible doesn't tell us that she asked forgiveness from God, but we know that David did. God did indeed forgive them because later on, Bathsheba gave birth to a son named Solomon, who was in the lineage of Jesus Christ!

Do you think that you have committed a sin so great that God will not forgive you? That He could not love you after what you have done? That is just not possible because God not only loves, but He is love! He can and He will forgive, and you don't have to live your life in condemnation anymore. He's waiting to hear from you!

NOTES

MAY 15

Elizabeth, the Favored Mother

"Let the favor of the Lord our God be upon us, and establish the work of our hands upon us; yes, establish the work of our hands!" ESV

Psalm 90:17

I want to mention three mothers found in the New Testament. The first one I think of is Elizabeth. She is the wife of Zecharias and the mother of John.

Even though Zecharias and Elizabeth were old and past child-bearing age, God made it possible for them to have a baby, whose name would be John. Upon becoming pregnant, we find her response to it in Luke 1:25 NIV, "The Lord has done this for me, she said. In these days he has shown his favor and taken away my disgrace among the people."

Not only was Elizabeth the mother of the forerunner of Jesus, but she was also the one to whom Mary shared the news that she would give birth to the Saviour. She was truly favored by God!

None of us know exactly how we will be used by God. He chose Elizabeth to be the mother of the one that would announce Jesus to the world. But He also chooses us for amazing things as well. Don't reject the call of God; you never know when He will show us His favor and we will be the witness of Jesus that someone needs to hear. What a privilege!

MAY 16

Mary, *the Blessed Mother*

"And the angel came in unto her, and said,
Hail, thou that art highly favoured,
the Lord is with thee:
blessed art thou among women."
Luke 1:28

I cannot imagine how Mary felt when she saw the angel, Gabriel, and he began to talk to her. How did she really feel when he told her that she would soon become the mother of the Son of God?

We can see in verse 28 of the first chapter of Luke that she was highly favored and was blessed among women. That's why she was chosen to be the mother of Jesus! Mary didn't waver in her decision to follow God. We find her response to Gabriel's announcement to her in Luke 1:38, "And Mary said, Behold the handmaid of the Lord; be it unto me according to thy word. And the angel departed from her."

Is that your response when He calls you? Do you answer Him with, "I will do what you have called me to do" or do you try to convince God that someone else would be better for the task at hand? We need to take Mary's lead and trust that He will guide us where He wants us to go and will continue to be with us along the way. There's no other choice that we should make other than to follow where God chooses for us to go. Don't you agree?

MAY 17

Eunice, the Faith-Filled Mother

"I am reminded of your sincere faith, a faith that dwelt first in your grandmother Lois and your mother Eunice and now, I am sure, dwells in you as well." ESV

2 Timothy 1:5

There is not very much at all about the mother of Timothy in the Bible. She is only mentioned by her name in the above verse. It tells us that she was taught about God by her mother, Lois, and she followed her example and taught Timothy about Him as well.

She's also alluded to in Acts 16:1 as the mother of Timothy, without giving her name. This verse lets us know that she was Jewish and was a believer. Even though her name is only listed in one place in the Bible, her influence was great on her son. Because of Eunice and her mother, Lois, Timothy grew into the man that was chosen as a traveling missionary and became a companion to Paul.

I pray that my life has influenced my children and grandchildren to live for God their entire lives. I want them to know that He will guide and direct them in the path that they should take. Can your children and grandchildren say that about you?

MAY 18

Mother of David, the Shunned Mother

*"For the Lord will not reject his people;
he will never forsake his inheritance."* NIV

Psalm 94:14

There are many mothers that their names are not given in the Bible. But they are nonetheless important. For the next several days, we will be looking at some of them. The first one I'd like to look at is the mother of David.

Her name is never mentioned in scripture, but Jewish history tells us that it was Nitzevet. Several scenarios are given by different theologians of the relationship between her and her husband, Jesse. But for some reason, neither she, nor her son, David, were considered an important part of the family and they both were shunned by them.

David tells us in Psalm 86:16 that his mother served God and he obviously learned to do the same through her. "Turn to me and have mercy on me; show your strength in behalf of your servant; save me, because I serve you just as my mother did." NIV

That's just how Christian mothers have trained their children throughout history; they train by example. Even though they may be shunned in the world, they make sure their children know God for themselves and will be fully accepted by Him. Can you say that you are training your own children in this way?

MAY 19

The Widow at Zarephath, the Trusting Mother

"Thou wilt keep him in perfect peace, whose mind is stayed on thee: because he trusteth in thee."

Isaiah 26:3

We are not told the name of this mother. Neither are we told what happened to her husband, nor how long she had been a widow. We do know that she had a son. She first comes on the scene during the time of a famine.

God instructed Elijah to go to Zarephath and that there would be a widow there that would sustain him. He did indeed find her and asked her for some water and a morsel of bread. She then told him that she was going to fix food for her and her son and then they would starve to death. Elijah asked her to first fix him a cake, which she did. Because she trusted Elijah and did what he had asked, God gave her an unending supply of oil and meal until the famine was over.

Later, her son became very sick and died. Because of her trust in Elijah and in his God, she went in search of him. Upon finding Elijah, he went with her, prayed over her son, and he was restored to life. This proved to her that she could truly trust Elijah, as well as God.

We can also trust God during the famine times that we encounter. No matter what we face or where we find ourselves, we can trust that He will be with us every step of the way. What a comfort it is when we learn this important lesson. He is trustworthy!

MAY 20

Mother of the Living, the Sacrificing Mother

Then the king answered and said, Give her the living child, and in no wise slay it: she is the mother thereof.

I Kings 3:27

There were two mothers that came to Solomon, seeking his wisdom. They each had a child and during the night, one of them rolled over onto her own child and accidently smothered him. So while the other mother slept, she switched the babies.

They each claimed that the baby that was alive belonged to her. Solomon listened to each one's story, and then asked for a sword to be brought to him. He said to divide the baby and each one could have half. One of the mothers agreed that this was a good idea, but the true mother cried out to give him to the other mother. At this point, knowing that this was truly the mother, he ordered that the baby be given to her. This mother knew her child and she knew the other mother was lying. She was willing to sacrifice her motherhood for the sake of saving his life.

The Bible does not record who this baby became because his mother saved his life. And neither do we know who our children will be; that is not our decision to make. Our job is to train them up in the admonition of the Lord and when they are old, they will not depart from it. Trust God with the future!

MAY 21

The Mother of the Boy with the Lunch, the Caring Mother

"No one should seek their own good, but the good of others." NIV

I Corinthians 10:24

I have wondered a lot of times about this mother. She packed the lunch for her son, not realizing that her labor of love would be used to display a miracle at the hands of Jesus.

We all know the story. Jesus had taught the people, healing the sick, all day! Evening came and He knew they were getting hungry. So He told the disciples to go and buy food for them. (John 6) They encountered a young boy that gave them his lunch. Jesus blessed this and fed over 5,000 that day with two loaves and five fish. And there were twelve baskets of food left over!

This young boy's mother is never mentioned in the Bible but there are lots of questions in my mind about her. Was she actually in the crowd that was fed that day? She was certainly part of the miracle. Was it her idea for her son to give his lunch to the disciples or did he do that on his own? What did the disciples do with what remained? I've wondered if they gave the leftovers to the young boy; did they help him carry it home? What did the mother think of that?

Have you ever been part of a miracle for someone else? This mother did not know that, because of caring for the needs of her son, she would also be meeting the needs of so many more. Who knows? You may even wake up in the morning and be used by God to be a blessing to others without you even knowing about it! All it takes is to be willing to be a useful vessel for Him and heed His voice. May our prayer be, "Lord, use me for your glory. Allow me to be a part of a miracle for someone today!"

NOTES

MAY 22

The Mother From Nain, the Thankful Mother

"Blessed be the Lord, who daily loadeth us with benefits, even the God of our salvation. Selah."

Psalm 68:19

One day, as Jesus and His followers were entering the town of Nain, they met a funeral procession of the son of a widow who lived there. Scripture does not give us very much information about her. What we do know is that Jesus had compassion on her because her only son had died. He stopped the procession and told her not to weep. What He did next surely brought her great joy, but also gave fear to some. He touched the casket and told her son to arise. He sat up and began to speak!

I'm sure this mother experienced intense grief by losing her only son. This was followed by a sense of awe as her son was given back to her. But she also glorified God for what she had just received according to Luke 7:15.

We must never forget to give God praise for His grace, His goodness, His kindness, His benefits, His __________.

(Fill in the blank for your own situation).

He deserves all the praise!

MAY 23

The Secure Mother

"I can do all things through Christ which strengtheneth me."
Philippians 4:13

For the remainder of the month of May, I want to talk about mothers in general. I would venture to say that most of us have questioned whether we even qualify to be a mother. There are so many responsibilities that a mother has and so many things that are expected of her.

But I believe that every mother has an intuition that is given to her when her baby is born. It just seems that she knows what to do when situations arise. I also believe that comes from God.

God made us to specifically know how to care for the little ones that He puts in our care. That is why babies are so attached to their mother in the beginning years of their life. The mother is usually the primary caregiver, and the baby will often look for her when he or she has a need.

Are you secure in your calling as a mother? Never doubt that you can take care of that baby; He has given you what you need to care for him or her. Trust that God knew what He was doing when you gave you that precious gift! You've got this, Mama!

MAY 24

The Appreciated Mother

"Thy father and thy mother shall be glad, and she that bare thee shall rejoice."

Proverbs 23:25

The story is told of a young boy that felt he should receive money for everything he did around the house. It read something like this:

For cutting the grass: $5.00
For cleaning up my room this week: $1.00
For going to the store for you: $0.50
Babysitting my kid brother while you went shopping: $0.25
Taking out the garbage: $1.00
For getting a good report card: $5.00
For cleaning up and raking the yard: $2.00
Total owed: $14.75

His mother read the list, turned it over, and wrote the following:

For 9 months I carried you while you were growing inside me: No Charge.

For all the nights that I've sat up with you, took care of your illnesses, and prayed for you: No Charge.

For all the trying times, and all the tears that you've caused through the years: No Charge.

For all the nights that were filled with dread, and for the worries I knew were and still are ahead: No Charge.

> For the toys, food, clothes, changing of diapers and even wiping your nose: No Charge.

The son read it, and with tears in his eyes, he wrote in big letters across his list, **"PAID IN FULL!"**

Mothers do much more than is noticed. If you still have your mother with you, give her a call and let her know how much you appreciate her. It'll make her day and bring a smile to her face!

MAY 25

The Understanding Mother

"Whoever is slow to anger has great understanding, but he who has a hasty temper exalts folly." ESV

Proverbs 14:29

There is a Jewish proverb that states, "A mother understands what a child does not say." That is so true.

There are times when a child will be going through something in their life and try to hide it from their mother. But she can usually see through that façade and know that there is something going on. And she will usually find out from them what it is.

It is always good to have a mother that will make time for you in those discouraging moments that we all go through. She will most likely understand what you tell her because she has probably been through it herself.

Even after you are an adult, having a good relationship with your mother is so important to her. Mothers tend to feel useless when her children don't make time for her. She feels that she is no longer needed in your life.

So decide today to contact your mother. Make it a daily habit. She is a very special person in your life, and she needs to hear from you. She will always be your mother and she will always need your love.

MAY 26

The Encouraging Mother

"Therefore encourage one another with these words." ESV

I Thessalonians 4:18

No matter how old your children are, they need encouragement. And that coming from their mother (or father for that matter) makes it all the better.

Encouragement, especially to a child, is very important. It gives them self-esteem and will let them know that they can do what they thought was impossible if they know that those closest to them have faith in what they do.

Here are a few ways you can give encouragement to your child:

- ◊ Show interest in what they are interested in
- ◊ Stop what you are doing if they want to spend time with you
- ◊ Talk with them often about what they want to talk about
- ◊ Plan times to spend with them doing what they want to do
- ◊ Tell them how well they are doing in school
- ◊ Hug on them and tell them you love them…often!

This is a short list; come up with your own list that will suit your children. You will be amazed at how they will respond to you when they hear your encouragement. They need to know that you are proud of who they are.

This quote from Chuck Swindoll really says it all, "Encouragement is awesome. It can change the course of another person's day, week, or life." Be an encourager to your children today-it'll make a big difference!

MAY 27

The Grateful Mother

"Children are a gift from the Lord;
they are a reward from him." NLT

Psalm 127:3

Being a mother is one of the most precious callings in the world. It is also one of the most challenging.

The first few months of mothering is a time that this new little one depends on the mother for almost everything. I know there are people that help with him or her but most of the time, their physical needs are supplied by the mother. It gets tiring but what a reward comes with it.

A mother's many jobs include being a comforter, a nurse, a teacher, a consoler, a protector, a fixer, a cook, a caregiver, a housekeeper, a taxi driver, a psychologist, a discipliner, among many others. And a lot of these come with seemingly no appreciation for all she does.

I am so grateful to God for the two children that Rick and I had the privilege of raising. To me, there is no greater privilege than to be a mother. My heart is overwhelmed as I see them and their families all serving God in some capacity. I just pray that I had a small part in getting them to the place they are today.

Even though you may be going through a hard time right now as a mother, you still can be grateful for the blessings that God has given you in your children. Never look at them as a burden, but as a blessing. One day you will be able to see the reward for your labors as they grow into who God has made them to be. And your heart will be filled with peace and joy because you are their mother!

MAY 28

The Loving Mother

"Most important of all, continue to show deep love for each other, for love covers a multitude of sins." NLT

I Peter 4:8

A mother's heart is filled with love for each of her children. It's amazing how she can have so much of it in her heart for them, no matter how many children she has.

It doesn't matter their ages; a mother's love remains. It has been said that a child will pull on their mother's apron strings when they are young, but as they grow older, they will pull on their mother's heart strings. A mother will love their children throughout their lives.

It is very important that our children know that we love them. Even when they make mistakes, and they will make them, they need to know that we still love them and that nothing can take that love away.

One of the greatest challenges of a mother is to cut the apron strings and allow their children to "fly on their own." When a mother eagle thinks it's time for their young to learn to fly, they will nudge them out of the nest and swoop under them to catch them until they do learn. That's the way it is with us. We gently push our children to try out their wings, knowing that if they fall, we will always be there to catch them.

Love your children, teach them in the ways of the Lord, then allow them to fly to greater heights than you will ever go. That is what true motherly love is all about.

MAY 29

The Listening Mother

"Understand this, my dear brothers and sisters: You must all be quick to listen, slow to speak, and slow to get angry." NLT

James 1:19

There are several traits of a great mother; one important one is to have a listening ear. As your children grow older and face issues in their lives, they will be more apt to discuss things with you if they know you are always willing to listen to them when they want to talk.

Here are several things that a listening mother should do:

- ◊ ***Don't do all the talking.*** Allow your child to talk too.
- ◊ ***Really listen.*** They probably have some legitimate concerns.
- ◊ ***Don't interrupt while they are talking.*** What they have to say is important.
- ◊ ***Take an interest in what is being said.*** Look at them while they are talking to you.
- ◊ ***Take time to explain*** if their ideas are good ones or bad ones. Don't just say, "Because I said so" or "Because I'm older than you and know what should be done."
- ◊ ***You are the authority and what you say is the final word.*** But this is better accepted if they know you will listen when they talk to you.
- ◊ ***End your discussions with prayer*** if there has been a problem that needed to be addressed, as well as a hug, and an "I love you!"

These are just a few basic instructions on how to listen when your children want to talk to you. Knowing they can come to you with the small stuff, will make them know that you will be available to talk when the big stuff comes along.

Remember that **LISTEN** and **SILENT** are spelled with the same letters! Now that's something to ponder on.

MAY 30

The Far-Sighted Mother

"She opens her mouth with wisdom, and the teaching of kindness is on her tongue." ESV

Proverbs 31:26

When we see the phrase, far-sighted, we often relate it to the eyes. This devotion is not about the physical eye, but the mind's eye.

When I say, the far-sighted mother, I mean that this mother can see the qualities and traits in each of her children and what they can become in their future. She knows the potential that lies within each one to reach the goals that they will eventually set for themselves.

A lot of times, especially as the children grow older, they feel that they are a failure or can't seem to find direction for their lives. It is in those times that the far-sighted mother can begin to plant seeds of expectancy and possibilities in their minds. They will soon gain the confidence they need to believe in themselves.

Build confidence in those children at a young age. With your words of encouragement, they will learn that they can fulfill whatever God has placed in their hearts. What you saw in them when they were young will become reality!

MAY 31

The Special Mother

"He healeth the broken in heart, and bindeth up their wounds."
Psalm 147:3

I want to dedicate this devotion to those special mothers that were not able to hold their precious little one in their arms or that only had them for a short time.

To those mothers who had miscarriages, I don't have the answer to your questions. I don't know why you did not carry them full-term. I don't know why you suffered that tremendous loss. I don't know why you have to face the times that you put on a smile when your friends give birth, but your heart is breaking in two because you didn't. The thing I do know is that God sees you and feels every pain that you are feeling. It is so important to allow Him to help you through this process.

To those who are grieving the death of their child. I don't know why that precious little one only lived for a little while. I don't know why that child passed away at such a young age, leaving you with the many questions about them in your mind. I don't know why you must deal with the hurt you feel when you see other mothers carrying and loving on their own child, and you no longer can! The thing I do know is that God cares. Even when you feel like He is nowhere around, He is carrying you through this difficult time.

Even though you are not able to hold and nurture your baby, you are still a mother, a special mother. You will one day be able to see your baby again if you have accepted Jesus as Lord and Savior. Climb up in His lap, lean against His chest, and allow Him to heal your hurting heart. You don't have to carry that heavy burden alone. He's waiting on you with open arms; He's nearer than you think!

NOTES

JUNE 1

Eugene Peal, the Godly Father

"In all things shewing thyself a pattern of good works: in doctrine shewing uncorruptness, gravity, sincerity,"

Titus 2:7

You should have just finished reading the devotions for May that were about mothers. We are going to do the same for fathers since this month has been set apart for honoring them. I will begin with my own father.

Eugene Peal was a very unique man and he was a Godly man. Anyone that knew him would tell you that. My dad was quite the intercessor! As I already mentioned in the devotion on April 24, the minimum that he prayed every day was six hours! He believed in prayer and everyone in our family trusted in those prayers. He was the first one we turned to when we had difficult times in our lives because we knew he would take it to the Lord.

My dad had polio when he was just a child, but that never hindered him from doing what needed to be done. He even helped my mom build our house, climbing on top of it to put up the rafters and roof. They also built two different churches during their years of ministry. So, polio was not a hinderance when it came to working for God. There's so much more I could say about this wonderful man, but this book would not hold all the great attributes.

What kind of heritage are you leaving for the next generation? Can they see Jesus shining through you and can they turn to you when they need spiritual guidance? If not, start today. Get into the Word of God and begin to pray every day. Then you will have something to leave your family when your time comes to move to Heaven. That's what it's all about!

JUNE 2

Rick Clendenen, the Loving Father

"Beloved, let us love one another: for love is of God; and every one that loveth is born of God, and knoweth God."

I John 4:7

My husband, Rick, was a very loving father, father-in-law, and grandfather. He loved his family with all his heart, and every one of us felt that love coming from him. That is one reason why Rick's death was so overwhelming to each of us.

In one of his Father's Day messages, Rick brought out requirements for a loving father. I'd like to present them to you here:

- ◊ **He has a love relationship with Jesus.** This certainly describes Rick. His love for Jesus, above any other, could be plainly seen by all who knew him.
- ◊ **He makes his family a priority.** Rick's priority list began with Jesus, but his family was next. We were extremely important to him, and he had a deep love for us.
- ◊ **He teaches his family the love of God.** This was just what Rick did. He trained us and taught us about the ways of the Lord.
- ◊ **He is consistent.** We never had to worry about Rick acting one way in front of others and a different way in front of us. He was the same whoever he was with.
- ◊ **He listens to his children.** This was something that Rick definitely did. He told them that he was available anytime they needed him. And he would listen to what they had to say.

- ◊ **He makes the salvation of his family his ultimate goal.** Rick was successful in this requirement. He lived his life in such a way that his family wanted to serve God, just as he did.

Anyone that knew Rick Clendenen, knew that he was a person who loved. He loved Jesus first, then his family, and then so many others that found their way into his heart.

Take his example and love those around you. Only then, when they know you love them, can you lead them to Jesus.

JUNE 3

Richie Clendenen, the Humble Father

"He guides the humble in what is right and teaches them his way." ESV

Psalm 25:9

A humble father seeks no praise even though he does so much for others. He knows that he is not perfect but strives to be the best that he can be. A humble father will put the needs of his children above his own personal needs. A humble father values his time but does not mind giving of that time to his children.

My son, Richie, is such a humble man in his approach to being a father to Trey and Liam, his two sons. Richie is particularly good at spending time with both of them individually. Instead of "me" time, he has "we" time. Letting them know how important they are to him, either by word or by action, is something that they will always remember! That is an attribute of humility.

Richie has had a tender heart and a humble attitude toward people since he was a child. Not only is it evident in his time with his sons, but it also shows in his position as pastor. He deeply cares for the people in the church as well as those in the community. He wants no accolades for whatever he does for any of them; he does not do any of it to be noticed. That is being humble.

A humble father knows that he must have God's help because he cannot meet all the needs of his children without it. And that is the secret to being a humble father: Always depend on God to do what you cannot do!

JUNE 4

Landon Owen, the Dedicated Father

"Those who fear the Lord are secure;
he will be a refuge for their children."

Proverbs 14:26

Landon is my son-in-law and is dad to my granddaughter, Kyndal. He is a great father and has always been. Since her birth, my husband and I have often commented on how dedicated he is to her.

According to the Cambridge Dictionary, the definition of dedicated is, "believing that something is very important and giving a lot of time and energy to it." This perfectly describes how Landon feels about his daughter. He is absolutely dedicated to Kyndal.

Landon took the job of being a father very seriously; he has spent valuable time with her from the time she was born. He has attended important programs at school, helped her with homework, went out of his way to make sure her needs were met. He supported her in her sports adventures and attended her games. But not only is he dedicated to all that she participates in, he is adamant that she will be in church, and he is dedicated to training her to live for Jesus. This is the most important thing a father could do for their child.

If you had a dedicated father, then take time to thank him for all he has done for you. If your father was absent, then you need to know that your Heavenly Father will always be there for you. He will be your everything if you will allow Him to be. Just remember this: He not only believes, but He knows that you are especially important and He is willing to give His time and energy to you. He loves you that much!

JUNE 5

God, the Heavenly Father

"O Lord, there is none like thee, neither is there any God beside thee, according to all that we have heard with our ears."

I Chronicles 17:20

The most important father anyone should have in their lives is God, our Heavenly Father. We must remember that we are nothing without Him!

Even though He knew of the pain and extreme suffering that Jesus would endure, He loved us so much that He sent His only begotten Son to earth so that we may have a way of escape from this world of sin. For that, we can be eternally grateful.

There are many, many attributes of God, the Father. Here is a list of just a very few of them, along with scripture references that you can read:

- ◊ **Love**-1 John 4:7-8
- ◊ **Compassionate**-Psalm 86:15
- ◊ **Faithful**-1 Corinthians 1:9
- ◊ **Merciful**-Psalm 103:8
- ◊ **Good**-Psalm 145:9
- ◊ **Righteous**-Psalm 145:17
- ◊ **Caring**-1 Peter 5:7
- ◊ **Powerful**-Psalm 147:5
- ◊ **Ever Present**-Proverbs 15:3

This is only a brief list describing God the Father. Take time and make your own list of what He means to you. And then, you, too, can sum it all up into one phrase: God is everything! Everything you will ever need, in every situation that you face, everywhere that you go, He is with you.

What a great assurance to know He is all these things and much, much more! Thank you, God for being a wonderful Father! I would not want to do life without You!

JUNE 6

Adam, the First Father

"So God created man in his own image, in the image of God created he him; male and female created he them."

Genesis 1:27

We all know that Adam was the very first father as recorded in the book of Genesis. Being formed by God, he and his wife, Eve are the only humans without mother and father.

God gave Adam the task of naming every animal as they passed before him, making him the first zoologist. He was also the first landscaper and horticulturist, as he tended the plants and trees, as well as taking care of the garden.

Because Adam and Eve both ate of the forbidden fruit, sin entered the earth, and Adam became the first man to sin. As we all know, this caused them, for one thing, to be banned from the Garden of Eden forever. It was after this occurred that Adam became the first father when Cain, and subsequent children, were born.

Adam seemed to have it made while he and Eve were in the Garden of Eden. But the deceiver finally persuaded them to believe a lie and they lost everything: their home, their uncomplicated way of life, abundant food, and most important sweet daily communion with God. Adam and Eve lost all of this, but God still took care of them. It is the same with us. Even though we choose to stray from God, He is there to forgive us and bring us back to right fellowship with Him. Choose today to turn from your sin and turn to God.

JUNE 7

Noah, the Persistent Father

"To those who by persistence in doing good seek glory, honor and immortality, he will give eternal life." NIV

Romans 2:7

God spoke to Noah about building the ark; he chose to obey His word and began to work on it. Historians do not agree on how long it took Noah and his sons to build the ark, but from what I could find in my research, it was between 75-120 years.

No matter how long it took, that is a long time to work on a project! As we read in Genesis 6:8, Noah found grace in the eyes of the Lord. He was a just man and God chose him to build the ark.

Noah obeyed what God told him and he was certainly persistent in following God's instruction. Who of us would work for that many years, seeing no end in sight? I tend to believe that Noah did not waver from his calling because he was the one that received the word from God. His three sons most likely trusted their father enough to help him continue the work.

We can learn from Noah that when we have a word from God, we should be persistent in following what He tells us to do. And, if we are, we will see results and victory from obeying that Word. It is as simple as that!

NOTES

JUNE 8

Abraham, the Faith-Filled Father

"That your faith should not stand in the wisdom of men, but in the power of God."

I Corinthians 2:5

Not only do we find the story of Adam in the book of Genesis, but we can also read about Abraham. He was the faithful patriarch of Israel and was known as the father of the faithful.

Here is a list of Abraham's attributes, found in Genesis 22:1-18:

◊ **He was a man of prayer.** Vs. 1-2-Abraham had talked with the Lord enough to know His voice when He spoke His name.

◊ **He was obedient.** Vs. 3-Abraham was willing to submit to the will of God.

◊ **He was a leader in worship.** Vs. 4-5-Abraham was willing to take his responsibility as a leader in worship.

◊ **He was trustworthy.** Vs. 7-8-Abraham had so won the confidence of Isaac, that just a spoken word was enough to calm his heart.

◊ **He had proper priorities.** Vs. 9-10-Abraham had his life in proper priority; God was first and then his family.

◊ **He produced sacrificial provision.** Vs. 10-12-Abraham had provided all that he was able to provide, and God provided the rest.

◊ **He was a man of blessing.** Vs. 17-18-Abraham, because of his relationship with God, has been remembered as the father of the faithful.

These are not only attributes of Abraham but are fitting examples of a faith-filled father. They are fathers that will see victory in their lives, as well as the lives of their families.

~ Rick Clendenen

JUNE 9

Isaac, the Trusting Father

"But blessed is the one who trusts in the Lord, whose confidence is in him." NIV

Jeremiah 17:7

Not only was Isaac a trusting father, but he was first a trusting son. We know the story of how God tested Abraham's faith and asked him to sacrifice his son, Isaac. I have often thought about what was on Isaac's mind when his father placed him on the altar in place of the animal. But God found Abraham faithful and provided a ram for the sacrifice, instead of Isaac. He could have easily run away; Abraham was over 100 years old at this time and he would not have been able to chase him down. But he trusted Abraham and obeyed what he said.

The Bible does not tell us much about the childhood, or early adulthood, of Isaac. What we do know is that Abraham sent his servant to choose a wife for his son from the land where they were from. Neither are we told if Isaac was aware of this venture. But he did trust the servant because he took Rebekah as his wife. And it seems that he trusted God throughout his life.

Trust, especially in God, is something that a father must teach to his children. The way to do that is to portray it in front of them. If they see that you trust God, then they will learn that they, too, can trust Him in everything that they face.

JUNE 10

Jacob, the Changed Father

"Therefore if any man be in Christ, he is a new creature: old things are passed away; behold, all things are become new."

2 Corinthians 5:17

The name, Jacob, means supplanter, or "something or someone who wrongfully takes the place of another." Jacob used deception much of his young adult life to "wrongfully take the place of another."

We can read in the Bible the story of Jacob buying Esau's birthright with a bowl of porridge. (Genesis 25) And again, when Jacob deceived Isaac to receive the father's blessing from him. (Genesis 27) Also, after he left home, married, and had children of his own, Jacob deceived his father-in-law. (Genesis 30) So Jacob lived much of his life as a deceiver.

But his life changed when he encountered and wrestled with the angel of God. Not only was his physical body changed by his hip being out of joint, but he received a new name, Israel, and his attitude toward his life was changed.

No matter what you have done in your life, God can forgive you and just as He did for Jacob, He will change you for the better. What you were before submitting to Christ will no longer define you because you have become a new creature in Him. Thank God that He knows what we can become even before we know it and He is there with us to help us have that changed life in Him.

JUNE 11

Joseph, the Desiring Father

"Delight thyself also in the Lord; and he shall give thee the desires of thine heart."

Psalm 37:4

Joseph was the favored son of Jacob because he was the son of his old age, according to Genesis 37:3. Because of that his brothers hated him. They ended up selling him to some traveling merchants and lying to their father about what had happened to him.

Joseph then found himself in Egypt. He was sold as a slave, lied about, and was sent to prison. He was forgotten when two other prisoners were released. After interpreting Pharaoh's dream, he was eventually promoted to second in command. It was during this time that he married and had two sons.

There came a time that Joseph revealed himself to his brothers when they came to buy grain during a famine, and their entire family moved to Egypt to be with him.

It must have been a glorious reunion when, after so many years, Joseph was finally able to see his aging father. I am sure that many times throughout his life in Egypt, he had longed for the day that he could introduce his two sons to his father, the grandfather that they had never met. And the desire to have him speak a blessing over them was fulfilled before Jacob died.

Have you considered saying a prayer of blessing over your children and grandchildren? I believe that God will honor that action as you lay your hands on them and bless them. You will never know what it will do for their future.

JUNE 12

Moses, the Protective Father

"In the fear of the Lord one has strong confidence, and his children will have a refuge." ESV

Proverbs 14:26

Moses had a unique life. We know that Pharaoh's daughter found him in the river, in a waterproof basket, and claimed him as her own. He was raised by his parents for the first part of his life, and then lived in the palace for several years. He spent some years in the desert, in which he found his wife, and had two sons.

When God called him to be the deliverer of the children of Israel, after making several excuses to God of why he could not do as He asked, he finally consented to follow His commands. He and his family went back to Egypt. At some point Moses sent his wife and sons back to Jethro, his father-in-law's home, according to Exodus 18:2. When Pharaoh finally released the Israelites, and they were in the wilderness, Jethro brought them back to Moses.

We are not told in scripture why Moses sent them to Jethro, but one speculation is that he wanted to protect them from the dangers they could possibly be facing while in Egypt.

Is that how you feel about your family? Are they foremost in your mind when any kind of uncertainty is lurking near your door? I can tell you this: God expects you to take care of them and be their protector. A protective father, or mother for that matter, will do what is best for the family to keep them safe from harm.

JUNE 13

Elkanah, the Committed Father

"And whatsoever ye do, do it heartily, as to the Lord, and not unto men;"

Colossians 3:23

We are not told very much about Elkanah in the Bible. What we do know is that he was a committed person in how he lived his life.

He was faithful in his worship of the Lord. Each year he would travel to Shiloh from the mountains of Ephriam where they lived. It was evident that he was committed to his faith.

Elkanah had two wives, Hannah and Peninneh. Whenever he would make the yearly trip, he always took his wives and children with him. He was committed to his family.

We all know the story of how Hannah prayed for a baby and God answered her prayer. What was Elkanah's response to it? We do not know for sure, but it makes sense that he would have given glory to the Lord. He was committed to his God.

We all need to be as committed as Elkanah to our faith, to our family, and to our God. If we are, then our lives will be a witness to others, and they will desire to draw closer to Him as their commitment level increases.

JUNE 14

Job, the Praying Father

"...The effectual fervent prayer of a righteous man availeth much."

James 5:16b

From the first verse in the book of Job, we find out that he was a perfect and upright man, one that feared God and eschewed (avoided) evil. He was also a wealthy man and in verse three of the first chapter, Job is called the greatest of all the men of the east. And he had seven sons and three daughters.

As we read further, we see that his sons would often hold feasts and invite their sisters so they could eat and drink together. These would last for several days. After each one, Job would pray over them, saying, "It may be that my sons have sinned, and cursed God in their hearts." Job did this continually.

When we read of Job, we only think about the trials that he went through in the testing of his faith. But his continual prayers for his children was a particularly important task that he did. He was concerned about his children, and he covered them in prayer.

How much do you pray over your children? Do you pray continually as Job did for his? You will never know, until you get to heaven, just what they have been spared because of your continual prayers. Make it a priority in your life!

NOTES

JUNE 15

King Saul, the Jealous Father

"For where you have envy and selfish ambition, there you find disorder and every evil practice." NIV

James 3:16

It was not God's perfect plan for the Children of Israel to have a king, but they rebelled against Him, so He gave them what they asked for. God chose King Saul to fulfill that request.

Saul's son was Jonathan. He always thought that he would follow in his father's footsteps and become king himself one day. But things did not turn out the way he thought they would. When he was troubled in his spirit, Saul would have David to play his harp, which would bring a calm to him. He eventually found out that David and Jonathan had become close friends, as close as brothers.

Saul first became jealous of David when they would come back from a battle as the people rejoiced and sang about Saul slaying his thousands and David, his tens of thousands. He wanted more accolades for himself than for anyone else.

And then, he was jealous of the relationship between Jonathan and David. He saw that his own son was defending David and supporting him, despite his father's attitude against him. That bothered him greatly. In the end, King Saul lost everything, even the life of his son, as well as his own.

We must never allow jealously to be a part of our relationship with our children. There will be others that will help to fashion their lives. But no one will ever take the place of the father and mother if we become the parents that God has called us to be.

JUNE 16

David, the Encouraging Father

"[11]For you know how, like a father with his children, [12]we exhorted each one of you and encouraged you and charged you to walk in a manner worthy of God, who calls you into his own kingdom and glory." ESV

1 Thessalonians 2:11-12

King David had many children, but he was an encouraging father to Solomon. David thought that he would be the one that would build the temple. God had a different idea; He told him that Solomon would build it.

The Bible tells us in 1 Chronicles 22 that God had spoken to David, telling him that he had shed too much blood in the wars he had been in to build the house of God in His name. So therefore, he charged his son, Solomon with this task.

Although it was his desire to build it, David submitted to God's direction. He was an encouragement to Solomon by collecting the materials needed for the building of the temple. He encouraged him by giving him the instructions on how to get it done.

Are you encouraging your children to seek God in all they do? Are you willing to step back and let God use them in the way He sees fit? God truly knows the future; it is our job as parents to encourage our children to listen to God and allow Him to show them the way along life's road.

JUNE 17

Zacharias, the Faithful Father

"Moreover it is required in stewards, that a man be found faithful."
I Corinthians 4:2

Zacharias was a righteous man who honored God. He and his wife had prayed to have a child. One day, while he was performing his priestly duties, Gabriel appeared to him in the temple. He told Zacharias that his prayers had been heard and he and his wife, Elizabeth would have a son that would be a witness for the coming of the Son of God. And his name would be John.

When Gabriel spoke to him, Zacharias doubted his word because they were old and past the child-bearing age. Because of his doubt and unbelief, he was struck dumb until the baby was born.

Since he was a priest, I am assuming that Zacharias was faithful to continue to serve in the temple of God, even though he could not talk. But when the baby was born, and the people thought that he would be named after himself, he asked for a writing tablet. He wrote, "His name is John." As soon as he declared the baby's name, his mouth was opened, and he spoke and began to praise God.

Zacharias knew that John would be an especially important person as he grew, so I am certain that he was faithful to teach him the ways of the Lord. I wonder how many times he told John about the encounter he had with the angel before he was born.

Being a faithful father is a high calling. Those children were placed in your care, and you need to tell them about your experiences with God. In doing so, it will create a desire in them to live for Him. Be faithful to God and watch your children learn to do the same.

JUNE 18

Joseph, the Training Father

"As arrows are in the hand of a mighty man; so are the children of the youth."

Psalm 127:4

Joseph was the earthly father of Jesus. The angel, Gabriel, visited Mary and told her that she would be the mother of the Son of God. This would be a virgin birth as the Holy Spirit came upon her and overshadowed her. She was engaged (or betrothed) to Joseph, but not yet married.

When she told Joseph about what had happened, he knew that under the law she could be stoned to death. So, he planned to divorce her privately. An angel visited Joseph as well and told him to marry her, which he did. Thus he became the earthly father to Jesus.

As Jesus was growing up, Joseph trained him to be a carpenter. I can just imagine Jesus sitting on a bench, watching his earthly father work with the wood, and being amazed at how it turned out. Joseph loved Him enough to teach Him his profession. I am sure he trained Jesus in many other ways as well.

We need more fathers today that would take a stronger interest in their children and would take the time to invest in their young lives. What a difference it would make in the next generation.

JUNE 19

Jairus, the Believing Father

"And all things, whatsoever ye shall ask in prayer believing, ye shall receive."

Matthew 21:22

Jairus was a ruler in the synagogue, and he had a twelve-year-old daughter that was very sick. He approached Jesus and fell down at his feet, pleading with Jesus to come to his house and heal her.

He knew that his daughter was at the point of death, but he also had faith and believed that Jesus could heal her if He would come and lay His hands on her. Jesus did not hesitate and went with him.

On the way, someone from the ruler's house came and told him that his daughter had died. Jesus heard these words and told the father, "Be not afraid, only believe." (Mark 5:36)

When they arrived at his house, Jesus had everyone to leave except the parents and Peter, James, and John, who had come with him. Jesus simply took her by the hand and said, "Talitha cumi," meaning "Damsel, I say unto thee, arise." And she did just that!

Because of her father's belief in the power of Jesus, she was healed. What wonderful things can be accomplished if we just believe that it can be done through Jesus. Two simple steps: BELIEVE and RECEIVE. Then we will see victory in the situations that we face!

JUNE 20

The Father of the Prodigal Son, the Expectant Father

"My soul, wait thou only upon God; for my expectation is from him."

Psalm 62:5

The story of the prodigal son is found in Luke 15:11-32. Although the father's name is not given in the Bible, it is a familiar story and is a parable that Jesus told. I will call him an expectant father.

He had two sons. One day the youngest son asked his father for the inheritance that he was to receive. The father's initial response was not recorded; it only states in the twelfth verse that "he divided unto them his living." The youngest son left a few days after and eventually spent it all.

He then decided to return home and ask his father if he would accept him back as a servant and not a son. But when he reached his home, his father ran to meet him. There was no condemnation, no shaming, no reprimanding; he only showed love to his rebellious son that had returned home a different man.

I can just imagine that father looking down the road several times every day, with an expectancy that his son would one day return. And then what he had been expecting finally happened! In verse twenty, we read, "And he arose, and came to his father. But when he was yet a great way off, his father saw him, and had compassion, and ran, and fell on his neck, and kissed him."

If you have wayward children that are away from God at the moment, just continue to pray that God will touch their spirits. Live with expectation that they will one day return to you and to God. That day will come!

JUNE 21

The Father of the Demon-Possessed Boy, the Desperate Father

"And call upon me in the day of trouble: I will deliver thee, and thou shalt glorify me."

Psalm 50:15

This story is found in three of the Gospels: Matthew, Mark, and Luke. In all three accounts, this father is in the crowd and cries out to Jesus asking for him to heal his son.

The father informs Jesus that his only child was being vexed by a spirit in which he would foam at the mouth. The spirit would try to throw the possessed son in the fire or the water to destroy him. This father was desperate for a cure.

Jesus asked for this boy to be brought to Him. As he was coming toward Jesus, the spirit attacked the possessed boy, and he began foaming at the mouth once again and wallowing on the ground. Jesus rebuked the spirit, and it left the boy. He was delivered to his father, completely healed.

This was a desperate father for sure. He sought out the one Person that he believed could and would heal his son. And that is exactly what happened. How would this boy have lived his life if his father had not been desperate enough to find Jesus and ask for help? Do you believe that God will answer your desperate cry for help? He is always ready and willing to hear your prayer and supply your every need!

NOTES

JUNE 22

The Involved Father

"Lo, children are an heritage of the Lord: and the fruit of the womb is his reward."

Psalm 127:3

Every couple, before they get married, have their own individual ideas of what each one's responsibilities should be. Sometimes, these things are ironed out fairly quickly, but other times, they last for years.

It is the same with parenting. Some fathers feel like it is the mother's job to take care of the baby. But I want to tell you fathers a little bit of advice. Your wife needs you to be involved in every aspect of raising your children. And your child needs to know that they can depend on you, as well as their mother, to meet their needs.

What a joy and a wonderful surprise it would be to your wife if you would tell her to go shopping for a couple of hours while you keep the baby (or kids). If you would do this every so often, it would improve your marriage, while giving you time to bond with your children.

As your children grow, they will be more apt to come to you with problems that they are facing if you have made them a priority in your life. Spending time with them will let them know that you think they are important. Children are a blessing from God. Take time from your schedule and involve yourself in their lives!

JUNE 23

The Patient Father

"Be completely humble and gentle;
be patient, bearing with one another in love." NIV

Ephesians 4:2

Being a patient father takes lots of work on his part. Fathers (and mothers, for that matter), having been through life longer than their children, know the pitfalls and bumps in the road that is just ahead of them. But you must realize that these hindrances are what is required for them to learn.

When your child begins to learn to walk, for instance, he/she will fall many times before they are steady enough to take steps without assistance. A patient father does not reprimand that child the first time they fall or when they hurt themselves and cry. He patiently consoles him/her, and then sets him/her up on their feet to try again. And eventually, the child learns to walk by themselves.

When it comes time to teach your child to ride a bike, you do not take the bike away the first time a fall occurs. There is no scolding because the art of riding the bike was not mastered. No, you patiently help him/her get back on with your support until the confidence to learn to ride returns.

As they get older, you do not demand that they do new things your way. A patient father slowly allows him/her to make their own decisions and if failure comes, he is there to offer encouragement to try again.

All of these take a lot of patience, as well as many other areas the father and mother will face as parents. But it can be done. Ask God for the wisdom to know when to release them at just the right time. Pray constantly that they make the right decisions. Be there for them when they make wrong ones and guide them in the ways of God. Be patient with them as they learn.

JUNE 24

The Teaching Father

"You shall teach them diligently to your children, and shall talk of them when you sit in your house, and when you walk by the way, and when you lie down, and when you rise." ESV

Deuteronomy 6:7

A father not only needs to strive to be all of these attributes in this month's devotions, but he also needs to be a teaching father.

My husband, Rick, was always looking for teachable moments to share with our children when they were young. One such moment happened when they were in their early teens.

He saw a bundle of popsicle sticks on the table beside him and he removed one of them. He then bent it to where it was broken but still together. He asked Richie and Renee how it could be stronger than it had ever been. Richie's reply was, "Duct tape" while Renee answered, "Super glue."

Rick pulled two other sticks out of the bundle and put them on either side of the broken one. And he said, "This stick is twice as strong as it once was. If you will stay in church, then when you go through times of brokenness, your brothers and sisters in Christ will come along side you, making you stronger than you were before."

There are always opportunities that will come that you can use as an object lesson to instruct your children about the things of God. Be aware of these moments and teach the lessons to them. These "spur of the moment" teachings will stick with them throughout their lives.

JUNE 25

The Blessed Father

"Your wife will be like a fruitful vine within your house; your children will be like olive shoots around your table." NIV

Psalm 128:3

Children are a blessing from God. Even though there will be trying times, especially to new parents, you are still blessed to be chosen to be the father and mother of that precious little one.

We are told in Psalm 127:4-5a, (ESV) "[4]Like arrows in the hand of a warrior are the children of one's youth. [5]Blessed is the man who fills his quiver with them…"

In Mark 10:13-16, we see Jesus' feelings about children. In these verses, the disciples rebuked the mothers for bringing them to Jesus. This greatly displeased Him, and He said to bring the children to Him. Verse 16 tells us, "And he took them up in his arms, put his hands upon them, and blessed them."

Again, in Matthew 18:1-6, the disciples asked Jesus who was the greatest in the kingdom of Heaven. Jesus' answer I am sure, amazed them. He called a little child over to Him and told those with him that whosoever humbles themselves as that child, he it is that is the greatest. And in verse 6, He made a strong statement about children, "But whoso shall offend one of these little ones which believe in me, it were better for him that a millstone were hanged about his neck, and that he were drowned in the depth of the sea."

So, you can see how very important Jesus considers children to be. You should consider yourself blessed to be a father (or mother). Do not ever think of your children as a burden, think of them as a blessing!

JUNE 26

The Appreciative Father

"Children are a gift from the Lord; they are a reward from him." NLT

Psalm 127:3

A good father is very appreciative for his family. He considers his children, as well as his wife, as a gift from God. And that is just what they are.

This father appreciates the fact that God chose him to be the leader of his family and he strives to raise his children to be more than what he has been. As the song says, "You raise me up to be more than I can be!"

Reed Markham has been a professor at several colleges and is an author. He made a wonderful quote about fathers: "The thrill of being a great father is not seeing your children go on to become successful adults. The thrill of a great father is the journey, experiencing your child's successes along the pathway to their greatness."

What a true statement! The father that is present to experience those successes with their children is the mark of a good father. He appreciates those times, knowing that he had a part in his children reaching their greatness.

Are you appreciative of your children? Do you look forward to spending time with them? Are you watchful of how you live your life in front of them, knowing what an influence you are making on them? Just remember that they are watching you and desire to be just like you! Appreciate them and be the Godly example that they need to see.

JUNE 27

The Respectful Father

"Respect everyone, and love the family of believers. Fear God, and respect the king." NLT

I Peter 2:17

I have seen quite a few fathers who show disrespect to those around them who share a different viewpoint than their own. Too many of those fathers do not realize that when they are disrespectful of others, there are little eyes that are seeing it and little ears that are hearing it.

It is a father's responsibility to train their children to respect their elders and those in authority over them. To do that, the fathers (and mothers as well) need to make that a practice themselves.

If you disrespect the pastor, for instance, then your children will disrespect him. If you are disrespectful to their teachers, then they will also disrespect them. This is a big one: If you disrespect their mother, then they will show the same disrespect to her. (And vice versa) Showing respect for others will certainly show up in the attitudes of your children.

Leviticus 19:32 NLT tells us, "Stand up in the presence of the elderly, and show respect for the aged. Fear your God. I am the Lord." And, in 1 Timothy 5:17, ESV "Let the elders who rule well be considered worthy of double honor, especially those who labor in preaching and teaching."

So, we can see that there are those in whom we should show honor and respect. Your children should be taught to respond in the same manner. Be careful what you say and do; they are watching!

JUNE 28

The Moral Father

"He that walketh uprightly walketh surely: but he that perverteth his ways shall be known."

Proverbs 10:9

Being a moral father is so vitally important, especially in our society today. The attitude of the world is anything goes! But that is just not true!

One definition I found for moral behavior is simply obedience to God's commands. Not half-hearted, but full obedience, because half-hearted obedience is disobedience!

We read in John 14:15, "If ye love me, keep my commandments." So, if we do not live a moral life, does that mean that we do not love God? Hmmm! That is something to think about. To me, this means if you love God, then you will keep His commandments, resulting in living a moral life. Also, in 2 Timothy 2:22, ESV it says, "So flee youthful passions and pursue righteousness, faith, love, and peace, along with those who call on the Lord from a pure heart."

Living morally is so important for children to see. What they see in the world is certainly not people living moral lives. Train them to live for God by living morally in front of them and they will be more likely to follow you than following the world.

JUNE 29

The Cool Father

"Fathers, do not provoke your children to anger by the way you treat them. Rather, bring them up with the discipline and instruction that comes from the Lord." NLT

Ephesians 6:4

Kids are the most truthful creatures on the planet! It is a fun thing to hear responses from them when asked questions. Here are some answers from kids, ages 2-16, when asked, "Why do you think Dad is cool?"

- ◊ "Because I can beat him at games." — age 13
- ◊ "Because he is super fun." — age 15
- ◊ "He is very good at just about everything." — age 16
- ◊ "He follows what God tells him to do." — age 11
- ◊ "He lets us sleep in … sometimes." — age 14
- ◊ "Because he's good at stuff." — age 5
- ◊ "Cause he is." — age 2
- ◊ "Because he holds me." — age 4
- ◊ "He's a good role model." — age 13
- ◊ "He takes me on daddy-daughter dates." — age 4
- ◊ "He wears hats." — age 9
- ◊ "He loves me forever no matter what." — age 7

Have you ever wondered what your children would answer to the above question? Do you feel like a cool father? Do your children think you are a super fun dad, a good role model, good at "stuff"? Can they say that you follow what God tells you to do, that you hold them, take them on daddy-daughter dates? Do they know that you will love them forever no matter what?

It is not too late to start doing things with your children. Whether you know it or not, they enjoy spending time with you. You will never regret it; it will never be a waste of your time!

JUNE 30

The Spiritual Father

"Remember your leaders
who taught you the word of God.
Think of all the good that has come from their lives,
and follow the example of their faith." NLT

Hebrews 13:7

The concept of being a spiritual father is new to some people. I want to be truly clear, a spiritual father does not take the place of your own father. There is no one that could or should take your father's place. But a spiritual father raises up spiritual sons, often working alongside the natural father.

My husband, Rick, became a spiritual father before he even realized what it was. It began with two of his nephews. Every time he was with them, he taught them a new lesson that he had learned himself. They were like little birds, grasping at every word that he spoke. And then as the years passed, several others were added, with him always teaching them. He would tell each one, "I will teach you if you will teach what you learn to at least two others." Before he passed away, he had around seventy men and women that considered him to be their spiritual father.

Not only was Rick a spiritual father, but he also thought of two important men in our lives as his spiritual fathers. And I feel the same about them. The first one was Dr. JT Parish. We are so thankful for the mentoring that this man of God did for us and our children. God brought him into our lives in a very desperate time and he has remained with us to this day. The other man is Dale Yerton. Through a series of circumstances, Rick asked him to mentor him, or be a spiritual father to him, in missions. He did just that, but he became much more to us. He has also remained faithful to us.

God will bring people into your life to be the spiritual father (or mother) that you need. And as you grow in the Lord, he will bring those that you can mentor as well. It is a great blessing that you are missing if you are not searching for spiritual fathers and spiritual sons. What you learn from the fathers, you can give to the sons. It is a continual process that will bring many rewards.

NOTES

JULY 1

Freedom

"Stand fast therefore in the liberty wherewith Christ hath made us free,
and be not entangled again
with the yoke of bondage."

Galatians 5:1

July is the month that we celebrate the freedom of our nation; therefore we are talking about freedom this month.

The definition of freedom, according to The Cambridge Dictionary, is: the condition or right of being able or allowed to do, say, think, etc. whatever you want to, without being controlled or limited.

Even though as Americans we are free to do what we want, there are boundaries. For example, a criminal may want to steal and kill, but there are laws that govern against that and there are punishments for not following them.

The same is true for Christians. We do gain freedom when we accept Jesus as Lord and Saviour. But that does not give us the right to sin just because the Bible says we are free. We are not free to sin, but we are free to stand in the liberty that Jesus has given us. We are free to enjoy living a Christian life. We are free to worship God and attend the church of our choice. We must not take that freedom and turn back to a life of bondage to sin.

Let's delve into the subject of freedom that we receive from Jesus when we give our lives totally to Him. Christ has indeed made us free!

JULY 2

Jesus Purchased Our Freedom

"Trust in him at all times, you people; pour out your hearts to him, for God is our refuge." NIV

Psalm 62:8

In Biblical times people were not able to have a personal relationship with God. They would have to go to the temple once a year and bring a sacrifice for the atonement of their sins. The high priest would then enter the Holy of Holies in their stead, taking with him the sacrificial blood to sprinkle on the mercy seat of the Ark of the Covenant, as well as burning incense while there. By doing this, his own sins, as well as those of the people, were atoned for one year. It would then be repeated annually at the Feast of Atonement.

It is so different with us today. Jesus willingly came to earth, died an excruciating death on the cross, and rose again so that we could have access to the throne room of God anytime. He became our sacrificial lamb!

I am so thankful that He would do all of that because He loved us so much! It is His desire for us to have a relationship with Him. He wants to hear from us often: in worship, in thanksgiving, in praise, and simply just talking with Him. He wants to be our best friend.

Are you thankful for the freedom that we have to spend time with Him personally? I sure am. Make time for God all throughout your day. He is right there with you; you can talk to your best friend anytime you desire!

JULY 3

Real Freedom

"If the Son therefore shall make you free, ye shall be free indeed."

John 8:36

We are born in bondage in need of a Saviour. Christ's attempt to free us is in vain unless we accept it! Although this is not an exhaustive list, here are five things from which Christ has liberated us:

◊ **Sin**-Romans 6:17-18. Without Jesus there is no escape from sin!

◊ **Fear**-2 Timothy 1:7. Fear is Satan's number one tool to defeat the children of God. Fear cost the children of Israel the Promised Land. Thank God, Jesus has freed us from the spirit of fear.

◊ **Doubt**-John 20:27-29. Christ lived, died, and rose again to increase our faith and diminish our doubt!

◊ **Sickness**-1 Peter 2:24. Christ did not only make atonement for our soul, but also the healing of our physical body.

◊ **Death**-Romans 6:22-23. Our victory over death is through Jesus Christ.

Through the atonement of Christ, we have an escape from every bondage known to mankind. Galatians 5:1 tells us, "Stand fast therefore in the liberty wherewith Christ hath made us free, and be not entangled again with the yoke of bondage."

~ Rick Clendenen

JULY 4

Freedom in America

"Let us go to his dwelling place;
let us worship at his footstool!" ESV

Psalm 132:7

The first amendment of the Constitution of the United States says: "Congress shall make no law respecting an establishment of religion, or prohibiting the free exercise thereof; or abridging the freedom of speech, or of the press; or the right of the people peaceably to assemble, and to petition the Government for a redress of grievances."

This gives us the freedom of religion, of speech, of the press, of assembly, as well as the freedom to petition. For example, we, as Americans, have been given the freedom to worship God in whatever way we desire without fear of government interference, as well as assembling as a body of believers.

I am thankful for our forefathers taking the initiative to make sure that we have those freedoms. It is certainly not the case in many other countries. Let's worship God together as we assemble in the church of our choice and thank Him for the freedoms that we experience in our country.

JULY 5

Freedom of Choice

"For where two or three are gathered together in my name, there am I in the midst of them."

Matthew 18:20

As we saw in yesterday's devotion, the Constitution of our country assures us of the right to assemble as a church and worship God as we wish. We even have the freedom to choose which church we want to attend.

The thing that we must consider, though, is that we all need to be a part of a church that preaches the truth of God's Word. There are those that preach and teach a different Gospel than that of salvation through Jesus Christ. Jesus plainly tells us in Acts 4:12, "Neither is there salvation in any other: for there is none other name under heaven given among men, whereby we must be saved." Jesus is the only way of entering Heaven.

You also have the freedom to choose whether you are even going to attend church. The decision for a child of God should be an easy choice to make: Go! It is there that you learn from His Word, you worship Him for who He is, you fellowship with other believers, and you can see the lost experience the New Birth found in Jesus. Just to name a few reasons why you should attend church.

One of the most important reasons is that you are being an example to your children. You train them by what they see you do. If it is your desire to see them become stable Christians on their own, then show them by being faithful with your church attendance. It will be a help to you, as well as to them.

JULY 6

Choose to Obey

"The Lord is not slow in keeping his promise, as some understand slowness. Instead he is patient with you, not wanting anyone to perish, but everyone to come to repentance." NIV

2 Peter 3:9

It is Christ's desire for everyone to be saved and for none to spend eternity in the flames of Hell with Satan. It should be the desire of each of us as well.

The Lord places people in our path every day. We should have the attitude of Jesus and be concerned about their souls. The Holy Spirit within you will prompt you who to encounter with the Gospel message.

You are free to choose to obey Him or to continue walking the path you are on with no concern for others whatsoever. But, if we want to truly imitate Jesus, as we are supposed to do, then we will be ready and willing to speak to them and hopefully, lead them to accept Him as Lord and Savior of their lives.

How many lost opportunities have you encountered and allowed to pass you by? I know I have had many! There is nothing we can do about that now, except to ask forgiveness from God and to obey the next time we are given the chance to be the mouth of Jesus. Commit your ways to Him and be a willing vessel!

JULY 7

Freedom From Sin and Death

"For the law of the Spirit of life in Christ Jesus hath made me free from the law of sin and death."

Romans 8:2

Sin entered our world through Adam and Eve when they disobeyed God's instruction, as well as when Cain killed his brother, Abel. But our way of escape from the destruction of sin was given to us through the death, burial, and resurrection of Jesus Christ.

We are told in James 1:14-15, "[14]But every man is tempted, when he is drawn away of his own lust, and enticed. [15]Then when lust hath conceived, it bringeth forth sin: and sin, when it is finished, bringeth forth death." So, we see that the natural progression of sin is:

- ◊ **Temptation**
- ◊ **Lust**
- ◊ **Sin**
- ◊ **Death**

But we have forgiveness of sin through Jesus. As we receive it from Him, we will experience eternal life in Heaven with Him. Thank God for the way of escape from the sin in this world. Accept His forgiveness today!

NOTES

JULY 8

Freed From the Slavery of Sin

"Jesus answered them, Truly, truly, I say to you, everyone who practices sin is a slave to sin." ESV

John 8:34

It has been said that sin will take you further than you wanted to go and will keep you longer than you wanted to stay. If you continue in sin, it will come to the point that sin will so enslave you that you will see no way out.

A person being a slave to sin means that he/she has no will of their own but is compelled to follow the leading of the devil. He/she doesn't have the power within themselves to leave the lifestyle of sin.

But Jesus is the way of escape for those who practice sin; He gave His life to deliver those that are a slave to it. His power is greater than that of the devil. As we accept Jesus, sin's power over our lives will be broken. Romans 6:6, NLT "We know that our old sinful selves were crucified with Christ so that sin might lose its power in our lives. We are no longer slaves to sin."

I don't want sin to have power over my life. I gave that permission to Jesus when I accepted His offer to be free from the slavery of sin. I pray that you have made that decision as well and you can say that sin no longer rules your life.

JULY 9

Set Free to Follow Him

"Being then made free from sin, ye became the servants of righteousness." NLT

Romans 6:18

"I am free to do what I want because Christ has set me free?" I have heard people say this statement; have you? Jesus has indeed set us free but there are some rules that we must follow. They are commonly called, "The Ten Commandments."

In Judges 17, we read about a man named Micah. He secretly stole silver from his mother. He admitted to stealing it and returned it to her. She then took the silver and had an idol made from part of it. In the first few verses, we see that Micah broke three of the Ten Commandments:

- ◊ **Do not steal**
- ◊ **Honor thy father and mother**
- ◊ **Do not worship anything but God**

Verse six tells us why Micah thought that his actions were OK. "In those days there was no king in Israel, but every man did that which was right in his own eyes." He felt that he was free to do what he wanted to do; he did what was right in his own eyes! God did not condone what he did, and neither will He reward us when we go against His Word.

If we are going to wholeheartedly follow Him, we will, by our own choice, not do what we think is right but do what He speaks. We have been set free to follow Him!

JULY 10

Free Yourselves

"People who conceal their sins will not prosper, but if they confess and turn from them, they will receive mercy." NLT

Proverbs 28:13

Jesus died so that we may be free from sin and be able to enjoy all that He has to offer us. He has done His part; have we done ours?

To accept the freedom that we receive from Jesus, our job is simply to believe, ask, and receive. But we have further responsibilities after that occurs.

In Hebrews 12:1, we read in the NLT version, "Therefore, since we are surrounded by such a huge crowd of witnesses to the life of faith, let us strip off every weight that slows us down, especially the sin that so easily trips us up. And let us run with endurance the race God has set before us."

This verse tells us to **free ourselves** from those weights that slow us down and trips us up. Those that keep us from approaching the Heavenly Father. We can't continue to take pleasure in those sins that are thrown across our paths by Satan and his imps. It is up to us to choose not to indulge in them; Jesus is not going to magically make them disappear. We must make that choice and follow through with it!

Free yourselves from those weights. Cast them aside and flee from them. And then run, with endurance, the race that Jesus has for you to run. Then you will receive Heaven as your reward!

JULY 11

Free to Worship

"O come, let us worship and bow down:
let us kneel before the Lord our maker."

Psalm 95:6

There is a chorus that we used to sing in church. It goes like this:

Set free to worship, I'm set free to praise Him
I'm set free to rejoice around the throne
I'll laugh, I'll dance, I'll shout and sing
Hallelujah, praise the Lord, let the Heavens ring
Set free to worship, I'm set free

To freely worship God in various ways is a privilege that not everyone has. My husband, Rick, has visited many countries where it is against the law to be a Christian. He has seen those that have had arms and legs broken, shoulders dislocated, and even worse, some have lost their lives just for professing Christ. He has also been to places where they must meet secretly and only have a very few minutes to worship together. If they are found by the local police, they will be among those that are severely beaten and possibly killed.

It'd be a good idea to think of these things the next time you worship God with other believers. Consider that we can freely worship God while the worship of other brothers and sisters in Christ must be done in secret, or they will face severe consequences.

While worshipping, some people may laugh, some may dance, some shout, "Hallelujah" or "Praise the Lord." Don't criticize them; just worship God in the way you feel comfortable and allow them to do the same. The secret is to worship God in your own way.

JULY 12

Freed by God's Grace

"For we are God's handiwork, created in Christ Jesus to do good works, which God prepared in advance for us to do." NIV

Ephesians 2:10

We all have a job to do in the Kingdom of God and it is by His grace that we can accomplish that to which He has called us. We have the freedom to answer that call or to be disobedient. But by God's grace we can and should make the right choice to follow His leading.

The above verse says that we are God's handiwork. He made us and He has put within each of us the ability to do what He desires us to do. It further states that we were created in Jesus to do the work that God prepared in advance for us to do. You will never be satisfied or fulfilled in your life until you discover just what your calling is and begin to do it, with God's help.

You may be called to be a worship leader, or a musician, or a janitor, or a nursery worker. You may be called to be a cook, or a decorator, or a massage therapist, or a computer programmer. You may even be called to be a doctor, or a nurse, or a lawyer…the list could go on and on. The secret is to diligently seek God and He will let you know what your particular calling is. And then to do it with all your might. In doing that, you are glorifying God.

Are you fulfilling that calling that God prepared just for you? Don't try to do someone else's job, you will never be happy. There is no better satisfaction in life than to be in the center of God's will, doing what He has prepared you to do. By His grace, you can be who God says you are!

JULY 13

Are You Truly Free?

"I will walk about in freedom,
for I have sought out your precepts." NIV
Psalm 119:45

What does "being free in Christ" mean to you? Do you think it means that you can accept Jesus and then be free to live your life any way you want?

According to the above scripture, that is not what it means. If you have truly accepted Christ as Lord and Savior, you will want to walk in His ways. That means that you will seek out his precepts, or study the scriptures, and live according to them. Then you will be able to walk about in freedom, knowing that the life you live will be submitted to Jesus and His ways, and not your ways.

Isaiah 55:9 tells us, "For as the heavens are higher than the earth, so are my ways higher than your ways, and my thoughts than your thoughts." As you accept Jesus, and learn more of His ways, then others will begin to see more and more of Him shining through you.

That's the kind of life I want to live; I want to represent Jesus in all I do. Draw as close to Jesus as you can, and you will feel His freedom as you follow in His footsteps. Your wants will come in line with His wants for your life!

JULY 14

Free Gift of Salvation

"Yet God, in his grace, freely makes us right in his sight. He did this through Christ Jesus when he freed us from the penalty for our sins." NLT

Romans 3:24

I have heard this phrase all of my life, "free gift of salvation," but it is not totally true. We don't have to pay for it so, in that sense, it is free to us. But it did cost Jesus His very life, and He freely gave it.

That was the purpose of Him leaving Heaven and coming to earth. He knew all along that He would give His life for the salvation of mankind. That is the only way that we can receive eternal life through Him. He suffered a cruel death because He loved us so much. He wanted us to have a way of escape from sin and the plan of salvation was put in motion as He was nailed to the cross.

How could we not want to accept this free gift of salvation from Him and spend our lives serving Him? How could we not want to share with others how they can do the same thing?

Let's all make it a priority to tell others about what Jesus did for them and lead them to salvation through Him. Jesus not only died for us, but He also died for all mankind. It's up to us to tell them!

NOTES

JULY 15

Free to Love Like Jesus

"34So now I am giving you a new commandment: Love each other. Just as I have loved you, you should love each other." NLT

John 13:34

There are people in this world that say they love Jesus, but their actions prove differently. Let's say that a drunkard wanders into your church and sits down beside you. Instead of showing him Christ's love, you turn up your nose and move to another seat. That is definitely not loving Jesus! And that, in itself, is a terrible representation of who Jesus is.

On the other hand, a true lover of Jesus sees that same man and realizes that he is someone for whom Jesus died. He will invite him to sit with him, with the possibility of leading Him to Christ later in the service. These are the ones that don't have to say that they love Jesus, it can be seen in all that they do.

I have heard it said by waitresses that Sundays are not their favorite days to work because the "so-called" Christians are their worst patrons. This does not show the love of Jesus either. My husband, Rick, would always ask the servers for their name when we would be at a restaurant. When speaking to them, he would use their name frequently and would complement them on the great job they were doing. This, my friend, is loving like Jesus.

We are free to treat other people however we want, but if we are going to represent Jesus, then we must love like He did (and still does). We never know what is going on in other peoples' lives; our kind words may be the only ones they hear on that day.

Start today to speak to people you meet. Compliment the servers, the lady behind the check-out, the people sitting at the table beside you… It'll brighten their day as you love like Jesus and represent Him to them.

JULY 16

Freedom From the Fear of Death

"O death, where is thy sting?
O grave, where is thy victory?"

I Corinthians 15:55

There are a lot of people in our world that fear death. Some of it is fear of the unknown. Some of it is questioning where they will spend eternity. They may have questions, such as, "Have I really done my best for Jesus?" "Will I go to Heaven when I die?" "Am I really saved?"

These are all legitimate questions that many have asked themselves. And these are placed in your minds by the father of all lies, that is, the devil. But we can know for sure that we are going to Heaven and be free from those fears. When we accept Jesus as Lord and Savior, and continue to live for Him, we will be with Him forever when it is our time to take our "Heavenly flight." That's a settled fact!

Hebrews 2:14-15 tells us that Jesus, by His death, freed us from the slavery that was caused by our fear of death. As Christians, we do not have to fear it. In the opening verse above, we see that death has lost its sting and the grave has lost its victory!

There is nothing to fear when death comes to us. We will all face it at some time in our lives. But we are freed from the fear of death when we accept salvation through Jesus. Praise God for that freedom!

JULY 17

Freedom From Worry

"Can any one of you by worrying add a single hour to your life?" NIV

Matthew 6:27

According to the Merriam-Webster Dictionary, the definition of worry is, "mental distress or agitation resulting from concern usually for something impending or anticipated."

A lot of times worry comes when we don't even know the outcome of a situation, we just think we know how it will turn out. And it does cause mental stress, which will, in turn, affect our physical body.

Worry does not come from God. As a matter of fact, God tell us in 1 Peter 5:7, NLT "Give all your worries and cares to God, for he cares about you." He cares so much about us that He tells us to give Him ALL our worries and cares. We just need to trust Him.

Are you allowing worry to dominate your thinking? Do you worry about things to the point that it has made you physically sick? If you answered yes to these questions, then you need to stop and give it to Jesus. As the old hymn says, "All to Jesus, I surrender; I surrender all!"

JULY 18

Free of Stress

"Commit to the Lord whatever you do, and he will establish your plans." NIV

Proverbs 16:3

I have been pondering about this thing called stress and I want to ask you a question. Can you really live free of stress in your life? I want to share with you what I have come to realize about the stress that I have allowed to settle in my life. I have stressed over so many senseless things. I say, "I have…" because I have put this on myself for years.

One example is constantly being late to places because I try to do too much before leaving for the appointment or whatever I had planned to do next. I carry too much stress over leaving those things undone. The truth of the matter is, they can wait until I get back; I don't have to get them done right away.

This leads me to stressing over the traffic. Sometimes I blame the other people and try to tell them how they need to "get out of my way." (I'm just trying to be honest here.) I need to remember that they have as much right to be on the road as I do. Other times, I stress over myself because it is my own fault for being late.

There is stress of all kinds and some of it is legitimate, such as serious illness, death, grief. But no matter what we are going through, we can look to our Heavenly Father, and He will give us rest. We **can** live free of stress. Thank you, Jesus, that you give peace in every situation. And when we accept Your peace, the stress must go!

JULY 19

Freedom to Choose Your Path

"You make known to me the path of life; in your presence there is fullness of joy; at your right hand are pleasures forevermore." ESV

Psalm 16:11

I saw a Facebook post this morning from a spiritual son of ours that caught my attention. It got me to thinking about God giving us free will to choose the path we will walk on. With his permission, here is his post:

"God has good things in store for you! He has a path that leads to blessing and fulfillment. It's up to you to choose that path. There is a way that seems right to man but the end is death. Yet, there is a way in God that leads to life. He won't "make you" do anything. You must choose and follow. Choose life!!!"

I totally agree with Josh. You can choose the path of blessing and fulfillment, or choose to walk away from God, which will lead to death. It is definitely your choice, and He gave you the freedom to choose your path.

If you are smart, you will choose the path that God has laid before you, that is life. It is your choice—Choose wisely!

JULY 20

Coming to Christ with Freedom and Confidence

"In him and through faith in him we may approach God with freedom and confidence." NIV

Ephesians 3:12

What a wonderful thought that we can freely come to God with any need or concern that we may have and know that He hears us. Not only that, but we can talk to Him and worship Him at any time of the day or night, knowing that He will listen.

Just spending time with Jesus is a refreshing to the soul. There are several scriptures in the Bible that remind us of this very thing. One of my favorites is Psalm 23:3, "He restoreth my soul: he leadeth me in the paths of righteousness for his name's sake."

He is ready and willing to listen as we bring our requests and petitions before Him. According to Matthew 6:8, He knows just what we need before we even ask. But He wants us to ask! Hebrews 4:16 ESV tells us, "Let us then with confidence draw near to the throne of grace, that we may receive mercy and find grace to help in time of need."

Do you struggle talking to Jesus? Do you ever wonder if He really wants us to come to Him? I can tell you that He wants us to feel free to come and converse with Him at any time. And when we do, we can have the confidence that He is right there waiting on us to have sweet communion with Him. Revelation 22:17 NIV, "The Spirit and the bride say, Come. Let anyone who hears this say, Come. Let anyone who is thirsty come. Let anyone who desires drink freely from the water of life."

JULY 21

Experience That Freeing Feeling

"Out of my distress I called on the Lord; the Lord answered me and set me free." ESV

Psalm 118:5

We all have had different experiences in our lives. Some even faced severe trauma. But whatever you have gone through, you can free your mind from those things that have affected you for years.

Whether it be grief, abuse of any kind, disillusionment, discouragement, whatever you are currently facing, you can be free from the torment of guilt and shame that constantly cloud your mind and hold you captive. Jesus came to proclaim liberty to the captives as we can read in Isaiah 61:1.

God doesn't want you to relive those things every day. You can be free from your mental captivity through Him. There is a peace in Him that will replace the struggle in your mind. You may feel free from it instantaneously or it make take some time. Seek out a mentor that you can talk with and that will pray with you. Let them help you learn to let it go and be free from the pain it has caused you.

Jesus is right by your side and desires you to experience that freeing feeling as you turn it all over to Him. "So if the Son sets you free, you are truly free." John 8:36 NLT You don't have to bear it alone any longer!

NOTES

JULY 22

What Worship Will Do

"Let all that I am praise the Lord; with my whole heart, I will praise his holy name." NLT

Psalm 103:1

As most of you know, my husband, Rick, passed away in 2020. There are days that I think I am doing pretty good with the grief, and then, every so often, it will hit me in the face, and it seems that what I was facing was so very heavy on my heart.

I was battling with some of those feelings recently. So, I decided to turn on some worship music and allow God to touch me like only He can do. As I listened and worshipped Him, I could sense those feelings that were bombarding my mind dissipate as my heart was filled with His love.

What a freeing feeling to be able to forget about those pangs of grief that were coming against me and bask in the presence of the Almighty God. I simply cannot put into words how the unspeakable joy and the peace that passes understanding made me feel on that day.

You can feel that too as you turn all the distress that is going on in your life over to your loving Father. Allow Him to fill you with His joy and peace and you will find yourself coming out of the doldrums that are trying to plague you. Worship the joy giver and the peace maker and you will soon feel the release of those contrary feelings take flight!

JULY 23

Worshipping God Frees Your Mind

"So that we would not be outwitted by Satan; for we are not ignorant of his designs." ESV

2 Corinthians 2:11

In yesterday's devotion, I told you about how worship cleared my mind of grief that I was experiencing. It will also free you from other things as well.

As you worship Him and consume your thoughts with the goodness of God, you will soon discover that your mind will be free from those negative things that come against you. Just thinking about how much He really loves you and what all He has done for you, simply because of that love, should give you peace in your mind.

Worry, concern, grief, fear, temptation, and discouragement are only a few of the weapons that the devil uses against you to turn you away from your Heavenly Father. But as you worship and give praise to God, those things don't stand a chance! For you, with God on your side, can fight and win any battle with which the devil comes against you.

So, when anything that is contrary to the Word of God comes against you, turn on some worship music and get in tune with Him. You'll soon see that your mind will be free from all distractions as you realize that God is with you and will lead and guide you in every situation in your life.

JULY 24

Believe the Lie or Accept the Truth

"Lead me in thy truth, and teach me: for thou art the God of my salvation; on thee do I wait all the day."

Psalm 25:5

Did you realize that for there to be a lie, there must be a truth first. The Bible is full of God's promises, but it is the plan of the devil and his imps to lie to you so that you will not accept them as truth. You have the free will to decide if you are going to believe the lie or accept the truth?

- ◊ The enemy will tell you that you are weak; God tells you that His strength is made perfect in your weakness. (2 Corinthians 12:9)
- ◊ The enemy will tell you that your past defines you; God tells you that all things have become new. (2 Corinthians 5:17)
- ◊ The enemy will tell you that God does not love you; God tells you that His love is everlasting. (Psalm 103:17 ESV)
- ◊ The enemy will tell you that you have gone too far to be saved; God tells you that He is faithful and just to forgive your sins. (1 John 1:9)
- ◊ The enemy will tell you that you are alone; God tells you that He will never leave you nor forsake you. (Hebrews 13:5)

These are a very few of the lies that the enemy tries to put in your mind. Do your own research and seek out your answers in the Bible to combat these lies. You will feel a great freedom in your heart and mind as you discover that the truth of God defeats the devil's lies every time!

JULY 25

Living a Lifestyle of Freedom

"But now that you have been set free from sin and have become slaves of God, the fruit you get leads to sanctification and its end, eternal life." ESV

Romans 6:22

What a wonderful statement: Living a lifestyle of freedom! I heard this at church recently and it struck a chord in my heart. You may be asking what that means. Let's look at it.

The world would say that it means you can live as you please. You don't have to have permission from anybody to do anything. You can go where you want to go, do what you want to do, be with whomever you want to be with. Even to obey whatever laws you want to obey.

For a Christian, living a lifestyle of freedom is totally different. It means that where you were once in bondage to sin, you are now liberated from that old sinful nature, and you are no longer enslaved by it. You were once ruled by sin and had no power within yourself to overcome it. But you are now free from the grip that sin had placed on you. From the moment that you accepted Jesus as Lord and Savior of your life, the chains of sins that were on your heart were instantly broken and you were loosed from them.

Be free from sin's clutches that have gripped you and experience the freedom that comes from Jesus and Him alone. I can assure you that there's nothing like it.

JULY 26

Free Your Heart from the Clutter

"Above all else, guard your heart, for everything you do flows from it." NIV

Proverbs 4:23

Do you remember how you felt when you surrendered your life to Jesus and accepted Him as Lord and Savior? I was only twelve years old when I became a Christian, but I remember feeling a great peace as the weight of sin on my heart was lifted.

It was 56 years ago (at the time of this writing) that I made that all important decision. There have been times that distractions came and just as we read about the church at Ephesus in Revelation 2:1-4, those were times in my life that I had lost my first love, that love that only should be given to my Lord and Savior. Oh, I still loved Him, but I had allowed other things to clutter my heart and take precedence over spending time with Him.

When distractions come, they are so subtle, that we don't even realize they are taking away from our love for Jesus. We must stay aware and not allow those things to distract us from our devotion to Him.

Take a survey of your own life today. Clean out the shelves of your heart, freeing it from the clutter and distractions, and making sure you have once again given Jesus first place. He is waiting on you!

JULY 27

Be a Useful Vessel

"Create in me a clean heart, O God;
and renew a right spirit within me."

Psalm 51:10

It should be the desire for all of us to be a vessel that God can use. And that vessel should be pure and clean, free of anything that would take your focus away from Jesus.

My husband, Rick, has traveled the world and has drunk from every kind of vessel imaginable. He would tell the stories of different types that he was given to drink from in the different places he would go.

He went to a place where he was served Diet Coke in a zip lock bag. To drink it, he was told to bite the corner of the bag. He was at another place where the only place to get a drink of water was a bucket in the middle of the village and everyone drank from a gourd. We can drink from all kinds of vessels, from paper cups to plastic bottles to fine China teacups. Each one is useful in their rightful place, but we want them to be pure and clean, free from dirt or anything else that would be harmful to us.

That's how we should be, too. We need to keep our lives free from the distractions of this world if we want to be a useful vessel for God. We must be constantly aware of things that would mar our lives and keep ourselves free from them. I want to be a useful vessel for Him; don't you?

JULY 28

Freedom to Forgive

"Forbearing one another, and forgiving one another,
if any man have a quarrel against any:
even as Christ forgave you, so also do ye."

Colossians 3:13

There are often situations that we encounter where people will hurt us, and we hold offenses against them. Sometimes our attitude is, "I want them to hurt as much as they hurt me." "I don't think they should be let off the hook that easily." "I would be giving in to them if I just forgave them."

You may be asking, "Why should I forgive them—I am still reeling from what they did to me." The answer is because Jesus told us to forgive and that should be enough of a reason why we should.

We are told in Luke 17:1 that offenses will come. But it's up to us how we choose to handle them. We mustn't allow them to dwell in our heart and fester in our minds. We can be freed from them as we choose to forgive.

It is a difficult thing to do, but the Bible tells us that we must forgive. It really doesn't matter what they did, what matters is if we decide to follow what Jesus tells us to do! The joy of the Lord will be restored to us when we choose forgiveness instead of clinging to the offense!

JULY 29

Freeing Your Hands of Offenses

"But if ye forgive not men their trespasses, neither will your Father forgive your trespasses."

Matthew 6:15

In yesterday's devotion, we talked about how Jesus tells us that we must forgive others that have caused us hurt. Jesus also told us in the above verse that for us to receive forgiveness from Him, we must first forgive others.

I heard a statement that said, "Living in the freedom of Christ includes our forgiveness of others!" We must pray this prayer: Forgive me, Lord, to the extent of how I forgive others. If we can just remember that bit of wisdom, then we would more freely forgive those that we hold offenses toward.

If you are carrying offenses in your hands, then you will have nothing to hold the blessings that God wants to give you. It's time to release those offenses, ask God for forgiveness, and give them to Him, never to pick them up again.

It is your choice to live a life of unforgiveness or to be blessed and receive forgiveness from God for yourself. Get rid of the offenses and grudges that you now hold and enjoy the freedom God has waiting for you!

JULY 30

A Debt I Couldn't Pay

"For the wages of sin is death, but the free gift of God is eternal life in Christ Jesus our Lord." ESV

Romans 6:23

It is so easy now days to go deeper into debt that you ever thought you would go. Commercials and ads about credit cards are so enticing. The thing they leave out is the fact that you end up paying back a much larger amount than you first spent. And it takes many years to pay them off.

Of course, there are some large expenditures that are necessary, such as, a car, a house, school loans, etc. These will also take years to make the last payment. Doesn't it feel wonderful, though, when that happens? You are finally free from that debt!

But there is a debt that we could have never paid on our own and that is the debt of sin. Nothing that we had, nothing that we could ever do, could free us from it. If we could have paid that debt ourselves, then the plan of salvation would not be needed and Jesus' sacrifice would have been in vain. But, praise God, there is a way of escape. There's a chorus that we once sang that tells us how we've been freed from this debt.

He paid a debt He did not owe; I owed a debt I could not pay
I needed someone to wash my sins away
And now I sing a brand-new song, Amazing Grace
Christ Jesus paid a debt that I could never pay

Thank you, Jesus, that you paid that debt for all mankind with your death, burial, and resurrection. Jesus loved us and gave His life so that we would no longer be under that debt of sin. We are free from that debt because it has been paid in full!

JULY 31

Sweet Peace of God

"And the peace of God, which passeth all understanding, shall keep your hearts and minds through Christ Jesus."

Philippians 4:7

I have talked about having freedom from various things in the devotions for this month. In this last one for July, I'd like to discuss the freedom to experience the sweet peace of God.

Since I've been a Christian, I have not always lived as close to God as I should have, nor always done the things I should have done, but I have never regretted making that decision!

There is another old song that carries with it such a great message. The last line simply says, "The longer I serve Him, the sweeter He grows." What a great statement! Jesus dwells in my heart and He gives me sweet communion when I take the time every day to meet with Him. I feel a freedom to worship Him like I never have before.

You can experience that same freedom. You can only feel it when you allow Jesus to have complete control of your life. There's such a peace that comes when you realize that Jesus is with you and will never leave you nor forsake you. Give Him your everything; He will replace it with His peace as you free your mind and worship Him. You will discover that experiencing Him will free you to be at peace!

NOTES

AUGUST 1

We All Have a Story

"He comforts us in all our troubles so that we can comfort others. When they are troubled, we will be able to give them the same comfort God has given us." NLT

2 Corinthians 1:4

We all have our own story, and no one's is the same. The question is are you hiding your story, or do you tell it to others so that they may come to know Christ because of hearing it? Every song that was written came from an experience that the composer had faced. The words came from their very heart and soul in hopes that the song would actually help someone else that was on the same journey that they had been on.

What is your story? Have you tried to write it down so that others may hear it and be inspired by it? Have you orally told someone how you came to the saving knowledge of Jesus Christ? By telling your story to others, it not only builds your faith, but it may give you the opportunity to lead them to Jesus.

Although we may not be happy with the situations that we face, it can always be used for the glory of God. He will put people across your path that need to hear your story. You just may discover that your stories are similar, and you will be able to tell them that they can make it…because you did!

In the next few weeks, I am going to look into the stories behind some of the songs that we sing. Hopefully, it will be inspiring to you to begin to tell others of your story.

AUGUST 2

Amazing Grace

"For God saved us and called us to live a holy life. He did this, not because we deserved it, but because that was his plan from before the beginning of time—to show us his grace through Christ Jesus." NLT

2 Timothy 1:9

This hymn was written by John Newton in 1772. He lived with both of his parents until his mother passed away while his dad was away at sea. The purpose of his dad's trips was to travel the coasts of Africa and capture slaves to be sold for profit. When Newton grew older, he went into the same "business" as his father.

On one such trip, he and his crew encountered a huge storm, causing some of his men to be swept overboard. The storm was so severe, it seemed that they would all drown. Newton battled the storm for eleven hours, during which he cried out to God, "Lord, have mercy on us." No one else was lost on the ship as the storm eventually calmed. This happened on March 21, and he proclaimed that day as "a day set aside for a time of humiliation, prayer, and praise." In this experience, he found God.

That would be his last trip to seek out slaves for his personal gain. When he made it back home safely, he decided to study Greek and Hebrew. He was able to give his testimony in several places, and was eventually ordained and began his own church. God had totally changed him from a man who was an advocate for the slave trade to a man actively working towards abolishing it.

We are no different than John Newton. Our story is different from his, but God's grace is still amazing to take us from a live of sin and completely change our mindset to live for Him. Praise God for His amazing grace!

Information from: Geneva.edu/blog/uncategorized/hymnology-amazing-grace.

AUGUST 3

There is Power in The Blood

"But if we walk in the light, as he is in the light, we have fellowship one with another, and the blood of Jesus Christ his Son cleanseth us from all sin."

I John 1:7

Lewis Edgar Jones wrote this hymn in 1889. Composing hymns was just a hobby to him, but he ended up writing over 200. Many of them were written after listening to various pastors' sermons. "There Is Power In The Blood" was his most famous and has been published in many hymnals.

Jones lived on a farm with his family until he was 21 years old. He went into business for a while but then attended the Moody Bible Institute in Chicago, IL. After attending a camp meeting in Mountain Lake Park, MD, he was so moved by the sermon on a particular night that he composed this hymn. It has been a favorite of many people over the years.

In this hymn, he speaks about what the blood of Jesus did for him and will do for us:

◊ Frees us from sin as we win victory over evil

◊ Freedom from passion and pride, receive cleansing

◊ Become white as snow as our sin stains are gone

◊ Enables us to do service for Jesus, singing praises to Him

These are only a few of the benefits that we receive when we decide to follow Jesus. If you haven't already done so, be washed in His blood today and begin to receive that cleansing flow that will wash you clean. His red blood will take a black heart and turn it white as snow!

Information compiled from: Hymnary.org/text/would_you_be_free_from_the_burden_jones ; DianaLeaghMatthews.com/theres-power-in-the-blood/#.YmK6J4XMJKg ; Hymnstudiesblog.wordpress.com/2013/02/19/there-is-power-in-the-blood/

AUGUST 4

It Is Well with My Soul

"Beloved, I pray that all may go well with you and that you may be in good health, as it goes well with your soul." ESV

3 John 1:2

The words to this hymn were written by Horatio Spafford in 1873 with the music written by Philip Bliss added later. This was written after a few years filled with tragedy. Horatio was a successful lawyer, as well as a real estate investor, and was a devout Christian. He also experienced deep tragedy, all within a few years. First, in 1871, their four-year-old son contracted scarlet fever and died. Just a few months later, they lost a large portion of their property holdings from the great Chicago fire.

In 1873, thinking that a trip to Europe would be a help to his family, Horatio put his wife, Anna, and their four daughters on a ship. He was to meet them after tending to some business. While on the voyage, the ship struck another and quickly sank. All of the daughters drowned, but Anna survived. She sent a telegram to Horatio stating, "Saved alone!"

Horatio immediately left to sail to his wife. When the ship neared the place where his daughters had died, he wrote the words to "It is Well with My Soul." Instead of dwelling on the tragedies that he had experienced in the past few years, he chose to focus on the faithfulness of God in the midst of it.

What a testimony and what an amazing song. To be able to say that it is well with your soul is not an instant thing. It takes years of trusting God in every situation that you face, no matter if the result is what you wanted or not. God knows what is best…trust Him with everything in you!

Information from: AmericanSongWriter.com/it-is-well-with-my-soul-behind-the-song-horatio-spafford-philip-bliss/

AUGUST 5

Blessed Assurance

"And we desire that every one of you do shew the same diligence to the full assurance of hope unto the end:"

Hebrews 6:11

When Fanny Crosby was just a baby, she contracted a cold infection which settled in her eyes. The doctor put a poultice on them, but this was a medical error that caused immediate blindness. She was taken to a famous surgeon in New York hoping to find help for Fanny. But it was too late; the damage was permanent.

Fanny never looked at her affliction as a disability, she considered it a blessing. She once made the statement, "Do you know that if at birth I had been able to make one petition, it would have been that I should be born blind?" When asked why, she replied, "Because when I get to heaven, the first face that shall ever gladden my sight will be that of my Savior!"

One day, in 1873, while visiting a friend, Mrs. Joseph F. Knapp, she asked Fanny to listen to a new melody she had just composed. She asked her what she thought the tune was saying. These words came out of Fanny's mouth:

Blessed assurance, Jesus is mine
Oh what a foretaste of glory divine
Heir of salvation, purchase of God
Born of His Spirit, washed in His blood

Fanny Crosby was used of God to write many hymns despite the fact that she was blind. This is such a powerful story behind the hymn, Blessed Assurance. She knew where her strength came from, and she did not let her blindness stop her from what God called her to do. What a blessing she has been to millions of people! She never allowed anything to hinder her from her God given gift; can you say that about yours?

Information from: PhamoxMusic.com/blessed-assurance-hymn-and-the-story-behind-it/ ; St-Ignatius.net/fanny-crosby-and-the-story-behind-blessed-assurance/

AUGUST 6

Just As I Am

"There is therefore now no condemnation for those who are in Christ Jesus."

Romans 8:1a

This hymn was written in 1835 by Charlotte Elliott. As a young woman, Charlotte was a portrait artist as well as a writer. Her health began to fail by the time she was 30 and she became an invalid, with a lot of physical pain, for the remainder of her life. Because of this, she became very discouraged.

When Charlotte was 33 years old, a preacher from Switzerland, visited the family. While there, he counseled with her concerning her spiritual and emotional problems. He said to her, "You must come just as you are — a sinner, to the Lamb of God that takes away the sin of the world."

Charlotte never forgot what her new friend had spoken to her. Fourteen years later she penned the words to "Just As I Am." The music to this hymn as we know it today was composed by William Bradbury and has been used hundreds of times during altar calls.

Aren't you thankful that we can come to Jesus just as we are, and He will accept us into His family? We only need to realize that His blood was shed for our salvation. Our job is to accept what He did for us and believe He has saved us from our sin. Oh Lamb of God, I come. Have you made that decision?

Information from: MightyIsTheLord.com/articles/2014/07/27/just-as-i-am-the-story-behind-the-song

AUGUST 7

His Eye Is on the Sparrow

"[29]Are not two sparrows sold for a farthing? and one of them shall not fall on the ground without your Father. [30]But the very hairs of your head are all numbered. [31]Fear ye not therefore, ye are of more value than many sparrows."

Matthew 10:29-31

The words to this hymn were written in 1905 by Walter and Civilla Martin. It was first written as a poem and the following day, was sent to George Gabriel who composed the music.

The Martins had gone to visit friends, Mr. and Mrs. Doolittle, in Elmira, New York. Mrs. Doolittle had been bedridden for close to 20 years and her husband, being crippled, was confined to a wheelchair. When Walter and Civilla visited with their friends, they saw that, despite their disabilities, they lived a happy, Christian life, giving inspiration and comfort to all who knew them.

Walter asked them the secret to their bright hopefulness, and this was Mrs. Doolittle's response, "His eye is on the sparrow, and I know He watches me." From that statement was born the hymn, "His Eye Is On The Sparrow."

No matter what we go through in our lives, no matter what we face, we can be assured that God is watching over us. If He has His eye upon the tiny, little sparrow, we can know, beyond the shadow of a doubt, that His eye is on us!

Information from: UmcDiscipleship.org/resources/history-of-hymns-his-eye-is-on-the-sparrow

NOTES

AUGUST 8

Sweet Hour of Prayer

"The Lord is nigh unto all them that call upon him, to all that call upon him in truth."

Psalm 145:18

William Walford was a blind, wood carver with an extraordinary memory. He wrote poetry and at times, spoke at the church where he attended. He would commit scriptures to memory as others would read to him and was able to quote them, including chapter and verse. He constantly dwelled on them in his mind, thus experiencing sweet communion with the Lord.

One day, sometime during the mid-nineteenth century, he was visited by Thomas Salmon, who was from New York, and William quoted to him a poem about prayer that he had committed to his memory. Thomas could see the beauty and significance of the poem and wrote it down for William. Three years later, when he returned home, Thomas showed it to the editor of the New York Observer, who then published it in his newspaper. After William's death (1850), it was set to music by William Bradbury in 1861 and became a popular hymn, being translated into several foreign languages. He never saw what an impact his simple poem made around the world.

What sweet communion with the Lord is available to us if we just take the opportunity and time to talk to Him through our prayers. It's the place where we can go to find relief from the cares of this world! Are you spending that much needed time with the Lord?

Information from: DianaLeaghMatthews.com/sweet-hour-prayer/#.YnK5hofMJKg

AUGUST 9

What a Friend We Have in Jesus

"Come unto me, all ye that labour and are heavy laden, and I will give you rest."

Matthew 11:28

This hymn was born through lots of struggles and grief by Joseph Scriven from Dublin, Ireland. The date it was written is unclear.

Joseph attended and graduated from Trinity College in Dublin and planned to marry his childhood sweetheart. Tragically, the day before the wedding, his fiancé was riding a horse, on the way to visit him. The horse was spooked by something he saw and bucked her off into a river and she drowned.

He felt he could no longer live there because of his grief, so he moved to Ontario, Canada. He soon became engaged again but sadly, tragedy struck him again. She contracted pneumonia and died shortly before the wedding.

Through everything he encountered in his life, he continued to find solace with Jesus, his best friend, by his side. He wrote "What A Friend" as a poem and sent it to his mother, never knowing that it would one day become a well-loved hymn.

This hymn reminds us that no matter what we go through in our lives, we can always turn to Jesus for comfort. We will miss that peace by bearing the pain ourselves because we don't carry everything to God in prayer. What comfort is available to us if we simply take it to God.

Information from: ReasonableTheology.org/hymn-story-friend-jesus/

AUGUST 10

There is a Fountain

"On that day a fountain will be opened
to the house of David and the inhabitants of Jerusalem,
to cleanse them from sin and impurity." NIV

Zechariah 13:1

The hymn was written by William Cowper from Berkhampstead, England. He was the fourth child born to Rev. John and Ann Cowper. However, before he was born, all three of his siblings had died. Then, within the next five years, he had 2 other siblings that did not survive. Finally, a brother was born and survived. But the mother soon passed away.

At age 6, William was sent away to boarding school, where he was bullied by his peers and disciplined harshly by his teachers. He attended Westminster from age 10-18, in which he was happy for most of those years. But he then suffered serious battles with depression and tried suicide three different times. He was declared insane and sent to an asylum. The caretaker there was an evangelical Christian and through him, William accepted Jesus as Lord and Saviour.

He struggled for the rest of his life with depression, but he wrote "There is a Fountain" during one of his happy times. Although he often felt that he was unworthy of salvation, he realized that Christ's blood completely cleanses us. Do you truly believe that? You should because that's the reason Jesus died—so that we can be cleansed from our sins. Thank God for His fountain filled with blood!

Information from: Judsonu.edu

AUGUST 11

The Old Rugged Cross

"And being found in human form,
he humbled himself by becoming obedient
to the point of death, even death on a cross." ESV

Philippians 2:8

"The Old Rugged Cross" was written by George Bennard in 1912 after being heckled by some young people at a revival meeting. That they would have such disregard of the Gospel greatly troubled him, and he began to study about Christ on the cross. This led him to write the first verse and chorus of this hymn. Several months later, he finished the song.

Upon completion of it, George presented it to the pastors where he was holding a series of meetings and they were brought to tears, asking him to present it to the church. Needless to say, it was received very well. The evangelist, Billy Sunday, eventually heard it and frequently incorporated it into his ministry.

This is one of the most well-known hymns today, as well as one of the most cherished in the Christian faith. Even though it was a horrible suffering for Jesus, I am so thankful that He loves us enough to have endured the cross and was raised from the dead so that we might experience salvation through Him.

Information from: FamilyRadio.org/devotional/history-behind-old-rugged-cross/

AUGUST 12

Rock of Ages

"The Lord is my rock, my fortress and my deliverer; my God is my rock, in whom I take refuge, my shield and the horn of my salvation, my stronghold." NIV

Psalm 18:2

Augustus Toplady wrote "Rock of Ages" in 1763. Augustus was 16 years old when he accepted Christ as Savior while attending a meeting in Ireland. Although, he had already been preaching for four years and writing hymns for two years!

Legend says that he was traveling through the countryside of England, a fierce storm came up and he sought out shelter from it. He came upon a cleft in a large rock and was protected from the storm. He supposedly wrote out the song while there on a playing card that was in his pocket. This hymn has been a favorite for many years.

Rocks are strong, solid, and unchanging. It means the same when you call a person a rock. You've heard the expression, "He/she has been my rock." But the greatest rock we can lean on is Jesus Christ! No matter the situation that we are going through, no matter what circumstances we are currently facing, Jesus will be our rock. Is He your rock? Lean on Him today and you will survive every storm that comes along.

Information from: DianaLeaghMatthews.com/rock-of-ages/#.YokOjHXMK00

AUGUST 13

I Surrender All

*"My son, give me thine heart,
and let thine eyes observe my ways."*

Proverbs 23:26

The lyrics for this beloved hymn was written by Judson Wheeler Van de Venter and was put to music by Winfield S. Weeden.

Even though Judson was raised in a Christian home, he did not accept Christ until he was 17 years old. He went on to graduate from the university with a degree in art and secured a job as a high school art teacher and administrator. He also studied and taught music, as well as sang and composed music. He became involved in the music ministry at his church. But he struggled within with the challenge of continuing to teach or to choose Gospel ministry. This struggle lasted for five years. This is how he described it:

"For some time, I had struggled between developing my talents in the field of art and going into full-time evangelistic work. At last the pivotal hour of my life came, and I surrendered all. A new day was ushered into my life. I became an evangelist and discovered down deep in my soul a talent hitherto unknown to me. God had hidden a song in my heart, and touching a tender chord. He caused me to sing."

Are you struggling with a choice that God has laid before you? I can tell you that you won't be truly happy until you decide to surrender everything to Him. He has called you; give Him your all today!

Information from: AuntyFaith.com/2020/01/15/the-story-behind-the-hymn-i-surrender-all/

AUGUST 14

Tis So Sweet to Trust in Jesus

"Lord Almighty, blessed is the one who trusts in you." NIV

Psalm 84:12

Louisa M.R. Stead wrote this hymn during a difficult time in her life. It is a hymn that is loved by all.

Louisa was born in England and became a Christian at age nine. She felt a strong call to be a missionary when she was a teenager. Around the age of 21, she immigrated to America and soon attended a revival meeting in Urbana, Ohio. In that meeting, she decided to go to China to do missions work. Her health became an issue, and she wasn't able to go. She eventually married a man named Stead.

One day, she and her husband decided to take their young daughter to the beach and have a picnic together. While there, Mr. Stead heard the cries of a young boy that was drowning. Without giving it a thought, he ran to the water to rescue him. He was unsuccessful in saving him and they both drown.

In facing this tragedy, Louisa wrote this hymn. She learned that she could continue on with her life by trusting in Jesus. Just by simply taking Him at His word, she could trust that He would take care of her. The same is true for you. Jesus gave us His Word and I believe it! Do you believe?

Information from: GodlyEssence.com/my-story-my-song-tis-so-sweet-to-trust-in-jesus/

NOTES

AUGUST 15

I Have Decided to Follow Jesus

"And ye shall be hated of all men for my name's sake: but he that endureth to the end shall be saved."

Matthew 10:22

This hymn is based on the last words from a man named Nokseng from the Garo tribe in Assam, India. Because of a great revival that occurred in Wales around 150 years ago, there were several missionaries that went to spread the Gospel to northeast India. One of them led Nokseng and his family to Jesus. Upon hearing about the conversion of this family, several tribe members became Christians.

When the chief of the village heard about it, he had Nokseng and his family brought before him. He told him to deny their faith, or they would be executed. Nokseng told him, "I have decided to follow Jesus; no turning back, no turning back." To which the chief ordered the two children to be killed. He then asked him if he would deny his faith since his children were now dead. Nokseng told the chief, "Though no one joins me, still I will follow, no turning back, no turning back" and the chief ordered his wife to be killed. Once more, the chief ordered Nokseng to deny his faith and his last words were, "The cross before me, the world behind me, no turning back, no turning back." To which the chief also ordered his death. The chief was so greatly touched with Nokseng's faith, that he chose to accept Christ, and the entire village did as well.

What a testimony this new convert had as he refused to deny Jesus. Can we say that we will stand for Him even though death is staring us in the face? Jesus must take precedence in our hearts, both in life and in death. He is that important!

Information from: BelieversPortal.com/the-true-story-behind-the-hymn-i-have-decided-to-follow-jesus/

AUGUST 16

His Name is Wonderful

"For unto us a child is born, unto us a son is given: and the government shall be upon his shoulder: and his name shall be called Wonderful, Counsellor, The mighty God, The everlasting Father, The Prince of Peace."

Isaiah 9:6

Some hymns do not have a long story of how it was written. This one is one of those, but it is interesting story. It was written by Audrey Mieir in 1955. The words came to her as she was watching a Christmas program at her church in Duarte, California.

Audrey was inspired as she saw the children dressed as the different characters in the story of Jesus' birth. At the end of the program, the pastor read the above scripture and with hands raised to heaven, he said, "His name is Wonderful!"

These words from her pastor set her mind awhirl and she wrote the chorus to this hymn in the flyleaf of her Bible. The remainder was written within the next few days, giving a fuller description of just who Jesus is!

Jesus is certainly wonderful to me, but He is so much more. As a matter of fact, there are not enough words to describe who He is. Do you feel the same about Him? He would love to hear you tell Him just what He means to you. Give it a try!

Information from: Crosswalk.com/church/worship/his-name-is-wonderful-11562301.html

AUGUST 17

I Love to Tell the Story

"Day after day, in the temple courts and from house to house, they never stopped teaching and proclaiming the good news that Jesus is the Messiah." NIV

Acts 5:42

Katherine Hankey was born into a wealthy English family in 1834. From an early age, it was her desire to tell the poor and downhearted about Jesus and to see them come to Him.

While she was young, she began holding Bible studies around London. When she turned eighteen, she also held Bible classes for the "factory girls" that lasted for several years.

On a mission to Africa in 1866, she became seriously ill. The doctors informed her that she would need extensive bed rest and was told that she could not teach her Bible classes for a year. While recovering, she wrote two long poem about Jesus. Some historians say that they were each 50 stanzas long.

Some of the words from the first poem was taken for the hymn, "Tell Me The Old, Old Story", written at the beginning of her convalescence. She titled it "The Story Wanted." The words to "I Love to Tell the Story" was taken from the second poem that was written ten months later, which she titled "The Story Told." This hymn was later set to music by William G. Fischer.

I'm sure Katherine had much more to tell her Bible classes about what she had gleaned during her recovery. God certainly uses those times to download many lessons to us during our trials. What has He taught you recently? Have you told anybody? You never know who needs to hear it!

Information from: PracticalBiblicalInsight.blogspot.com/2009/06/hymn-history-i-love-to-tell-story.html ; Wikipedia.org/wiki/I_Love_to_Tell_the_Story

AUGUST 18

Because He Lives

"Yet a little while, and the world seeth me no more; but ye see me: because I live, ye shall live also."

John 14:19

This song was written by Gloria Gaither in the late 1960s during an uncertain, fearful time in her life. Bill, her husband, was recovering from mononucleosis and she was expecting their third child. At the same time, they and their church were facing unfounded accusations, bringing on discouragement. Added to all of this, Gloria was being tormented with fear of the future and bringing another child into a sin-crazed world.

One day, as she was sitting in her darkened living room, there came a calm and peaceful rest over her. Her fear and torment were replaced with the joy that only comes from God.

In her own words, this is how she described that time in her life. *I can't quite explain what happened at that moment, but suddenly I felt released from it all. The panic that had begun to build inside was gently dispelled by a reassuring presence that engulfed my life and drew my attention. Gradually, the fear left, and the joy began to return. I knew I could have that baby and face the future with optimism and trust. It was the Resurrection affirming itself in our lives once again. It was LIFE conquering death in the regularity of my day.*

Out of this was born the song, "Because He Lives." You too can realize that joy and peace when you see that you can face tomorrow because He lives in you. Life is indeed worth living just because He lives!

Information from: BelieversPortal.com/story-behind-because-he-lives-hymn/

AUGUST 19

Turn Your Eyes Upon Jesus

"Unto thee lift I up mine eyes, O thou that dwellest in the heavens."
Psalm 123:1

Helen Lemmel was the daughter of a Methodist minister, as well as an established hymn writer and a soloist. In 1922, after reading a booklet written by Lilias Trotter, entitled "Focussed", and hearing of her life story, she wrote this hymn. The original title of it was "The Heavenly Vision" but is most known by the first line of the refrain.

Lilias Trotter was born into an upper-class family in London and lacked for nothing. Sadly, her father passed away when she was twelve years old which devastated her. It was at this time that she came to accept Jesus as her Lord and Savior. She later felt the call to do missions work in Algeria.

At some point during this time, Lilias wrote the booklet which was an inspiration to Helen Lemmel. The following is the section that inspired her to write "Turn Your Eyes Upon Jesus": *Turn full your soul's vision to Jesus, and look and look at Him, and a strange dimness will come over all that is apart from Him, and the Divine "attrait" by which God's saints are made, even in this 20th century, will lay hold of you. For "He is worthy" to have all there is to be had in the heart that He has died to win."*

Having never met Helen, Lilias Trotter did not know that her writings would have such a great influence on so many others through the writing of this hymn. And neither do we know what influence we exhibit and just what it will do. Are you living a life that will lead others to look into the face of Jesus? Be careful what you do--there is always someone watching!

Information from: CastlefieldsChurch.org.uk/turn-your-eyes-upon-jesus-the-story-behind-the-hymn/

AUGUST 20

Great Is Thy Faithfulness

"[22]It is of the Lord's mercies that we are not consumed, because his compassions fail not. [23]They are new every morning: great is thy faithfulness."

Lamentations 3:22-23

Although many hymn are written out of dramatic circumstances, this one was inspired by the daily faithfulness of God realized by the author.

Thomas Obadiah Chisholm was born in Kentucky and became a teacher at the age of sixteen, even though he was not able to continue his own education into high school or any further training.

At twenty-one years of age, Thomas became the associate editor of the local newspaper. It was six years later that he accepted Jesus as Lord and Savior during a revival meeting. He became a minister in the Methodist faith and was pastor for a short time. Poor health forced him to resign that position. In 1953, he retired and moved to a Methodist Home for the Aged in New Jersey where he spent the rest of his days.

In 1941, Thomas wrote to a friend, mentioning that his income had not been large at any time of his life due to his health issues. But he also wrote of the unfailing faithfulness of God in the letter. The date of the writing of this hymn is unclear but he certainly experienced God's faithfulness throughout his life.

I can say that God has been faithful to me. And I have found that His mercies are new every morning. Do you know that you can experience God's faithfulness too? I cannot make it with Him; I hope you feel the same.

Information from: BelieversPortal.com/story-behind-great-is-thy-faithfulness-hymn/

AUGUST 21

As The Deer

"As the deer pants for streams of water,
so my soul pants for you, my God." NIV

Psalm 42:1

This hymn is one of my all-time favorites. The music is soothing for the soul and the words are straight from the Bible, touching my very heartstrings.

It was written by Marty Nystrom in 1984 after a trip to Christ for the Nations Institute in Dallas, TX. He had met a girl and the relationship did not work out as he had thought. This left him with a broken heart. His roommate encouraged him to fast and pray over the situation, in order to turn himself back to God.

During this time, he sat down at a piano and noticed a Bible there, open to Psalm 42. After reading the first verse of that chapter, he composed this hymn. He thought that the hymn was just for him, and he kept it to himself for a while. But before leaving Dallas to return back home, he did share it with one person, who introduced it to the students at the school. It became a well-loved hymn around the world.

How many times have you found yourself discouraged, despondent, disillusioned, or disappointed over situations that arise in your life? God is your answer, no matter what you are going through. Thirst after Him just as the deer pants and thirsts for the water. He will be a refreshing to your soul if you'll just go to Him.

Information from: CountryThangDaily.com/psalm-deer-marty-nystro/

NOTES

AUGUST 22

I Need Thee Every Hour

"Do not be anxious about anything, but in every situation, by prayer and petition, with thanksgiving, present your requests to God." NIV

Philippians 4:6

This hymn was written by Annie Hawks in 1872. By the time she was 14 years old, she already possessed a gift of writing poetry and was sending them to a variety of newspapers on a regular basis.

As a prominent writer of gospel songs, her pastor, Dr. Robert Lowry, saw her gift of writing poetry and was a great encouragement to her to continue with her writings.

Here is her own account concerning the writing of this song: "One day as a young wife and mother of 37 years of age, I was busy with my regular household tasks during a bright June morning [in 1872]. Suddenly, I became so filled with the sense of nearness to the Master that, wondering how one could live without Him, either in joy or pain, these words were ushered into my mind, the thought at once taking full possession of me -- I Need Thee Every Hour..."

I can fully understand the words of this song, especially since my husband, Rick, has passed. Even though grief is difficult, and it takes time to go through it, God is with you through it all and He will continue to be with you as you turn to Him. He will answer you every time you call on Him, even if it is every hour of every day; He will never tire of hearing from you!

Information from: Umcdiscipleship.org/resources/history-of-hymns-i-need-thee-every-hour

AUGUST 23

This Is My Father's World

"The earth is the Lord's, and the fulness thereof; the world, and they that dwell therein."

Psalm 24:1

This hymn was written as a poem by Maltbie L. Babcock and was later set to music by Franklin L. Sheppard. Maltbie was born into a socially prominent family and did not waste any of the many opportunities to succeed that he had been given. He was a baseball player, varsity swimmer, and later, became an ordained Presbyterian minister and pastor.

Maltbie was also a skilled musician, and a great lover of nature. He was in the habit of taking morning walks to the top of a hill near Lockport, New York where he lived at the time. From here, he had a full view of Lake Ontario and the countryside.

When he would leave his house to go on these walks, he would tell his wife that he was going out to see his Father's world. While on one of them, and admiring everything around him, Maltbie was inspired to compose this hymn. He realized that the earth does indeed belong to the Lord.

No matter how bad things get in our world, we must remember that God is still the Ruler. There's no wonder that Maltbie wrote:

This is my Father's world, O let me ne'er forget
That though the wrong seems oft so strong God is the Ruler yet

Information from: UmcDiscipleship.org/resources/history-of-hymns-this-is-my-fathers-world

AUGUST 24

At Calvary

"And when they had come to the place called Calvary, t here they crucified Him, and the criminals, one on the right hand and the other on the left." NKJV

Luke 23:33

Dr. R. A. Torrey was president of Moody Bible Institute and received a letter from a pastor in Ohio, asking if they would accept his son. The father related to him that he was a troubled teen and felt that Moody Bible Institute would be just what he needed.

Dr. Torrey told him that they were not running a reform school. With much persistence, the man continued to ask, and Dr. Torrey finally gave in with the stipulation that he was to attend all the classes, obey all of the rules, and stop by his office every day.

So, William Newell was enrolled and faithfully followed all he was told to do, including visiting Dr. Torrey each day. In the process of time, Bill accepted Christ as Lord and Savior! He finished the school, graduated, and later became a teacher there himself. During this time, he wrote a meaningful poem, and said, "As I read what I had written, I realized that it was a word picture of what had happened in my life." He took the poem to the head of the music department who composed the music to the song.

Can you say, as did William that you spent years in vanity and pride, not knowing about Jesus being crucified and dying for you? And then that wonderful day when you went to Calvary and found liberty in Jesus. What a glorious day that was! I am so thankful for Calvary! Aren't you?

Information from: maxesmith27.wordpress.com/2010/06/06/at-calvary/

AUGUST 25

God Will Take Care of You

"I will be your God throughout your lifetime— until your hair is white with age. I made you, and I will care for you. I will carry you along and save you." NLT

Isaiah 46:4

This hymn was written by Civilla Martin, and the music was composed by her husband, William in the early 1900s.

At this time, William was a traveling evangelist while spending some time at the Practical Bible Training School in Lestershire, now Johnson City, New York. Before a certain preaching engagement which was many miles away, Civilla became sick, and William was trying to make the decision of whether to go to preach or to reschedule the meeting. Their young son told him, "Father, don't you think that if God wants you to preach today, he will take care of Mother while you are away?"

Because of his son's encouraging words, William chose to go to the engagement. By the time he returned home, she was much better and had written a poem, "God Will Take Care of You", to which he later added the music. It was the pure childlike faith of their child that inspired this song.

Do you believe that God will take care of you no matter what's going on in your life? I trust Him and absolutely know that He will do just that! Give Him your worry and then you, too, can believe that God will take care of you!

Information from: SermonWriter.com/hymn-stories/god-will-take-care/

AUGUST 26

He Leadeth Me

*"He maketh me to lie down in green pastures:
he leadeth me beside the still waters."*

Psalm 23:2

On March 25, 1862, a young preacher, Dr. Joseph Henry Gilmore, was filling the pulpit for the pastor there, who was away that night. He chose to speak on Psalm 23.

As he was preaching, he didn't seem to be able to get past verse two. This was during the dark days of the Civil War, and he felt led to focus on God's leadership.

After the service ended, Dr Gilmore and his wife were invited to one of the deacon's houses for a time of fellowship and refreshment. While others were talking with each other, he wrote the words to this hymn as a poem. He later gave it to his wife. Without his knowledge, she sent it in to a Christian publication. After which, William Bradbury, a hymn writer, added the music to the poem.

Three years later, William was preaching at another church that had just purchased new hymnals. As he looked through it to find out what hymns they were singing, he came across his very own poem. His wife explained to him that she had been the one that had sent it in.

I have chosen to be a faithful follower of Jesus, allowing Him to lead me. As you, too, make this decision, you can have such a peace that you are not making this life journey alone. He will be with you, leading you, wherever you go.

Information from: EnjoyingTheJourney.org/hymn-history-he-leadeth-me/

AUGUST 27

When The Roll Is Called Up Yonder

"And there shall in no wise enter into it any thing that defileth, neither whatsoever worketh abomination, or maketh a lie: but they which are written in the Lamb's book of life."

Revelation 21:27

This hymn was written by James Milton Black. He had a great interest in music at an early age and later became the church musician. He was also the youth leader and Sunday School teacher.

On day, he walked down an alley and met a fourteen-year-old girl; it was apparent that she was living a rough life. He found out that she had an alcoholic father. Having compassion on her, he invited her to Sunday School. She did come and faithfully attended his class.

It was his practice to have the children to quote a Bible verse when he would call the roll. One day, the young girl did not answer when her name was called, and James noticed that she wasn't there. This greatly concerned him. When he checked on her, he found that she was deathly sick with pneumonia. Even though James called the doctor, she died a few days later.

He was very saddened by her death and began to think about calling of the roll in heaven and how he wanted to make sure he was there to answer that roll call. He wrote this song in just 15 minutes.

Are you absolutely sure that you will be there when that most important roll call is made? You can be, you know. That is one roll call that you do not want to miss!

Information from: The-end-time.org/2019/11/24/story-behind-the-song-when-the-roll-is-called-up-yonder/

AUGUST 28

I Know Who Holds Tomorrow

"For I the Lord thy God will hold thy right hand, saying unto thee, Fear not; I will help thee."

Isaiah 41:13

Ira Stanphill, the author of this song, was a musician and minister. During his life, he served in nine different organizations as youth director, music director, and pastor. He preached at many places in the United States and abroad and he wrote over 500 songs.

He married Zelma, a preacher's daughter, in 1939, and she began traveling with him. Eventually, she decided that the ministry was not the life for her, and she left Ira. They divorced in 1951.

It was at this time that Ira went into a deep depression. One day, as he was driving home, he began to hum what would become this song. Upon arriving, he went straight to his piano and jotted down the words. Ira had learned that he could trust that the one who holds his tomorrow would hold his hand and go with him as he lived his life day by day.

I know who holds my tomorrow and every other day after it and that is Jesus! He holds yours as well. You may not understand why certain things happen, but you can trust that God will always be with you as you face every new tomorrow.

Information from: DianaLeaghMatthews.com/i-know-who-holds-tomorrow/#.YrfLsRXMKOO

AUGUST 29

Jesus Paid It All

"For ye are bought with a price: therefore glorify God in your body, and in your spirit, which are God's."

I Corinthians 6:20

This hymn was written in 1865 by Elvina Hall. She was sitting in a church service when the words came to her.

There was nothing special about this day when Elvina was at Monument Methodist Episcopal Church. As the pastor was preaching a rather lengthy sermon, her mind began to wander. She began to think about the cross and the sacrifice that Jesus had made for the world. Not having any paper to write on, she penned the words to this song on a page from the hymnal.

When the service ended, Elvina showed it to the pastor who was very impressed with it. He mentioned to her that the church organist had written a tune but had no words to go with it. His name was John Grape.

Elvina and John met, worked together, and "Jesus Paid It All" was birthed. After showing it to the pastor again, he convinced them to submit it to Professor Theodore Perkins, publisher of Sabbath Carols. He gladly published it, and it is still sung by many today.

Jesus indeed paid it all for our salvation with His very life. It was a debt that we would never have been able to pay. Our job is only to say, "Yes!" I am thankful for the day I made that decision to live for Him. Have you made that decision?

Information from: HymnCharts.com/2022/04/18/jesus-paid-it-all-2/

AUGUST 30

Victory In Jesus

"But thanks be to God, which giveth us the victory through our Lord Jesus Christ."

I Corinthians 15:57

The song was written by Eugene M. Bartlett, Sr. He was a singer, music publisher, producer, and songwriter.

Things were going very well for Eugene. He had married his sweetheart in 1917 and they had two children. He published hymns, as well as traveling and holding singing schools and conventions.

But at the age of 53, in 1939, Eugene suffered a paralyzing stroke, and he was basically bedridden. This naturally ended his traveling; these were some dark times for him. But he began to look back over his life, and thought about the night he was born again, and the wonderful life he had experienced since that time. With pen in hand, he began to write what became his most popular song.

We can all experience victory in Jesus just as Eugene Bartlett did. Just think about where God has brought you from and the many blessings you have seen that He has given you. He is always with us and will never leave us, no matter what we face in our lives.

Information from: BackstorySongs.com/2019/10/31/victory-in-jesus/

AUGUST 31

How Great Thou Art

"For the Lord is great, and greatly to be praised: he is to be feared above all gods."

Psalm 96:4

I can't end this section without writing about one of the greatest songs ever written. It is usually listed as second, next to Amazing Grace. Carl Boberg, a native of Sweden, wrote this as a poem in 1885, after being inspired by hearing the church bells during a thunderstorm. He first named it, "O Great God."

It was published but it did not catch on. But, three years later, someone matched the words with a traditional Swedish melody and Carl published the poem once more in his own newspaper in 1891, with the musical notation added.

A few decades passed and in the 1930s, this poem, with the music had traveled to different countries. An English missionary named Stuart Hine heard it in Russian while he was in Poland. He was so moved by it that he translated it into English and took it home with him to England. This is where it was renamed to "How Great Thou Art."

In the 1940s, Evangelist Dr. Edwin Orr heard it being sung by native tribal people in Assam, India. He also was moved by it, and he brought it to the United States. By 1954, George Beverly Shea picked it up and began singing it in the Billy Graham crusades.

Carl died in 1940, never knowing how much of an impression this hymn made on the world. Our own lives will make an impact to those around us without us even knowing it. The secret is to live our lives before others so that we represent Jesus. Our influence will be farther reaching than we will ever know, even to later generations. Live for Jesus, that's all that matters!

Information from: Crosswalk.com/faith/spiritual-life/the-story-you-don-t-know-behind-how-great-thou-art.html

NOTES

SEPTEMBER 1

Do You Really Believe?

"But my God shall supply all your needs according to his riches in glory by Christ Jesus."

Philippians 4:19

Do you make it a daily habit to read God's Word? The Bible has a lot to say; do you believe everything it says?

What about the above verse? Do you really believe that God will provide what you need when you need it? Or do you think it is just merely words to make you feel good?

This verse says that God will supply ALL our needs! He cares about every single need that we have, and He promises that He will give us what we need.

He doesn't say that He might meet our needs or that He would think about meeting our need. Neither did He say that He would pick and choose which need He would meet.

God also says that He would supply all our needs ACCORDING to His riches in glory by Christ Jesus. Do you realize that there is no end to God's riches? God will never run out of His supply to meet whatever need we may have.

So, take that to heart. The next time you have a need, whether it be financial, physical, spiritual, or any other, know that He will supply whatever it is that you need. Give Him your struggle by believing what He says and allow Him to give you His peace!

SEPTEMBER 2

God Always Knows What He's Doing

"For everything comes from him and exists by his power and is intended for his glory. All glory to him forever! Amen." NLT

Romans 11:36

I was reading about the creation in the first chapter of Genesis this morning and a thought came to me: God always knows what He's doing!

One thing that God did when He created our world was divide the light from the darkness. He knew that Nicodemus, for fear of being ridiculed by the other rulers, would one day come to Jesus by night to talk to Him. When He created the seas, He knew that Jesus would one day walk on the water and bid Peter to walk on it as well.

He knew when He created the birds of the air that the raven would one day bring food to Elijah. When he created the fish of the sea, He knew that one would be used to swallow Jonah in order for him to learn to obey what God had spoken to him. And most importantly, God knew when he created the trees, that Jesus would be crucified on a cross, made from a tree, that we may be saved.

The point is God doesn't do anything haphazard. He always has a plan in mind. It is our job to trust Him in all that we do and know that His plans are for our good. Can you say that you trust God? He does have a plan in mind for each of us; trust Him and see it come to fruition.

SEPTEMBER 3

I Do

"But whoso hath this world's good, and seeth his brother have need, and shutteth up his bowels of compassion from him, how dwelleth the love of God in him."

I John 3:17

The most common place you hear the response in the title is at a wedding when the bride and groom answer the question: Do you take this man (woman) to be your lawfully wedded husband (wife)? Do you promise to love and cherish them… And their answer is "I do." But as I ponder this, I have a few more questions to ask you.

◊ Do you care about your fellow Christian that is in need?

◊ Do you pray for more than just your family or close circle of friends?

◊ Do you love and do good to those enemies that hate you and despitefully use you?

God has a different idea about questions such as these than I had at a time in my life. I would not have been able to answer them with "I do". I once thought that it was my responsibility to take care of myself and not be concerned with what other Christians needed. It's a dog-eat-dog world; you have to take care of yourself because no one else will take care of you if you don't. Right??

Absolutely wrong! We are to have compassion for others' needs and not just for our own. Can you answer those questions with, "I do" as well as others that God may ask you? Look deep within your heart and make the decision to show His compassion to those He places in your path.

SEPTEMBER 4

Are You Thirsty for God?

"Blessed are those who hunger and thirst for righteousness, for they shall be satisfied." ESV

Matthew 5:6

On the way to church today I saw many people on the road that obviously had other things on their mind besides God. I saw some that were pulling a boat, heading toward the lake. It didn't seem that church was on their agenda for the day. I passed by McDonald's, and I saw 10-12 cars waiting in line at the drive thru. It seemed as though these people didn't plan to attend church either.

If these people only knew that they could turn to God, they would find satisfaction for the thirst in their souls. And then, their desire to learn more of Him would lead them to church as well as delving in His Word themselves.

This made me think about what Jesus told the Samaritan woman at the well. We find this in John 4:10, "Jesus answered and said unto her, If thou knewest the gift of God, and who it is that saith to thee Give me to drink; thou wouldst have asked of him and he would have given thee living water."

Do you thirst for more of God? If so, make it a priority to know Him better. One place to learn more about Him is a good, Bible-believing church. Start attending today!

SEPTEMBER 5

Results From Desperation

"And call upon me in the day of trouble: I will deliver thee, and thou shalt glorify me."

Psalm 50:15

Have you ever heard the phrase, "Desperate times call for desperate measures?" When I read this, there is one character that stands out in my mind. This woman had what the Bible calls, "an issue of blood" and she had been plagued by it for twelve years. She had spent all that she had seeing many physicians for her disorder.

When she heard about Jesus, she felt that she would be healed if she could only touch the hem of his garment. Since she had the issue with blood, she was considered unclean and anything she touched would also be unclean. (Leviticus 15:25-27) She was desperate for her healing, and she had great faith to see it accomplished. And that's just what happened. She received her healing because of her desperation and determination.

That is exactly how we should approach the Lord with our requests.

- ◊ Seek out Jesus.
- ◊ Have faith in Him that He can move on our behalf.
- ◊ Believe that He will meet our need.
- ◊ Give Him praise for the answer.

Be desperate and determined and God will supply your every need!

SEPTEMBER 6

In Training

"For this God is our God for ever and ever;
he will be our guide even to the end." NIV

Psalm 48:14

Do you realize that every one of us is in training? Things we go through, trials we encounter, lessons we learn are all training ground for what God has prepared for us to do in a specific season of our lives.

But there will come a time when the season we are in will change. And as it does, the past one is strengthening and training for the next one to come.

Sometimes I think that if I could have only realized this principle when I first became a Christian, I would be better prepared for this moment of my life. But on the other hand, if I had "known then what I know now," I may have given up on my journey.

I thank God that He sees the future and knows just how much to let us know. What a peace there is in knowing that He has already paved our way and is guiding our steps.

SEPTEMBER 7

Life's Journey

"But you know Him,
for He lives with you and will be in you." NIV

John 14:17b

Jesus has promised us that when He leaves He will send another Comforter. The Holy Spirit is that Comforter. Our life can be totally changed if we turn control over to God.

I liken it to you being in your car going on a journey. The Father, the Son, and the Holy Spirit are in the car with you and the Holy Spirit is driving. You have no idea of where you are going. But if you just sit back and trust the Holy Spirit to drive you (or lead the way for you), you will have a much smoother journey. It's when we try to take the wheel thinking that we know a better way that we get in trouble.

Life is full of potholes and detours. If someone else is driving the same route you are and are just ahead of you, they can let you know of those distractions before you reach them. If you listen to them, then you can avoid them.

Jesus has been through life as a man, and He knows about temptations that could hinder our journey. We must learn to put our trust in Him and wholeheartedly believe that He knows what is best for our lives.

NOTES

SEPTEMBER 8

It Takes Unity

"But can the ax boast greater power than the person who uses it? Is the saw greater than the person who saws? Can a rod strike unless a hand moves? Can a wooden cane walk by itself?" NLT

Isaiah 10:15

It has been said that "it takes two to tango". This phrase has been used to refer to arguing. It does take two to argue. If one person refuses to enter into the argument, then the other is just blowing off steam. The main point is that it takes two people to perform this task.

It can also work for good. As in the verse above, the ax cannot do anything by itself. Neither can the saw, the rod, nor the cane. The Bible also tells us in Ecclesiastes 4:9, "Two are better than one...." Have you ever seen an ax cut down a tree by itself? Have you seen a cane take off walking without a man to lean on it for support? Neither have I.

We are to be in unity with our brother. My husband's definition for unity as you can read in his book, Playing from The Second Chair, is "the allowance of diversity for the outcome of harmony." Unity does not mean for everyone to play the same instrument. Nor does it mean that everyone will possess the same talent. We must allow others to perform in the way in which God has called them and support them in it.

Support is an important part of unity. If it isn't "your time to shine", share in the glory of another. Then when you are in the spotlight, they will be able to share in your glory. Unity is a symphony!

SEPTEMBER 9

God Writes Our Stories

"The Lord keeps watch over you as you come and go, both now and forever." NLT

Psalm 121:8

Some people go through life never thinking about their future, only living for today. There are others that want to know what will happen in years to come and every little step it will take to get there.

Did you ever think that God is the author of the story of our lives, and He is the one that is writing our own personal book? He is the one that places us in the right place at the right time. He's the one that puts the right people in our path for the right purpose. He knows the beginning from the end so He is the only One that can write our story.

Parts of our story (our life) are sad; some are extremely hurtful. Some are very happy and joyful. But what we must learn in every area of our lives is to simply trust God. No matter the circumstances, we must cling to the fact that He loves us and will always be with us throughout every situation that we face.

What a comforting thought! No matter what our mind is telling us we just need to believe that He is guiding our every step. Then, at the end of our story, we will be in Heaven, living with Him forever. That's what I long for; don't you?

SEPTEMBER 10

It's In the Waiting

"Wait on the Lord: be of good courage, and he shall strengthen thine heart: wait, I say, on the Lord."

Psalm 27:14

Have you ever been in the valley of decision, and you are seriously praying for an answer from God? I certainly have. It's not always an instant answer; sometimes you have to wait for it.

The Bible tells us to wait on the Lord! That is often the hard part. If you're like me, I don't like to wait. When I want something, I want it now. If there's a place I want to go to, I want to go now. If I want to talk to someone about something I feel is important, I want to talk to them now.

But in life, we will do a lot of waiting. When a woman is pregnant, she will have to wait for that baby to be fully developed before she can hold him or her in her arms. When you start a new job, you will have to wait before receiving a promotion or before getting a raise until you have proven yourself to your boss. There's even waiting when you're driving, and you come to a traffic light that's red.

So it is when we are waiting on God for an answer to our prayer. But we should not just wait idly by during this time of waiting. It's now that we should get more into the Word, as well as our prayer closet and draw closer to God. And as we do, we can learn great things from Him.

If you are in a waiting period, just remember that God has heard your prayer, and He will answer you in His time. And know that He will strengthen your heart as you wait on Him.

SEPTEMBER 11

Are You Prepared for His Answer?

"Then you will call on me and come and pray to me, and I will listen to you." NIV

Jeremiah 29:12

Yesterday, we talked about waiting on God for the answer to our prayer. But are we prepared for the answer, no matter if it's yes or no? Or are we simply waiting for God to agree with us and give us His nod of approval?

I have been in that spot before when I have prayed to Him with a question on my heart. I wasn't really asking God for the answer, I just wanted Him to say, "Yes." I had to come to the place where I would be OK with it if His answer would be no.

Are you willing to receive God's "no" answer and continue on with your life in Him? Too many times, we blame God for not giving us the answer we want to hear and turn away from Him because of it. We must keep in our mind that He knows the road ahead and He knows exactly what we need for the journey. He also knows what we don't need and the harm it will cause us later on.

The secret is to trust Him, no matter if He says yes or no to our request. He truly does love us and wants what's best for us. Trust and love go hand in hand. Can you say that you trust God with everything? This is a question that we should all answer with a hearty "Yes."

SEPTEMBER 12

Forgiveness

"You Lord, are forgiving and good,
abounding in love to all who call to you." NIV

Psalm 86:5

Forgiveness is a two-way street. When God forgives us of our sins He forgets that sin. If you were to bring it up to Him later, He would simply say, "What sin?" That is such a marvelous concept!

But even though God forgives us, there is one person that we must forgive as well: the other person on the two-way street. That is us! Why hold yourself guilty if God has forgiven and forgotten?

When you know that God has truly forgiven you then forgive yourself and move on with peace in your heart.

God is good like that, you know! He's an everlasting Father that loves His children enough to help us live in peace with Him and with ourselves. I'm thankful we serve a forgiving God!

SEPTEMBER 13

Appointed Time

"For the revelation awaits an appointed time; it speaks of the end and will not prove false. Though it linger, wait for it; it will certainly come and will not delay." NIV

Habakkuk 2:3

The latter section of this verse can be viewed in two different ways. You can interpret "though it linger" as meaning that the revelation may linger. And this certainly may be true. We can trust that God will bring revelation although it may take a while to come.

But it also came to me that "though it linger" could mean that the "appointed time" will linger. In other words, I believe God has an appointed time for us to share revelation. God's timing is perfect. Not only does He have an appointed time, but we are to wait for His timing for it will surely come.

We have all heard the phrase, "a word in season." That means that there is a specific time that we are to share the revelation that we received from God, and we should linger until it's the right time. The lingering time will not last forever. We just need to learn to wait on Him to tell us the perfect time to release that word. And then, it will be received well and won't fall on deaf ears. There will be an appointed time!

SEPTEMBER 14

Steal, Kill, and Destroy

"The thief cometh not, but for to steal, and to kill, and to destroy: I am come that they might have life, and that they might have it more abundantly."

John 10:10

The devil is out to steal your soul, kill your influence with others, and destroy the life that you have in Christ. And even though nothing he does is good, he is very successful at his job!

He will disguise himself so that you will not know it is him that is attacking you. Or that it is even an attack at all. He, for sure, will not come at you in a red suit, with horns and a pitchfork!

The Bible tells us in James 1:17 NIV, "Every good and perfect gift is from above, coming down from the Father of the heavenly lights, who does not change like shifting shadows." So if good gifts come from God, then what is not good comes from Satan.

As you are reading this devotion, whether anyone is in the room with you or if you are alone, say out loud, "God-good; devil-bad!" Say it again several times until you get in down deep in your spirit. Pretty soon, you will be able to declare that God is good, and He gives good things! Aren't you glad that we serve a good God that will always give us good gifts?

NOTES

SEPTEMBER 15

Last Words That Will Last

"Then Jesus, calling out with a loud voice, said, Father, into your hands I commit my spirit! And having said this he breathed his last." ESV

Luke 23:46

The last words you hear someone say before they leave this earth are very important. Those words will not be asking about the weather, or who won the ballgame the night before. They will not be words about how much money you have or how big your house is. No! When you breathe your last breath, all of these material things will not matter to you.

Jesus made seven final statements while he was on the cross. We need to take heed to these important words with which Jesus left us.

- ◊ **Luke 23:34**-"Father, forgive them; for they know not what they do" Jesus was forgiving.
- ◊ **Luke 23:43**-"Today shalt thou be with me in paradise." Jesus was concerned.
- ◊ **John 19:26-27**-"Woman, behold thy son!" "Behold thy mother!" Jesus was loving.
- ◊ **Matthew 27:46**-"My God, my God, why hast thou forsaken me?" Jesus was obedient.
- ◊ **John 19:28**-"I thirst." Jesus was human.
- ◊ **John 19:30**-"It is finished." Jesus was confident.
- ◊ **Luke 23:46**-"Father, into thy hands I commend my spirit." Jesus was willing.

What a message that Jesus gave us while on the cross. We need to pay attention to the attitude that Jesus had as He was making these statements. We should strive to have these attitudes as well. Help me, Jesus, to represent you in all I do!

SEPTEMBER 16

Don't Be Troubled

"And Jesus answered and said unto her, Martha, Martha, thou art careful and troubled about many things:"

Luke 10:41

This is a familiar story in the Bible and is only found in the book of Luke. It is the story of two sisters that loved Jesus but responded in two totally different ways.

In verses 38-39, we are told that Jesus came to the house where they lived. Martha was busy with all the work that goes into serving guests in your home, while Mary was sitting at Jesus' feet. Being very frustrated with her sister, Martha took it to Jesus, asking Him to tell her to help. Jesus' response is recorded in verses 41-42.

One truth I get from this story is that people are different and respond in different ways. Each sister was using their particular talent to worship Jesus. Martha was a doer; she wanted to give Him her best by serving Him. Mary, on the other hand, was a hearer; she wanted to grasp everything that Jesus was teaching, sitting at His feet and learning from Him.

A word of advice to you: Don't be troubled with how others are serving God. Serve Him in your own way and allow others to do the same. If you follow this pattern, you will soon see that He will calm your hearts and bring peace to your troubled soul.

SEPTEMBER 17

God's Masterpiece

"I will praise thee; for I am fearfully and wonderfully made: marvellous are thy works; and that my soul knoweth right well."

Psalm 139:14

I once attended an evening church service and saw two young men perform a short skit before the pastor preached. One portrayed himself while the other portrayed God, having a hammer and a chisel. The first one talked about being God's workmanship and then "God" came out and began to chisel away at him to make him into the masterpiece He created him to be.

It was a very moving skit, and I began thinking about how I used to put myself down a lot of the time because I wasn't happy with the person I was. I then realized that I was not putting down myself, I was putting down one of God's workmanships.

I found the scripture listed above and I held onto it until I truly believed it in my heart. I may not be happy with some of my features, I may not look like a model, etc. but instead of dwelling on these areas, I choose to praise God for making me as I am for I am His masterpiece.

Do you truly believe that you are God's masterpiece? It's true, you know! He is the One that formed you and He is the One that considers you a masterpiece. Believe it!

SEPTEMBER 18

Work of Art

"For we are His workmanship,
created in Christ Jesus for good works,
which God prepared beforehand,
that we should walk in them." ESV

Ephesians 2:10

One definition of workmanship is a work of art or masterpiece. When an artist works on a piece, it is not considered a masterpiece until it looks exactly right in his eyes.

What others may see as a work of art, the artist sees imperfections and ways of improvement. I have painted several pieces; when others see a finished painting, I see how I could have done better with this or that.

Our granddaughter, Kyndal, has stayed with us on the days that her mother worked since she was a baby. As she became a little older, she always wanted to draw with her crayons. I still have the majority of those drawings and I treasure them; even though she is now fourteen years old. Other people may not see them as a work of art but that is just what they are to me.

That's the way that God looks at us. He does not see our imperfections and flaws; He only sees that we are a masterpiece. We are His masterpiece! Always keep in your mind that you are a work of art in God's eyes.

SEPTEMBER 19

He Bends Down and Listens

"[1]I love the Lord because
He hears my prayers and answers them.
[2]Because He bends down and listens,
I will pray as long as I breathe!"TLB

Psalm 116:1-2

Recently, these verses really touched my heart when I read them. It made me realize just how much God wants us to communicate with Him.

I know that He hears and answers us when we pray but verse two says that He "bends down and listens." That lets me know that He really desires to listen, that He's making the effort by bending down to us. That is a friend indeed!

There is no wonder that someone was so inspired to write:

What a friend we have in Jesus
All our sins and griefs to bear
What a privilege to carry
Everything to God in prayer

I honestly believe that I could not make it if I couldn't communicate with the Lord. And knowing that He desires to listen to me warms my heart and puts me at ease. I pray that you feel the same!

SEPTEMBER 20

Got Problems?

"Then said David to the Philistine, Thou comest to me with a sword, and with a spear, and with a shield: but I come to thee in the name of the Lord of hosts, the God of the armies of Israel, whom thou hast defied." ESV

I Samuel 17:45

We all have problems. We cause some of them ourselves, but some are given to us by the devil. It is his job to stop us from serving God. He sometimes places mountains (or problems) in front of us to detour us and eventually end our road to Heaven.

David was just a boy and Goliath was over nine feet tall in the above text. It was humanly impossible for him to defeat this giant. But David didn't go out to Goliath only by human strength. As he told him, he came to him in the name of the Lord of hosts. He even told him that he would cut his head off when all he had was a shepherd's staff, a sling, and five stones!! How could he cut off his head without a sword? He used the enemy's (Goliath's) own sword!

You can do the same with the problems that you face. Even though it seems impossible to overcome in your human mind, face those problems in the name of the Lord of hosts and He will help you tackle them. God will provide you with the tools necessary to cut off the head of those problems. It is God's desire for you to face them with victory in mind just as David knew he would see victory when he faced Goliath.

Got problems? You can have victory over them as you face them in the name of the Lord of hosts!

SEPTEMBER 21

Taking Down Your Goliath

"And David put his hand in his bag, and took thence a stone, and slang it, and smote the Philistine in his forehead, that the stone sunk into his forehead; and he fell upon his face to the earth."

I Samuel 17:49

In yesterday's devotion, I talked about the fact that we all have problems and how David faced his problem, Goliath, in the name of the Lord. Today, I want to talk about the steps to take in taking down our Goliath.

We all have Goliaths in our lives--problems that seem so large that there's no way to conquer them. They are so overwhelming that it seems these problems will conquer us. We must remember through these times that nothing is impossible with God. Our problems are small in God's eyes. The reason our problems seems large to us is that we can't see a way out, but God sees the answer. If we can only envision them from God's perspective, we can and will conquer them.

Here are some steps to consider:

- ◊ **Pick up the sling**. Or in our vernacular, take the bull by the horns.
- ◊ **Position the stone in the sling**. Allow God to speak to you through His Word and stand on that Word.
- ◊ **Aim**. Pray about the situation and do what God speaks to you.
- ◊ **Swing**. Allow the Holy Spirit to work in the situation.
- ◊ **Release**. Speak to the situation and release it into God's hands.

God will be with us through whatever problems we face just as He was with David. As you place your trust in Him, you will see the victory when you face your Goliath!

NOTES

SEPTEMBER 22

In The Storm

"Then fearing lest we should have fallen upon rocks, they cast four anchors out of the stern, and wished for the day."

Acts 27:29

This morning I've felt the presence of God in the midst of the storm. Thank God for His supernatural peace that passes understanding! That kind of peace that only comes from you!

God spoke to me this important truth: We must get peace in the boat before we can get peace over the storm. In other words, before you can have peace in what you are facing, you must have God's peace in your heart. We get this only through the Word of God; I call it faith anchors! A word from God changes everything!

Today I was reading Acts 27 about Apostle Paul facing a storm of unusual strength for many days. The verse above caught my attention. Paul had a word from God that anchored his soul in the midst of the storm! And with that word, came God's peace.

All of us will face some storms in our lives. But it's how we face the storm that makes the real difference! God's peace will come to us in our storms, just as it did with Paul. There's nothing that will take the place of that peace!

~ Rick Clendenen

SEPTEMBER 23

Who Is This Man?

"The disciples were amazed. Who is this man? they asked. Even the winds and waves obey him!"

Matthew 8:27

The familiar occurrence in the above verse is a little hard for me to understand. Jesus was asleep in the boat and a storm came up. The disciples awakened Him because they feared they were going to drown. After all the time that they had spent with Jesus, they did not trust that He was going to take care of them; they still felt that they would die in this storm.

But that is not what puzzles me the most. It is that they were amazed that Jesus could speak to the wind and the waves, and they obeyed Him! After all they had seen, having been with Jesus, they were awed that He could calm the storm they were facing. You would think that they would have faith that Jesus would handle this dire situation before them.

But then again, we are the same way. Jesus moves for us in difficult circumstances in which we find ourselves. And then when another situation comes that we think we can't survive, we oftentimes don't think He can take care of it. The same Jesus that met the first need, is able and willing to meet the next need that comes our way.

Jesus cares about every situation that we face, and He is ready to meet our every need if we just ask Him. There is nothing too difficult for Him to handle if we'll just turn it over to Him and believe that He will do whatever needs to be done.

SEPTEMBER 24

Peace and Calm

"And he arose, and rebuked the wind,
and said unto the sea, Peace, be still.
And the wind ceased,
and there was a great calm."

Mark 4:39

Today's devotion is from the same story as yesterday but this one has been written from a different perspective.

We live close to several lakes here in Kentucky. As a matter of fact, we're only a few miles from an area called LBL (Land Between the Lakes), which is a government owned game reserve between two of the largest man-made lakes in the world. The government even uses these two lakes to generate power for several neighboring states.

This morning, on the way to church, we passed over an extension of one of these lakes. I noticed how calm and still the water was. This made me think of my own soul. How that sometimes I can wake up and just be mad at the world for no apparent reason, such as this morning. No one had upset me the day before, I just woke up mad. And then I sat down, read my Bible, and spent some time with the Lord. Without realizing it, the angry feelings had dissipated.

Not only can Jesus calm the natural waters, but He will also calm the angry waves of your soul. Just spend time with Him each day and see what a difference He can make in your day!

SEPTEMBER 25

He Feels Our Pain

"And Jesus, moved with compassion, put forth His hand, and touched him, and saith unto him, I will; be thou clean."

Mark 1:41

Have you ever wondered why Jesus touched those He healed? I have always thought that He touched them because that's just what we do when we pray for someone. But consider this: Jesus touched them because He loved them and felt their pain.

When a relationship between a man and woman begins to blossom, you can see them, for example, holding hands as they take a walk. You have seen a mother tenderly touch the cheek of her baby, as she talks with them. You even see this in young children as they make new friends, putting their arms around each other's neck on the way to the playground.

I had never thought about Jesus touching people as He healed them until this morning. I believe He simply felt what they were experiencing in their bodies and wanted them free from that pain. He felt their infirmities and tenderly touched them to let them know that He loved them and wanted to heal them.

What an eye-opener! Jesus is touched by our infirmities (Hebrews 4:15) and therefore, we can really know that He loves us and "feels our pain"! Wow!

SEPTEMBER 26

We Are All Called

"I therefore, a prisoner for the Lord, urge you to walk in a manner worthy of the calling to which you have been called,"
ESV

Ephesians 4:1

Can you imagine Mary's feelings when she was told that she would be the mother of the Son of God? She was only a teenager at the time of the angel's visit. This week I have been thinking about Mary and how I felt as a teenager. I certainly was not ready to take on the responsibility that was placed on her.

For one thing, I was just not mature enough to be a mother, much less the mother of Jesus. Also, a teenager is not usually very wise in the ways of the Lord. I do believe that God speaks to people while in the early years, even earlier than teenagers. But it stands to reason that a woman is just wiser and has learned from more experiences if she becomes a mother, say in her twenties.

But on the other hand, think of just how Mary felt when she finally realized that God specifically chose her for this awesome responsibility! She must have been quite a young lady in His eyes for her to be the mother of Jesus.

The truth is God knew what He was doing then, and He knows what He is doing now. He has specifically called each of us; what are we doing with that call? He knows the very intents of our heart and He knows what we are capable of, even though we aren't aware of it ourselves. He chooses whom He will because He knows ahead of time what we can become. Trust Him and accept the calling He has placed on your life.

SEPTEMBER 27

Relationship With God

"A man that hath friends must show himself friendly: and there is a friend that sticketh closer than a brother."

Proverbs 18:24

How do you look at God? What kind of relationship do you think God really wants with you? Is He a God with a big stick expecting and waiting for you to "mess up"? Absolutely not! Is He a heavenly being that is so superior that He cannot be touched by your circumstances? Of course not! Is He waiting for you to make a mistake, just so He can judge and punish you for it? The answer is a resounding NO!

What He wants is for you to communicate with Him on an everyday basis, just as you would your dearest and closest friend. As a matter of fact, that is exactly what God wants to be: your closest friend. He wants you to talk with Him as if He is sitting right beside you. Because He is! He is with you wherever you go.

God knows you; He really knows you! You cannot hide your feelings, or anything else for that matter, from Him. He knows everything about you: the reasoning behind your every action, your purpose for everything you do. But the wonderful thing is that even though He knows it all, He still loves you and wants a relationship with you.

The way to begin in this relationship building process is getting to know God by spending time with Him. Spend time in His Word; not because it is a duty, but because it is what you want to do. Spend time just talking to God; not asking or petitioning, just simply talking to Him. If you will start here, then your relationship with God will grow and He will become to you a very dear and personal friend. This is God's desire.

SEPTEMBER 28

The Lord Has Need of You

"And they said, The Lord hath need of him."

Luke 19:34

The above scripture occurred before the triumphal entry of Jesus into Jerusalem. He had sent two of His disciples into the village to find a colt (donkey) that had never been sat upon. This is the statement that Jesus told them to tell anyone that asked why they untied the colt.

I was thinking about that statement this morning as I read it and wondered if Jesus ever said, "I have need of Debbie Clendenen." I believe He has, and you can insert your name there as well. I don't always know why He has need of me in a particular situation; I just need to not question Him but offer myself to be a usable vessel for Him.

That is a hard thing for me. I like to know what's ahead and the reasoning behind it. But that's not trust. Trust is doing just as the two disciples did: Obey without question, knowing that the Lord has need of you.

Lord, help me today to be ready when You have need of me so that I may be a vessel, ready to be used by You when those times come.

SEPTEMBER 29

Let Your Light Shine

"For at one time you were darkness, but now you are light in the Lord. Walk as children of light." ESV

Ephesians 5:8

I always thought this scripture meant to be a Christian in the midst of sinners. In one sense, this is what it means. How will they know unless we tell them about the saving grace of Jesus Christ?

But a more personal meaning is to let your light shine in the dark times of your life. Whether you know it or not, people are watching you and how you respond to your trials and tribulations. This is a prime opportunity for you to let your light shine while you are in your own personal darkness.

Not only can your life and your attitude be a witness to others during your trials, but you can be assured that your light will shine, no matter what circumstances you are facing.

We all experience dark moments when we struggle to see what is ahead of us. It is then that we can shine the brightest so that others can recognize the light of Jesus in our lives. Just remember: You can't tell if your light is shining until you are in the darkness! Be that light and shine for Jesus.

SEPTEMBER 30

Where Do You Find Yourself?

"Jesus went up on a mountainside and called to him those He wanted, and they came to Him. He appointed twelve..." NIV

Mark 3:13-14a

Take a moment and try to imagine living during the time that Jesus was on the earth. What a joy it would have been to follow Him into town after town, listening to Him preach the Good News to everyone that would listen.

Jesus had multitudes following Him wherever He went. He chose twelve from the multitude. From the twelve (the disciples), He had three (Peter, James, & John), from the three, He had one (John, the disciple that leaned on His breast).

In which group do you find yourself today? Do you follow Jesus, as the multitude, to see the signs and wonders? Or do you follow Him, eager to learn as did the twelve? Have you chosen to be in the inner group with Jesus, but follow Him from afar? Or have you decided to follow Jesus to the cross, letting the world know that you are His disciple?

Jesus is looking for us to become as John. No matter where you find yourself, the world knows whose disciple you are. It is your choice! The closer you get to Jesus, the more intimate the relationship with Him. Choose wisely!

NOTES

OCTOBER 1

Is It Vain to Serve the Lord?

"Ye have said, It is vain to serve God: and what profit is it that we have kept his ordinance, and that we have walked mournfully before the LORD of hosts?"

Malachi 3:14

In Genesis 6:14-18, we read that God commanded Noah to build an ark for the salvation of his family. Noah was faithful to do what God called him to do and his family was saved. Noah, is it vain to serve the Lord?

In the first few verses of Job, we find that he was a perfect and upright man that feared God and served Him. Verse 3 tells us that God had blessed him and that he was the greatest of all the men of the east. Job remained faithful even through his greatest time of testing; a time when he lost all that he possessed. But God remained faithful to him and in the end, gave him twice as much as he had at the beginning. Job, is it vain to serve the Lord?

What about the three Hebrew children in the fiery furnace because they refused to bow to anyone but God? He was in the fire with them, and they didn't even smell of smoke when they came out. Shadrach, Meshach, and Abednego, is it vain to serve the Lord? Think about Daniel in the lion's den. He refused to turn from God, and He delivered him. Daniel, is it vain to serve the Lord?

How about you? Has Satan tried to convince you because you're suffering persecution that it is vain to serve the Lord? If we will just be faithful to God, He will be faithful to us and bring deliverance to His people. When every knee bows and every tongue confesses Jesus is Lord, we will know that it was not vain to serve the Lord.

~ Rick Clendenen

OCTOBER 2

Where Are You Looking?

"[1]I will lift up mine eyes unto the hills, from whence cometh my help. [2]My help cometh from the Lord, which made heaven and earth."

Psalm 121:1-2

Are you looking back? Sometimes it is good to see where you have come from, but it is not good to stay there and live in regret. My husband used to say that if you live your life staring in the rearview mirror, that is a recipe for a wreck!

Are you looking down? Is your mind consumed with thoughts of what you have done wrong or what you could have done better? Don't allow the devil to tell you that you are not good enough or that you will never amount to "a hill of beans," as the old saying goes. He is a liar and the father of them!

Are you looking around you? The mess our world is in will discourage anybody. It seems as though people are falling by the wayside all the time and not turning their eyes to Jesus.

Or are you looking up? Those that are planted firmly in Christ Jesus know that we find our strength and encouragement in Him. We know that we can face anything if He is by our side.

Direct your eyes upward today as you ponder on the words of this old song:

Turn your eyes upon Jesus
Look full in His wonderful face
And the things of earth will grow strangely dim
In the light of His glory and grace.

OCTOBER 3

Mind Your Own Business

"If you suffer, however, it must not be for murder, stealing, making trouble, or prying into other people's affairs." NLT

1 Peter 4:15

There are people in this world that spend their time spreading gossip. The Bible calls them busybodies. (2 Thessalonians 3:11, 1 Timothy 5:13)

All my life I have heard people say, "Mind your own business!" But I never knew that it is in the Bible. In 1 Thessalonians 4:11, we read "Make it your goal to live a quiet life, minding your own business and working with your hands, just as we instructed you before." NLT

This is great advice, and we should keep it in the forefront of our minds when faced with hearing gossip from others or when we consider spreading it ourselves. My husband, Rick, said that if you're not part of the problem, or part of the solution, then you should remove yourself from the situation.

What do you do when you hear gossip? Do you participate in it by spreading it yourself? Or do you turn away from it? We should steer clear of any gossip and do just what God tells us in His Word: to mind our own business! If we want to be a follower of Christ, that is just what we will do.

OCTOBER 4

Desire to Learn

"As iron sharpens iron, so one person sharpens another." NIV

Proverbs 27:17

I have been reading about Elijah being taken up in a chariot of fire. Elisha knew this would be his last day with him and he didn't want to leave his side. Elijah asked him what he could do for him before he left. Elisha responded that he wanted a double portion of his spirit (or anointing) and become his successor.

Oh, if we could only grasp what Elisha felt and desire to sit at the feet of great men and women of God and want what they possess in their relationship with God. How I wish I would have recorded the many, many talks my husband, Rick and I had about the Lord. How I wish I had recorded all the times my dad would talk to me about the goodness of God.

God has been so good to me to have these two great men in my life. But I also have many others in my life that I can learn from, among those are my son, my son-in-law, spiritual fathers and mothers, spiritual sons and daughters…

I want to be like a sponge and soak in what the Lord speaks through them. How about you—are you seeking knowledge from those that God has given you? Spent time with them and soak in what God is speaking to them.

OCTOBER 5

The Future Is Coming

"Peace I leave with you; my peace I give you.
I do not give to you as the world gives.
Do not let your hearts be troubled
and do not be afraid." NIV

John 14:27

The future is on its way! Are you worrying about your future? Do you worry about what your world will look like five, ten, or even twenty years from now?

It has been proven that excessive worry will cause all kinds of medical conditions. It can harm your physical body as well as your mental state. And it will affect your spiritual life.

There's really no need to worry. If you're a child of God, just simply believe that He has everything under control. He knows what is going to happen next and He's not worried.

Give your worry to God and He will replace it with His peace! Wouldn't that be a wonderful exchange?

OCTOBER 6

Have Faith and Trust God

"Trust in the Lord with all your heart; and lean not on your own understanding."

Proverbs 3:5

Did you know that there is a difference between faith and trust? But they are both very important. Faith says, "I believe" but trust goes a step further and says, "I know".

Webster's Dictionary even defines faith as something that is believed, and trust is assured reliance. I believe God or have faith in Him that He will meet my need. But I trust Him with my entire life and know that He will take care of me.

It takes faith to believe a plane can fly but it takes trust to actually step on that plane. It takes faith to see your children begin to make their own decisions; it takes trust to know that even in their mistakes, they'll succeed. It takes faith in God to be saved but it takes trust to know that God will teach you how to live a Christian life.

Choose today to put your faith in the Lord Jesus Christ and you can then put your trust in Him to lead the way. It will be the best decision you will ever make!

OCTOBER 7

NOW Faith

"Now faith is the substance of things hoped for, the evidence of things not seen."

Hebrews 11:1

There have been many sermons preached, many lessons taught, and many books written on the subject of faith. I have heard the eleventh chapter of Hebrews called "the chapter of faith" or the "hall of faith." The above verse is the Biblical definition of faith. My definition is simply: Without doubt, I believe!

God is happy when we have faith. As a matter of fact, we find this in Hebrews 11:2. It is expressed better in the Amplified Version: "For by this [kind of] faith the men of old gained [divine] approval."

We also find in Hebrews 11:6 that without faith, it is impossible to please God. We can't even become part of His family without it. It all starts with faith, and it will continue throughout our lives.

We need to remember our faith of yesterday in order to have faith in our tomorrow. For this to happen, we must have faith today, as the scripture above say, "NOW faith…"

NOTES

OCTOBER 8

What Do You Call Him?

"Then he said to them, "But who do you say that I am?" And Peter answered, "The Christ of God." ESV

Luke 9:20

Mary gave birth to the Son of God and was told to name him Jesus. He is given many other names in the Bible but what do you call Him? Have you ever misused His name? How many times have we heard His precious name being flippantly thrown around or even used as a curse word?

Philippians 2:9 tells us that God gave Jesus "a name which is above every name." We should highly respect the name of Jesus and use it the way in which we are directed in God's Word:

◊ **Luke 24:47**-Preach repentance and remission of sin in His name

◊ **John 14:13**-Ask of the Father in His name

◊ **John 20:31**-Receive life through His name

◊ **Acts 16:18**-Command demons to flee in His name

◊ **Ephesians 5:20**-Give thanks in His name

These are only a few but if we use the name of Jesus in the proper manner, all these benefits will be ours. Otherwise, there will be consequences if we misuse it, according to Exodus 20:7 NLT, "You must not misuse the name of the Lord your God. The Lord will not let you go unpunished if you misuse his name." The choice is yours!

OCTOBER 9

God's Opinion Is Higher Than Ours

"For as the heavens are higher than the earth, so are my ways higher than your ways, and my thoughts than your thoughts."

Isaiah 55:9

I've been reading about Moses and his conversation with God at the burning bush this morning. God was calling him to lead the children of Israel out of Egypt and Moses was trying to tell Him why he couldn't.

Here are his responses to God's call and the fears that accompanied them:

- ◊ "Who am I to go before Pharaoh? Who am I to lead the people of Israel out of Egypt?" He had a fear of the past.
- ◊ "Who do I tell the children of Israel is the name of the one that has sent me?" He had a fear of inadequacy.
- ◊ "What if they won't believe me or listen to what I tell them?" He had a fear of rejection.
- ◊ "I've never been good with words, I am slow of speech, I get tongue-tied when I try to talk to people!" He had a fear of humiliation.
- ◊ "Lord, please send someone else." He had a fear of failure.

But God had an answer to all Moses' excuses. The truth is, God could see more in Moses than he could see in himself! And that's the way He sees us. Whatever excuses we give Him, His opinion of us is always higher than what we think of ourselves!

OCTOBER 10

Standing In God's Love

*"But God, who is rich in mercy,
for his great love wherewith he loved us"*

Ephesians 2:4

There's a song that we sing today that says, "My fear doesn't stand a chance when I stand in Your love!" Fear tries to tell you that there is no way you can do what God says you can do. But if you stand in God's love, you can conquer anything that comes to you.

You can replace the word "fear" with anything that is contrary to God's calling on your life. Here are some examples:

- ◊ **My PAST** doesn't stand chance when I stand in Your love!
- ◊ **My INADEQUACY** doesn't stand a chance when I stand in Your love!
- ◊ **My REJECTION** doesn't stand a chance when I stand in Your love!
- ◊ **My HUMILIATION** doesn't stand a chance when I stand in Your love!
- ◊ **My FAILURE** doesn't stand a chance when I stand in your love!

There is absolutely nothing that can stand in the presence of God's love; they simply don't stand a chance and cannot keep you from your destiny in Christ Jesus.

Allow God to work through your life to bless others. You can do it with His help. As Ephesians 6:10 tells us, "...Be strong in the Lord, and in the power of His might!"

OCTOBER 11

Overcoming Your Fears

"I sought the Lord, and he heard me, and delivered me from all my fears."

Psalm 34:4

There are some people that carry a lot of fear in their lives; some of them for many, many years. Fear is one of the main tools that the devil uses against the children of God. But we don't have to be a slave to those fears. If we want to overcome them, we need to do two things:

- ◊ We have to acknowledge them for what they are and where they come from.
- ◊ We must turn them over to God and follow His Word.

Sarah faced her fear of the unknown and followed her husband to a new land. Esther faced her fear of failure and saved the entire Jewish nation from death. The woman with the issue of blood faced her fear of rejection and received her healing. Mary faced her fear of ridicule and became the mother of the Saviour of the world.

As the song says, "I'm no longer a slave to fear. I am a child of God!" Let faith take the place of fear in your life and you will no longer be in its clutches!

OCTOBER 12

I Don't Know How to Pray

"And when you pray, do not heap up empty phrases as the Gentiles do, for they think that they will be heard for their many words." ESV

Matthew 6:7

Have you ever heard someone say, "I don't know how to pray?" Or "I don't know the words to say to God." I'm sure there are a lot of people that feel this way, especially new Christians. The fact of the matter is, there is no set way to pray.

The definition of the word, pray, from Merriam-Webster.com is, "to address God with adoration, confession, supplication, or thanksgiving." My definition is simply to talk to God. You don't have to use eloquent words when you talk to Him; He knows everything about you, and He knows that is not how you converse with others. I often think that if I begin to pray and say something like, "My most gracious and righteous Father, who abides in the Heavenlies among the cherubim and seraphim..." I can just imagine God saying, "Who is that talking to Me?" because that is not how I talk to Him. Sometimes, I just say, "I love you, Lord. I thank you for this day. I need Your help today." I talk to Him like I talk to a friend because He IS my Friend!

There are no magical words that you have to know to pray to God. The important thing is that you do pray, that you talk to your best Friend. He wants to hear from you. Make it a habit to converse with Him all throughout your day and you will see that your spirit will be revived, and your soul will be refreshed!

OCTOBER 13

Do You Love Your Judas?

"Even my close friend, someone I trusted, one who shared my bread, has turned against me." NIV

Psalm 41:9

Many of us have those in our lives that have betrayed us at one time or another. You can call them your Judas. What should our attitude be toward them when that happens?

Too many times we make excuses for why we can't, or shouldn't have to, love them. But you know what? None of those excuses will hold water!

We must remember what Jesus did and do likewise. He chose Judas to be one of his disciples. He got on His knees and washed his feet. He served communion to him. Jesus did it all knowing that Judas would soon betray Him.

I heard a statement today that we all need to remember: "The true test of Christianity is not how much you say you love Jesus, but how much you show that love to Judas!" That is a true statement and should hit home with all of us.

John 13:35 tells us, "By this shall all men know that ye are my disciples, if ye have love one to another." By loving your Judas, you show that you love Jesus!

OCTOBER 14

The Calling Still Remains

"For the gifts and calling of God are without repentance."
Romans 11:29

God has given each of us a job to do. He has **called** us, and it is our responsibility to do that job. It is not IF we decide to accept the call that matters. It is that even if we choose not to fulfill it, the call itself still remains.

Let's take Jonah, for instance. He thought he could go to another place to stay away from fulfilling his call. But God was with him wherever he went. He could not run far enough to get away from Him and His calling.

The above verse says that the gifts and calling of God are without repentance. This means that they will never by revoked by God and He will never take them away. His calling is sure, immovable, and will never be reversed.

Even if we choose to run away from God's instructions, like Jonah, the calling still stands. Be a responsible person and obey that which God has told you to do.

NOTES

OCTOBER 15

The Water Is Not Important

"Blessed are all who fear the Lord, who walk in obedience to him." NIV

Psalm 128:1

We read about Jesus walking on the water in Matthew 14:22-32. Jesus had gone to the mountain to pray, and a storm arose where the disciples were in their boat.

It was somewhere between 3 AM and 6 AM that Jesus went to them, walking on the water. The disciples were afraid, so Jesus told them who He was. Then Peter told Jesus if it was truly Him, to tell him to join Him, and Jesus simply said, "Come." Peter obeyed and stepped out of the boat.

The water was not important. What was important was his obedience. Peter didn't initially consider the water when he stepped out. Once he did, he was afraid, began to sink, and Jesus reached out to him. But the water was a stumbling block to the other disciples—a hindrance to their obedience.

Look not to the water—look not to the hindrances in your path. Look only to Jesus and obey His word to you. He'll lift you up when you feel that you're falling. The passage states in verses 30-31, that when Peter called for Jesus, he ***immediately*** stretched forth His hand—He ***immediately*** came to his rescue. Jesus will take you by the hand and lift you above your circumstances.

OCTOBER 16

Follow God's Will

"The world and its desires pass away, but whoever does the will of God lives forever." NIV

I John 2:17

The above verse tells us that "whoever does the will of God lives forever." This realization will bring such peace and joy to your soul. Even though following God's will is not always easy, it is rewarding!

I think too many people don't want to submit to God's will but wants God to adjust His will to fit their own agenda. I have been there...many times. But the tragedy is that in keeping this as our mindset, we miss the opportunity to know God more fully.

I want to totally submit to His will. I want to know Him more today than I did yesterday. I want to spend time in His Word and learn more truths about Him. I want to decrease and allow God to increase more and more in my life. I don't always succeed in doing all these things, but I do want Jesus to be seen in me and I want to be more like Him every day.

Do you feel this way about your life? Are you submitted to doing God's will whether or not it agrees with what you want to do? You will never be totally happy until you submit everything to Him.

OCTOBER 17

Give Jesus the Wheel

"But I trusted in thee, O Lord: I said, Thou art my God."

Psalm 31:14

I do not like to drive behind a van, SUV, or large truck where I can't see where I'm going. So, I usually try to pass them when I can on my journey so I will be able to see what's up ahead.

I often find myself in those types of situations and it is very frustrating. Today as I was driving, I felt the Lord speak to me, "That's how it is with life. You can't always see what is ahead of you. That's when you need to trust Me and not try to figure it out yourself."

A great peace came over me as I pondered those words and realized that He really does know what's ahead of me and He knows what's best for me. All I have to do is trust Him and give Him the wheel!

I wish I had learned this principle earlier in my life. I experienced a lot of bumps and bruises that I would not have had to suffer from if I had only given Jesus the steering wheel of my life. I should have known that I didn't have to know what was ahead in my journey. Thank you, Jesus, for loving me anyway. I give you the reins of my life and I trust you to guide me every step of the way.

OCTOBER 18

The Right Motives

"So, whether you eat or drink, or whatever you do, do all to the glory of God." ESV

1 Corinthians 10:31

Have you thought about why you chose to serve God? Do you have the right motives in mind or are you seeking glory for yourself? The above verse tells us that whatever we do, we should do it all to the glory of God.

Once you accept Jesus as Lord and Savior and begin living a Christian life, you have to guard against those things that the devil will bring to your mind. We are told in Ephesians 6:11, "Put on the whole armor of God, that ye may be able to stand against the wiles of the devil."

The word "wiles" means tricks, schemes, or strategies. The devil's main strategy is to turn us away from God and he will use anything in his arsenal to accomplish it. One thing he will use is the need for glory in the things that we do. We must recognize that is a trick of the devil. The way to fight against this tactic is to give God all the glory in everything we do.

Check your heart and make sure that you are not seeking the glory of man in what you do, but that you are giving any glory that you receive back to God. He is the One who deserves it all!

OCTOBER 19

What Type of Person Are You?

"Let us hold fast the confession of our hope without wavering, for he who promised is faithful."

Hebrews 10:23

We all go through difficult times in our lives. It has been my experience that in every crisis, there are three types of people that arise:

- ◊ **The HIDERS**, those that stick their head in the sand and ignore what's going on until everything gets back to normal!
- ◊ **THE HURLERS**, those that look for someone to blame because they're experiencing a change in their lives!
- ◊ **THE HEALERS**, those that realize that the crisis is opening a new opportunity for God to be seen and glorified!

In my devotion today, I read the account of David and Goliath found in the seventeenth chapter of 1 Samuel. Can you recognize these three groups within that story? Can you also see that David was the only one that fully seized the moment for God?

I'll leave it up to you to figure out which group you are in when you face a crisis in your life; choose wisely which one you'll join!

~ Rick Clendenen

OCTOBER 20

In Which Room Are You Living?

"I cry out to God Most High, to God who will fulfill his purpose for me." NLT

Psalm 57:2

We have all had times in our lives when we've pondered our past, our present, and our future. I want to relate that to three different rooms of our mind: memory, perception, and imagination.

Memory is our first room, the room of our past. Let's call it the back porch. Here we let our minds wander to how things used to be. It's OK to visit this room, but we cannot live on the back porch. If we live our lives focused on the past, we will never be able to look forward to our future.

The second room is our perception, or the present. Let's say it's your living room. Here is where we should be dwelling today, thinking on what we can do to help someone else along their way. Here is where we find out our purpose. If we still have breath, then we still have purpose.

The last room is our imagination. It is our future; I will call it the front porch. We sit here and ponder on what the future holds. Here we begin to seek God for ways that He can use us to be a servant for Him. But living here keeps us from serving God in the here and now.

We don't want to spend too much time on the back porch, stuck in the past, we will soon fill our hearts with **regrets** of things that we haven't done. If we live on the front porch, living in the future, all we will see is **reservations** of doing what God has called us to do. We can occasionally visit these two rooms, but we don't need to live in either one of them. We should live in the living room and fulfill His purpose for our lives. It is here that we will see **rewards**!

OCTOBER 21

Use Your Pain

"Who comforteth us in all our tribulation, that we may be able to comfort them which are in any trouble, by the comfort wherewith we ourselves are comforted of God."

2 Corinthians 1:4

Isn't it a horrible feeling when you have been physically hurt, and you see blood gushing from the wound? It is especially scary at the beginning because you don't know how serious it is.

Things can also happen to us emotionally that causes pain in our hearts and our spirits. It can hurt us deeply, a lot of times even more than the pain from the physical wounds.

But, in both cases, God wants to take our wounds and "make them all better." He wants to heal all of those, whether it be physical or emotional. You may carry scars but there can be healing for the wounds.

A very wise man once said, "Wounds ooze blood but scars ooze wisdom." You can learn from the pain that you experienced. You can either carry it your entire life, or you can seek God for His healing and minister to others that have gone through the same thing. Use it for God's glory and you will be blessed yourself!

NOTES

OCTOBER 22

All Because You Obeyed

"And through your descendants all the nations of the earth will be blessed—all because you have obeyed me." NLT

Genesis 22:18

In my devotion time recently, the verse listed above jumped out at me. God was speaking to Abraham after the potential sacrificing of Isaac. The words that leaped from the page to me was, "ALL BECAUSE YOU OBEYED ME."

As this was driving home the importance of obedience to me, I began thinking about what we are stealing from ourselves, our family, our community, our future generations when we refuse to be obedient. Then, I heard that still, small whisper tell me, "Your LACK of obedience can change generations too."

Oh, just to think that I could be the cause of what my future generation may have to endure simply because of my disobedience. I do not want that on my shoulders! I want them to see my obedience to God and the blessings that can bring.

The choice is ours to make. Who will be left behind because of our decision? Who will be brought into the fullness of God because of our decision? I pray that you will seriously consider this and make the right choice: Obey God and see your future generations blessed!

OCTOBER 23

Why Tithe?

"My covenant will I not break,
nor alter the thing that is gone out of my lips."

Psalm 89:34

Is tithing a Biblical principle? Yes, it is! We read the familiar passage in Malachi 3:10a, " Bring ye all the tithes into the storehouse, that there may be meat in mine house..." That is about as plain as it gets! Bring your tithe to the storehouse or the place you receive your sustenance.

In verses 10b-12 is found God's promises when you tithe.

- ◊ He will open the windows of heaven
- ◊ He will pour out a blessing that you can't contain
- ◊ He will rebuke the devourer
- ◊ Your fruit will not be destroyed
- ◊ Your vine will bear fruit
- ◊ All the nations will call you blessed

Those are some great promises! But to receive them, you must first choose to give the tithe to God. If you do, you will find that you will be able to do more with the 90%, than you would if you kept the 100%. God is faithful and His promises are sure!

OCTOBER 24

The Time to Tithe

"And in process of time it came to pass, that Cain brought of the fruit of the ground an offering unto the Lord."

Genesis 4:3

In Genesis 4, we read the account of Cain and Abel and the offering or tithe they gave to God. Verse 3 tells us that Cain waited to give to God ("And in the process of time…"), while Abel brought the first of his flock (Verse 4).

Let's consider this scenario. If a person comes to your house for a visit, what do you consider him/her? Let's say you are serving pie, to whom do you offer the first piece? Would it be considered a dishonor if you don't offer him/her any at all?

I'll answer them for you. He/she is called the guest of **honor** and you give him/her the first piece of pie out of **honor**! And yes, it would be dishonoring to not offer a piece to him/her.

We are told in Proverbs 3:9, "Honour the Lord with thy substance, and with the firstfruits of all thine increase:" Cain did not honor God because he gave his offering in the process of time. But Abel did show honor to Him by giving the first! So the time to give your tithe should be the first thing you do! By doing so, you show honor to God with the first fruits of your labor.

OCTOBER 25

Great Faith

"When Jesus heard it, he marvelled, and said to them that followed, Verily I say unto you, I have not found so great faith, no, not in Israel."

Matthew 8:10

We are told in Matthew 5:1 that Jesus taught the multitudes while sitting on a mountain. In verses 3-11, we read about the beatitudes in what is normally called, the Sermon on the Mount. But Jesus doesn't stop there. He continues to teach them through the entirety of chapters 5, 6, and 7.

As Jesus came down from the mountain, He headed toward Capernaum and a leper came to him, asking to be made whole. Jesus touched him and his leprosy left. After entering the city, He was then approached by a centurion whose servant was seriously sick. He simply asked Jesus to speak the word and his servant would be healed. As is recorded in Matthew 8:10, Jesus marveled at the centurion's faith and stated, "I have not found so great faith…"

While reading this portion of scripture, I thought about my own faith and what Jesus would say about it. Would He say that I have great faith as He said of the centurion? Or would it be as in the case of the disciples being afraid during the storm when Jesus told them, "O ye of little faith." What about you? How is your "faith meter"? We should all strive to have great faith and put our total trust in Jesus Christ!

OCTOBER 26

But If Not...

"[17]If it be so, our God whom we serve is able to deliver us from the burning fiery furnace, and he will deliver us out of thine hand, O king. [18]But if not, be it known unto thee, O king, that we will not serve thy gods, nor worship the golden image which thou hast set up."

Daniel 3:17-18

In the book of Daniel, we read that Jerusalem had been besieged by Nebuchadnezzar, king of Babylon, and he captured several of the young men to be brought there to serve in the king's palace. Among them were Shadrach, Meshach, and Abednego.

About this time, the king had a golden image built and ordered everyone to bow before it. If anyone refused, he/she would be thrown into a fiery furnace. Of course, these three Godly men chose not to bow, and they were brought before the king, who was extremely angry with them. Their answer for refusing to obey Nebuchadnezzar's command is found in the above verses.

Consider this question: What is your attitude toward God when He doesn't answer a prayer in the way you have asked of Him? These three men certainly did not want to be thrown in the burning furnace, but they trusted God enough to know that He was able to deliver them from the fire. And they added, "But if not..." If God chose to not deliver them from the fire, they emphatically stated that they would not worship anyone else but Him.

I pray that we can say that we have that much trust and faith in God. We most likely will not be thrown into an actual fiery furnace but we will face extreme struggles at times. But, like Shadrach, Meshach, and Abednego, we can know that God will carry us through them. And even though they may not turn out as we expect them to, we can still trust Him in those "but if not..." moments that we face. Trust God anyway, no matter the outcome of your situation!

OCTOBER 27

That's When the Angels Rejoice

"In the same way, I tell you, there is rejoicing in the presence of the angels of God over one sinner who repents." NIV

Luke 15:10

One of the ways that Jesus taught was by parables, and He used this method quite a bit. You can read them in Matthew, Mark, and Luke. According to Christianity.com, the definition of a parable is a simple story to provide a more profound lesson or teaching. Jesus took something that was common to his disciples and followers and taught them a life-lesson from it.

One of my favorite parables from Jesus' teachings is the lost coin. It is found in Luke 15:8-10. The woman had ten coins. I can just see her keeping them in a safe place and every so often, taking them out and examining each one. One day she discovered that one coin was lost. We are told that she lit a lamp and swept her house, searching diligently until she found it. She invited her friends and neighbors to come and rejoice with her that she had found the lost coin.

Jesus said that this is like unto a sinner who repents. As is stated in the above verse, there is rejoicing in the presence of the angels of God when a lost person finds salvation through Jesus Christ.

How does it make you feel to know that the angels were rejoicing when you accepted Christ Jesus as Lord and Savior of your life? Can you imagine the roar in Heaven when you made that all important decision? And they rejoice over every one of us in that same manner. It must mean we are very important to the inhabitants of Heaven; we can rejoice in that fact!

OCTOBER 28

God is Always Working

"...for your Father knoweth what things ye have need of, before ye ask him."

Matthew 6:8b

I was reading the story of the feeding of the five thousand from the sixth chapter of John. I began to think about what happened to the twelve baskets that were left over.

Have you ever thought about that? The scriptures don't tell us what became of them. But, if they gave them to the young boy that had the original basket of bread and fish, can you imagine the response of his mother when he came home with them? She may have even been in the crowd that was fed that day. Either way, she would have been amazed at this blessing!

Consider this: There were twelve baskets left over—one for each disciple. Think about what was going on in their minds. They had to have been in awe of what they had just experienced.

First, as they were getting food from the original basket to pass out to the people, the supply never ran out. Secondly, as they were handing out the food, their own baskets did not run out until all the people had enough. Lastly, as they were gathering the scraps that were left over, their baskets were filled again. All of this from two fish and five loaves of bread!

Do you have things in your life that you think are impossible to overcome? Do you feel that your needs are so large that they can't be met? All it takes is a child-like faith in a big God! He is a miracle worker, and He is always working in your behalf. Simply put your faith and trust in Him—He knows what you need even before you ask. And He will meet them when you do ask!

OCTOBER 29

Pure Worship

"Enter into his gates with thanksgiving, and into his courts with praise: be thankful unto him, and bless his name."

Psalm 100:4

There are many ways that we, as God's children, can worship Him. Some prefer to sit, with head bowed and eyes closed, quietly talking to Him. Others will stand, raising their hands, and shouting and singing praise to Him. Still others may want to leap, just as the lame man did when Peter and John walked by him at the gate of the temple, and he was healed. All of these are OK to do, just as long as the attitude is one of humility as we praise Him.

When we worship, are we completely honest about wanting more of God? Or is our worship only for what He has given us? Do we ever just worship Him to show how much we love Him?

God knows what is in our hearts. It would be a good idea if we would look deep within ourselves and make sure our desire is first and foremost for Jesus. The "things" will come just because He loves us and desires to bless us. But our worship must first be to God because of who He is and not for what He does!

I want to be that kind of person. One that totally worships God, not expecting anything, but to show how much I love Him. Is that also your desire? God longs to hear that kind of worship from all of us. He is certainly worthy of all our praise!

OCTOBER 30

The Process of a Miracle

"Behold, I am the Lord, the God of all flesh: is there anything too hard for me?"

Jeremiah 32:27

In the first chapter of Luke, we find where the angel, Gabriel, came to Mary with the news that she would be the mother of the Savior. Just a few days after, she went to visit her cousin, Elizabeth. Before Mary could tell her about what she had just experienced, the Holy Spirit revealed to Elizabeth that Mary was pregnant with her Lord.

What a confirmation to Mary that she was indeed carrying the Son of God in her womb! Elizabeth told Mary that she (Mary) was blessed because she believed God would do what He said. Oh, that we would take God at His word as Mary did and believe for the impossible!

We can read Mary's response in verses 46-55. Before the miracle was evident to others, she gave praise to God. This is a major key!

So, according to Luke 1, the process of receiving your miracle is this:

- ◊ **Give your life to Jesus**-Vs. 30
- ◊ **Believe that you are highly favored by God**-Vs 28
- ◊ **Believe the word from God**-Vs 38, 45
- ◊ **Believe that nothing is impossible with God**-Vs 37
- ◊ **When you receive your miracle, give praise to God**-Vs 46-55

OCTOBER 31

Finding Joy in the Journey

"You make known to me the path of life; in your presence there is fullness of joy; at your right hand are pleasures forevermore." ESV

Psalm 16:11

We are all on a journey as we travel life's road, and it is different for everyone. We don't know what we will face nor when our individual journey will end. But I can tell you that you can have joy as you travel this road, no matter what is thrown in front of you to hinder or even stop you from reaching your destination.

There will be tough times in your life. But you can still have the joy of the Lord in your heart as you encounter and pass through those times. Listed below are some encouraging scripture verses to hold on to during those difficult times that you are sure to face.

- ◊ **Romans 8:18**, "For I reckon that the sufferings of this present time are not worthy to be compared with the glory which shall be revealed in us."
- ◊ **James 1:2-3**, "[2]Consider it pure joy, my brothers and sisters, whenever you face trials of many kinds, [3]because you know that the testing of your faith produces perseverance." NIV
- ◊ **Psalm 30:5b**, "…weeping may endure for a night, but joy cometh in the morning."
- ◊ **Romans 12:12**, "Be joyful in hope, patient in affliction, faithful in prayer." NIV
- ◊ **Philippians 4:4**, "Always be full of joy in the Lord. I say it again—rejoice!" NLT

Research the Word of God for yourself and find other verses showing that you can indeed keep joy in your heart as you face trials in your life. Hang on to the truth that Jesus wants to fill you up with His joy, the kind of joy that is everlasting, no matter what you are facing. Thank you, Jesus, for that wonderful joy!

NOTES

NOVEMBER 1

Thankfulness

"Give thanks to the Lord, for he is good.
His love endures forever." NIV

Psalm 136:1

November is the month in which we celebrate Thanksgiving. It's a time that families gather and eat a meal usually consisting of their favorite meat, typically turkey and/or ham, with all the fixings that go with it. Each one makes their specialty, whether it be meat, vegetables, or dessert, bringing it to a specified location to share with their loved ones.

I've been around long enough to see those that were once young become the ones that are now cooking the meals. I'm sure this tradition will continue for years to come. I am thankful for those times; they are precious memories to me.

The devotions in this month will all be centered around thankfulness. Take a moment out of each day during this month and write down what you are thankful for. Then, on the last day, reread what you have written, and you will see just how good God has been to you. Thank Him for those blessings that He has given you. Why not practice doing it every day, not just in November. I can promise you that your days will go better when you have a heart full of thankfulness!

NOVEMBER 2

Thankful for My Salvation

"Behold, God is my salvation; I will trust, and not be afraid: for the Lord Jehovah is my strength and my song; he also is become my salvation."

Isaiah 12:2

The most important thing that anyone could ever do is to accept Jesus Christ as your Lord and Savior. I am so thankful for the night I decided to follow Him.

It happened during a revival that we were attending in Dover, TN when I was twelve years old. My mom and dad had actually built and pastored this church years before and they still had a relationship with those precious people. I felt the conviction of the Holy Spirit touch my heart as an older cousin asked me if I wanted to pray. I nodded and with her help, I prayed the sinner's prayer and accepted Jesus.

I wasn't a bad person before then. I attended church with my parents. I respected them and was obedient to them. I did not get into trouble at school. But none of that could save me; only when the blood of Jesus was applied to my heart was I truly saved.

I will forever be grateful to my cousin for talking to me that night. I have now lived for Jesus for 56 years and I will never regret making that decision. I love Him more today than I ever have, and that love grows every day. Thank you Jesus for saving me!

What is the story of your salvation? Have you ever written it down so that others can read it after you are gone to glory? It would be a blessing to them. Do it today!

NOVEMBER 3

Thankful for the Work of Jesus Christ

"Looking unto Jesus the author and finisher of our faith; who for the joy that was set before him endured the cross, despising the shame, and is set down at the right hand of the throne of God."

Hebrews 12:2

What would I do or be without Jesus? For that matter, where would any of us be without Him? I simply cannot understand why people want to live without Jesus in their lives!

I thank Him for His faithful, everlasting love for all mankind. The Bible tells us in Psalm 136:26 ESV, "Give thanks to the God of heaven, for his steadfast love endures forever." Jesus loves "little ole me" and gave His life as a ransom for my soul.

I thank Him that He was willing to suffer and die as a substitute for us. We were the ones that should have died on that cross because it was for our sins that He was there. In 1 John 2:2 NLT, we read, "He himself is the sacrifice that atones for our sins—and not only our sins but the sins of all the world."

I thank Him for His death, burial, and resurrection, which was the finishing touches in the plan of salvation. Thank God that it didn't end at the crucifixion and Jesus was left in the tomb. He was resurrected so that we may be free from the sin in our lives, and we can experience life in Him! "And if Christ be not raised, your faith is vain; ye are yet in your sins." 1 Corinthians 15:17

I fully embrace Your love and forgiveness for me. Thank you for providing that way of escape and the heavenly reward we will one day experience. I love you, Lord, with all my heart!

NOVEMBER 4

Thankful That the Veil is Torn

"For through him we both have access by one Spirit unto the Father."

Ephesians 2:18

The Bible tell us in Ephesians, chapter two, that Jesus, our High Priest, tore down the wall that separated Jews from Gentiles and opened up our access to God!

Do you realize that this is speaking of the veil of the temple? Do you know just how big this veil was? It was sixty feet high, thirty feet wide, and four inches thick! It took 300 priest to break it down or to put it back in place!

But God ripped it from top to bottom to make a way of access to Him all because of the finished work of our High Priest Jesus Christ! That's so amazing!

Now you can come boldly to the throne of God to find mercy and grace to help you in your time of need! For that we can be eternally thankful to Him!

~ Rick Clendenen

NOVEMBER 5

Thankful That Jesus is the Word

"And the Word was made flesh, and dwelt among us, (and we beheld his glory, the glory as of the only begotten of the Father,) full of grace and truth."

John 1:14

In John 1:1-2 we learn, "[1]In the beginning was the Word, and the Word was with God, and the Word was God. [2]The same was in the beginning with God." Then in John 6:63, Jesus says that His words are life. "It is the spirit that quickeneth; the flesh profiteth nothing: the words that I speak unto you, they are spirit, and they are life."

Have you had times that your mind was swirling with things going on around you? These feelings tend to place blinders on your eyes and make you believe that the peace of God is far from you. That's the time to get away from everyone and get into God's Word. It will bring you peace and give you a change of perspective.

The words of Jesus give life and will help you in any situation that you are facing. But it won't do you any good until you open the Bible and read the words that are within it. Don't allow the distractions of this world to keep you from finding the answers for which you are seeking. Make it a daily habit and allow the words of Jesus to speak life to you and your circumstances.

NOVEMBER 6

Thankful That I Can Trust Jesus

"And they that know thy name will put their trust in thee: for thou, Lord, hast not forsaken them that seek thee."

Psalm 9:10

I am so thankful that it is possible to trust Jesus even when things don't turn out the way I thought it would. I have prayed many prayers and God has answered everyone one of them. The answer was not always what I prayed for, but I learned that God's answer to our prayers come in three different ways:

Yes Wait No

When my husband, Rick, suffered a massive stroke in 2020, people all over the world were praying for his healing. Of course, it was my deepest desire that God would heal him, and he would be able to testify to that fact. But He had other plans for Rick than what we had.

That was, without doubt, the hardest thing I have ever had to endure. But Jesus was, and still is, with me. I had a choice to make: to turn against Him because He took my husband away from me, or to turn toward Him and embrace His love for me. I chose the latter. I have seen Jesus be faithful to others when they were going through a tough time and I knew, beyond the shadow of a doubt, that He would do the same for me.

Throughout my life, I had seen how Jesus has been with us in other difficult times and how He never left us. Without realizing it, I metaphorically placed those memories on a shelf in my heart and added many others along the way. When Rick passed away, I was able to review those memories and know that He was with me in every one of them and He would not leave me now. I have had some lonely and sad times, but I have felt Jesus with me the entire time. He has never let go of my heart nor my hand and I know that He never will.

I have news for you: He will do the same for you. You can trust that He will never leave you nor forsake you. Lean on Him in all you go through, and He will be right by your side through it all!

NOVEMBER 7

Thankful for Family

"The wicked die and disappear, but the family of the godly stands firm." NLT

Proverbs 12:7

God has been so good to me and has given me a great family. As I've said before, my parents were both Christians so therefore my brother and I were raised in a Christian home. We both married Christians and built our homes centered on God. We, in turn, raised our own children to love the Lord and they are all serving God in the church in some capacity. They now have children of their own that are being taught about the ways of the Lord.

Not everyone has a Christian heritage. But you know what? You can start now with your own family, teaching them about God, praying for them, being a Christian example to them. Then, one day, they too will accept Christ and when they start a family, they will train them, just as they themselves were trained to love Him and accept Him as Lord and Savior of their lives. That's the greatest thing you can do for your children, begin the Christian heritage that they need, especially in the day and time in which we live.

Keeping Christ first in all you do is the key to success. Being a Christian example to your children will be the beginning of a Christian heritage for them. Family is so very important. God placed you within your particular family unit for a reason. You may be the very one to lead them to Jesus. What a blessing that would be both to you and to them!

NOTES

NOVEMBER 8

Thankful for Pastors/ Pastors' Wives

"Take heed therefore unto yourselves, and to all the flock, over the which the Holy Ghost hath made you overseers, to feed the church of God, which he hath purchased with his own blood."

Acts 20:28

I have had quite a few pastors and pastors' wives throughout my life, and I am thankful for each one. They have all had a huge influence on me and have helped me in my Christian walk in many different ways. I greatly appreciate every pastor and pastor's wife that I was able to sit under and learn from.

A pastor does not have an easy job. It is not a nine-to-five job that they can go home and forget everything that happened that day; their parishioners are constantly on their minds. They have many sleepless nights and very busy days trying to be many things to many people!

A woman has to have a calling on her life to survive the life of a pastor's wife. At times, she will need to be his intercessor, his sounding board, his shoulder to cry one, his encourager, and much more, while still being mother to their children and homemaker in their home.

Last month was Pastor Appreciation, which is a good thing! But we need to let them know more than just in October that we love and appreciate them. You'll never know how a word of encouragement will uplift them both. Be the one who compliments, not the complainer! It'll help you and will certainly help them too.

NOVEMBER 9

Thankful for My Church

"I was glad when they said unto me,
Let us go into the house of the Lord."

Psalm 122:1

I have talked about attending church throughout this devotional and that's because it is very important to me, as it should be to you. I love my church and being there with my brothers and sisters in Christ. The main focus has always been Jesus. There is no competition with other churches. There are no arguments with other denominations over interpretation of scripture. It's just about Jesus and the salvation of souls.

It is also a place to come and worship God together. There is freedom there to worship Him in whatever way you feel comfortable. I have often thought about how people display their emotions when they attend their favorite sporting event. You will see some sit quietly and clap their hands. Or some go to the other extreme, stand, with hands raised, jumping, and shouting for their team.

People are the same in their worship to God. Here are a few ways in which we can worship Him and Biblical references to verify them:

- ◊ **Clapping hands.** Psalm 47:1
- ◊ **Raising hands.** Psalm 134:2
- ◊ **Praising God with a loud voice**. Luke 19:37
- ◊ **Bowing before God**. Psalm 95:6

I hope the church you attend allows you to worship God freely. And I pray that you are seeing souls saved there so that you can worship Him with them. Make it a habit to attend church and worship Almighty God for who He is!

NOVEMBER 10

Thankful for Godly Friends

"The heartfelt counsel of a friend is as sweet as perfume and incense." NLT

Proverbs 27:9

Godly friends are a treasure and I have been blessed to have some great ones. God placed them in our lives at just the time that we needed them.

There are two couples that my husband, Rick, and I considered as "our besties" and they have remained true to me since he passed away. They have never made me feel like a fifth wheel and have included me in outings. They were there for me during that difficult time of Rick's sickness and death and continue to call and make sure I am doing OK. They will never know how much I love and appreciate them.

God has also brought others to me that are friends as well. My husband, Rick, was counseling a precious lady that had lost her husband a short time before his own death. She has been such an encouragement to me, and I thank God for her and her new husband. I knew who she was, she had attended our church for years before she moved to another state. We actually became close by becoming friends on Facebook. It was just a natural transition to become friends when she moved back. She's now a great friend.

Still, there are others that are near and dear to my heart. I can call on any of them if I have a need and they will help me. What a blessed life to have so many that I can call a friend.

Have you thought about thanking God for the friends that He has placed in your life? It is such a solace to know that you don't have to go through life alone but can lean on them for strength when you are weak, comfort when you are hurting, and sincere happiness when you are rejoicing. True friendship is certainly a God-given blessing!

NOVEMBER 11

Thankful For Ministry

"Only fear the Lord, and serve him in truth with all your heart: for consider how great things he hath done for you."

I Samuel 12:24

My husband, Rick, and I were both called to the ministry before we were married, him to be a preacher and me to be a preacher's wife. Let me share the story to you.

We were both at a yearly youth camp; we were engaged to be married at the time. After several back-and-forth conversations with God about being called to preach, Rick finally submitted his will to Him and accepted the call one night of the camp. I was unaware that he was having this struggle, and I certainly didn't know that he chose to submit to God on that particular night. But at the same time, I told God that I would submit to Him to be a preacher's wife.

Our ministry has taken us to many places, both in the United States, and around the world. It was not always easy; we faced some hard times. But it was rewarding, and God blessed us.

Ministry doesn't always mean standing in the pulpit and preaching. Or to travel the world sharing the Gospel of Jesus Christ. Ministry can include working in the nursery at your church, cleaning the church, visiting the shut-ins, writing a card of encouragement to those that are discouraged, cooking a meal for a family in need, etc. All of that is ministry, and you will be rewarded for them just as much as the one who stands and preaches.

Are you fulfilling the ministry that God has prepared for you? He is calling you, are you listening? Better yet, are you obeying what He is telling you to do? Decide to be a blessing to someone every day and watch what God will do!

NOVEMBER 12

Thankful For Times of Refreshing

"For I will satisfy the weary soul,
and every languishing soul I will replenish." ESV

Jeremiah 31:25

We all have experienced times when our spirits are low, thus causing our emotions to be on edge. This can happen as a result of being too busy, facing hurts, disappointments, or grief, not spending time in the Word of God, not finding time for prayer and communion with Jesus, etc. There are a myriad of reasons why this occurs.

The good thing is that we don't have to stay in this frame of mind. Jesus is always right there with us, no matter what circumstances we face, and He wants to send refreshing to our souls that only He can give.

The secret to conquering these things and receiving His refreshing is to turn it all over to Jesus. Ask Him to help you get back on track. Here are a few scriptures that will help you in those low times.

- ◊ Too busy-Matthew 11:28
- ◊ Hurts, disappointments, grief-Proverbs 12:25
- ◊ Not reading God's Word-Psalm 119:105
- ◊ Not praying or communing with Jesus-Philippians 4:6-7

I am so thankful that we can come to Jesus at any time, and He will hear our cry. He will bring the refreshing to our souls that we so desperately need!

NOVEMBER 13

Thankful For the Joy of the Lord

"Rejoice in the Lord always: and again I say, Rejoice."

Philippians 4:4

Yesterday we talked about low times in our lives when we needed our souls to be refreshed by Jesus. Today, I want us to look at what happens when we receive that refreshing.

In Nehemiah 8:10, we are told that the joy of the Lord is our strength. As we get into the Word of God and ask for His refreshing, we will soon feel His strength come and we will be able to face our days with His joy.

Psalm 16:11 tells us that in His presence is fullness of joy. If your heart is full of His joy, there will be no room for sadness, depression, or any other adverse feelings to stay in your mind.

We read in 2 Corinthians 7:4 that we can be exceedingly joyful, even in our tribulations. Trials and tribulations will certainly come to us, but we can still have the joy of the Lord while we are going through them.

There are many more verses about the joy of the Lord in the Bible. Take the time to study it out for yourself. You will then see that you can indeed rejoice in the Lord always and have joy in your heart! Be full of the joy of the Lord, dear friends!

NOVEMBER 14

Thankful for Prayer

"I call upon you, for you will answer me, O God; incline your ear to me; hear my words." ESV

Psalm 17:6

In the devotion on October 12, we talked about not knowing how to pray. In that devotion, I gave the definition of the word, pray, from Merriam-Webster.com, "to address God with adoration, confession, supplication, or thanksgiving."

According to BillyGraham.org, prayer is defined as, "spiritual communication between man and God, a two-way relationship in which man should not only talk to God but also listen to Him." I like the further explanation that man should talk and listen to God. The truth is, God wants us to talk to Him, but He also desires to talk to us too.

I am so thankful for the privilege we have to go to Him in prayer. In early Bible times, there was no communication between God and man, only between God and the high priest. Jesus changed that for all mankind when He gave His life as a ransom for many. We can now go to God and commune with Him ourselves.

Is prayer part of your daily devotion time? Do you talk to God all throughout the day? He is waiting for you to communicate with Him, as well as listen to what He has to say to you. Thank you, God, for giving us the opportunity to converse with you whenever we desire!

NOTES

NOVEMBER 15

Thankful for God's Provision

"I have been young, and now am old; yet have I not seen the righteous forsaken, nor his seed begging bread."

Psalm 37:25

God is a good Father, and He provides for His children. We shouldn't allow worry to even cross our minds when we are in need. We can take our requests to our Heavenly Father, and He will make sure we are taken care of.

Life gets hard sometimes, but that doesn't mean that we should stop trusting God. What goes on in our world does not catch Him by surprise. He is the only One that we can depend on, and He will never let us down.

There was one time in our lives that we did not have food in the house to feed our family and we did not have the money to buy any. So we took our young children for a short ride in the car. When we arrived back home, there were several bags of groceries sitting on our front porch. We don't know to this day who left them there; we just know that God met our need.

Many times, God came through for us when we didn't know the way out of our dilemma. We had no clue what to do; we just trusted God for the answer. And He never failed us! You, too, can trust Him for your provision and needs. He will be there to help you; you can always count on Him!

NOVEMBER 16

Thankful for the Change of Seasons

"Thou hast set all the borders of the earth: thou hast made summer and winter."

Psalm 74:17

As I am writing this devotion, I can see out the window how the leaves have changed from green to different vibrant colors and it is beautiful!

Fall is my favorite time of year, right after the sultry heat of the summer and before the cold days of winter. The leaves have already begun to fall from the trees, signaling that winter is just around the corner. That is the way it happens year after year, one season changing into another. From winter to spring to summer to fall and then the cycle begins again.

I don't particularly care a lot for winter. I think it is because I do not drive in ice and snow, so I spend a lot of time in the house. But winter must come in order for the ground to produce new life in the Spring.

We all go through different seasons in our lives too, some being very hard. But we must choose to embrace whatever season we are in and learn from it before we can move on to the next one. Sometimes we have extremely hot summers or terribly cold winters. And in life, we have some difficult seasons; it is in those times that we learn the most.

God, help me to accept my season, enjoy the life You have given me, and be content until it's time to move on to the next season.

NOVEMBER 17

Thankful for the Bible

"Thy word is a lamp unto my feet, and a light unto my path."
Psalm 119:105

In reading from the Guinness World Records website, I realized just what an impact the Bible has made through the ages of time. It reads, "The best-selling book of all time is the Christian Bible. It is impossible to know exactly how many copies have been printed in the roughly 1500 years since its contents were standardized, but research conducted by the British and Foreign Bible Society in 2021 suggests that the total number probably lies between 5 and 7 billion copies."

There are several genres that can be found within the Bible. I have listed a few of them:

- ◊ History of creation-Genesis
- ◊ Narrative-Esther
- ◊ Music-Psalm
- ◊ Love story-Song of Solomon
- ◊ Future events-Daniel, Revelation
- ◊ Birth and Ministry of Jesus-Matthew, Mark, Luke, John
- ◊ Christian Living-Galatians, Ephesians, Philippians, Colossians

This only scratches the surface of what can be learned from reading the Bible. Read a portion of it every day. Develop your own reading plan. I read from the Chronological Daily Bible. You may want to read a different version each year. You can research the internet and find a plan that best suits your schedule. The main thing is to get into the Word and allow it to get into you. It will change your life for the better!

NOVEMBER 18

Thankful for God's Healing

"I shall not die, but live, and declare the works of the Lord."

Psalm 118:17

God has touched and healed my body many times. I am thankful that we can approach His throne when we need healing, and He will answer and move on our behalf. I want to relate a few healing stories that my family has experienced over the years.

When I was a young teenager, my mom was diagnosed with Tuberculosis and was sent to a TB hospital; she stayed there for 22 weeks. Everyday her prayer would be, "God, heal me for Your glory." One day, while looking out her hospital window, she saw a vision of Jesus in the clouds and He wrote in the sky, "I have healed you!" She received a miraculous healing that day.

In the early 1980's, I contracted Toxic Shock Syndrome and was admitted to the hospital. Within a few days, I was taken to the Intensive Care Unit because my condition had grown worse. While there, God spoke to me and said, "I am not finished with you yet." From that moment on, my condition changed for the better. I believe I was healed at the moment.

About that same time, after having several tests ran, my husband, Rick, was told that he had thyroid cancer. We were devastated at that news, but God spoke to him and said, "Are you going to believe the word of the doctor or the word of the Lord?" We chose to believe God's Word and he was healed!

God does not always speak to people when they are healed. Sometimes it's a simple touch from a believing saint. Or your own faith as you pray for yourself. And it's not always for the "big diseases" that God will heal. It is His desire for us to be healed so that we can declare His glory. Believe Him today and be healed by His power!

NOVEMBER 19

Thankful for Memories

"Dear children, let us not love with words or speech but with actions and in truth." NIV

I John 3:18

When someone that you were very close to dies, your mind will frequently think about times you spent with them. I am so thankful that God built our brains in such a way as to store memories that we can go back and visit.

I often allow my mind to remember places my husband, Rick, and I have been, people we've met, things we've done. But I don't linger there. For if I do, I will lose my focus of where I am headed today, and instead, wish for things of yesteryear. That is not how God intended for us to remember good times.

Some of my favorite memories with Rick are:

- ◊ Going on a cruise with friends
- ◊ Loving the people in the church we pastored
- ◊ Traveling together to various churches where he would preach
- ◊ Taking our grandkids on "Grandparents/Grandkids—No Parents Allowed" trips

But some of my most treasured times are when we were home. We used to watch Jeopardy on TV and I would even keep score. He would work on a message while I would research something for him that he would be speaking about. We did everything together and those are sweet memories.

What kind of memories are you making with your family? What will they remember after you have made your heavenly journey? Don't get so busy that you forget about the people that are most precious to you. Make sure that your family will smile when they remember the time spent with you. You are what is important to them.

NOVEMBER 20

Thankful for the Little Things

"But seek ye first the kingdom of God, and his righteousness; and all these things shall be added unto you."

Matthew 6:33

Did you know that God cares about the most minute things that are concerning to you? It's not just the "big things" that you face, but He cares about every aspect of your life.

I want to relate a personal story to you that will hopefully bring clarity on this subject. We were struggling financially; we had two small children and we had both been through serious illnesses. What extra money we may have had went to paying medical bills.

One day I wanted a certain kind of cookie. It was so much on my mind that I could almost taste it. I really liked them but hadn't had one in a long time. But God saw my desire and although I didn't pray for it, He answered that longing in my heart.

My aunt and uncle lived across the road from us at the time and she called me. She told me that she had bought a package of cookies that they didn't like, and she wanted to give them to us. When I went to get it, it was the very cookie that I had been wanting. Out of all the different kinds of cookies, God placed that very one in her hands so that I could learn that God cares about the little things!

That may sound silly, but it has stayed with me all these years. I thank God that He not only meets our needs, but He will sometimes give us our wants, even if it is something small. And the good thing is, as you put your trust in Him, He will do the same for you too!

NOVEMBER 21

Thankful for an Attitude of Gratitude

"O give thanks unto the God of heaven: for his mercy endureth for ever."

Psalm 136:26

Being thankful is an attitude that we should always have. When you think about what the Lord means to you, you can't help but have an attitude of gratitude. I am going to list scriptures here for you about thankfulness.

◊ 2 Samuel 22:50
◊ 1 Chronicles 16:8
◊ Psalm 7:17
◊ Psalm 30:4
◊ Psalm 50:14
◊ 1 Corinthians 15:57
◊ Ephesians 5:20
◊ 1 Thessalonians 5:18

This is not an exhaustive list by any means. Take some time reading through these; add your favorite verses about thankfulness to this list. Pretty soon, you will notice that your thoughts will be turned to those of gratefulness, and your problems will not be in the forefront of your mind. When you keep an attitude of gratitude in your heart, you will enjoy much brighter days.

NOTES

NOVEMBER 22

Thankful for the Simple Life

"Set your affection on things above, not on things on the earth."

Colossians 3:2

I can be considered a "plain Jane" kind of girl because I am thankful for the simple things in life. As of this writing, I am 68 years old and have never desired to live extravagantly. My husband, Rick, and I have always lived a simple, but very satisfying and happy life.

We have never lived in a large, elegant home, but ours has been filled with love and the peace of God. We've never driven glamorous, expensive cars. As a matter of fact, God has given us multiple really nice cars, in which one of them was brand new. We dressed nice but our clothes were not costly nor brand-name.

I said all that to say this: We did not need those expensive things to make us happy. "Things" do not bring true happiness; living for Jesus is where you will find peace and contentment.

If you are looking for that happiness, you won't find it in the things of this world. Life with Jesus will bring you more than they ever could. I may live a simple life, but I live happy; that makes all the difference!

NOVEMBER 23

Thankful for Jesus' Example

"He that saith he abideth in him ought himself also so to walk, even as he walked."

I John 2:6

It is my desire for people to see Jesus when they look at me, but my attitude and actions don't always show it. I strive each day to be more like Him.

Jesus faced a lot of hurtful things while He was on earth, just as we do. But He did not retaliate in anger against people as I want to do a lot of times. He was mocked, spat upon, betrayed, physically harmed, mentally hurt, was killed…He faced all kinds of situations where He could have allowed His emotions to get the best of Him. But He didn't! He loved the people that did those horrible things to Him.

You may say, "He was the Son of God; He had the ability to love and forgive." But He was totally man at those moments, and He felt all the pain that was associated with all He went through. He felt the shame, the disappointment, the frustration, the sorrow, the exhaustion, the agony… He felt it all, but He still loved those that caused it!

The good news is that He gave us the same ability to love and forgive! If we are going to represent Jesus in all we do, then we must love the ones that cause us pain, just as He did. I pray that, even though I am hurting, I can still love those people just as Jesus does. Can you pray that prayer?

NOVEMBER 24

Thankful for the Holy Spirit

"Now the God of hope fill you with all joy and peace in believing, that ye may abound in hope, through the power of the Holy Ghost."

Romans 15:13

The Holy Spirit is a very important part of my life. He lives inside of me, and I feel His presence every day.

There have been a lot of times in my life that I have been on the verge of making a wrong turn and the Holy Spirit has gently told me, "No! Don't go that way. There is danger ahead." I have not always obeyed what He has told me, but I have found out that He will guide me in the paths I should go if I will only listen and do what He says.

But that's not all that He does. He convicts us of our sins (John 16:8). He dwells in us (John 14:17). He teaches us all things (John 14:26). He guides us into all truth (John 16:13). He equips us with spiritual gifts (1 Corinthians 12:4-7). He gives us power (Acts 1:8). He gives us comfort (John 16:7).

His comfort has sure sustained me during the death of my husband. It has sustained me throughout his sickness, death, and even afterwards, while I'm learning to live out this new chapter of my life. I am so thankful that the Holy Spirit is a constant help to me and my family.

You, too, can make it through anything in your own life with the Holy Spirit's help. He will hold you up and carry you if you will just allow Him to. Turn to Him; He will be what you need when you need it!

NOVEMBER 25

Thankful for Godly Influence

"And be not conformed to this world: but be ye transformed by the renewing of your mind, that ye may prove what is that good, and acceptable, and perfect, will of God."

Romans 12:2

The definition for influence from dictionary.Cambridge.org is "to affect or change how someone or something develops, behaves, or thinks." I am thankful for those who had a Godly influence in my life.

I have seen individuals who have served God for sixty years or more. There must be something to a life with Christ for them to stick it out that long. They don't sing or preach anymore. It takes them a little longer to get to their seat; they have more aches and pains that they endure every day. But they remain faithful to God. They are faithful with their church attendance, with their prayer time and reading of the Bible. These people have more of a Godly influence than they will ever know.

I want my life to show others that I am faithful to God. I want to influence others that living for Him is satisfying and rewarding. People are always watching your life and how you respond to situations that you face. Are you influencing them in the ways of the Lord? Is it their desire to be like you "when they grow up" as the old saying goes? Live your life so that others will want to live for God; let them see Him in you!

NOVEMBER 26

Thankful for God's Protection

"But let all who take refuge in you rejoice; let them ever sing for joy, and spread your protection over them, that those who love your name may exult in you." ESV

Psalm 5:11

My husband, Rick, and I traveled thousands of miles throughout our ministry, especially in the latter years. God was with us in every one of those miles. I could tell you story after story of how He protected us as we traveled doing God's work.

There were also many international trips that were made that He took care of us. Even though on one of his trips his plane was struck by lightning, God was there, and he safely arrived at his destination. On another international flight, there was a situation that ended in airport security coming on the plane and escorting one of the passengers off before anyone else was allowed to deboard. God was certainly with them on that flight.

He kept us safe for all those years and He continues to do the same for me as a widow. I put my full faith and trust in God; I know that He goes with me and will protect me wherever I go. And He will do the same for you. He will be right there with you, too. Thank you, God, for Your divine protection!

NOVEMBER 27

Thankful for the Promises of God

"For all the promises of God in him are yea, and in him Amen, unto the glory of God by us."

2 Corinthians 1:20

The Bible is full of God's promises, and I believe every one of them. He does not lie; He will come through with every single promise that He has made to us.

The above verse tells us that the promises of God are yea and amen. According to Strong's Concordance, yea, in the Greek, simply means, yes, certainly, even so. Amen is truly, most assuredly, so let it be. To me, that means they are true, and you can absolutely believe them and take them to heart.

Here is a list, along with scripture references, of just a few of His promises that we can rely on:

- ◊ He will forgive our sins-1 John 1:9
- ◊ He will give us strength-Psalm 29:11
- ◊ He will give us rest-Matthew 11:28
- ◊ He will never leave us-Hebrews 13:5
- ◊ He will fight for us-Deuteronomy 3:22
- ◊ He will give us wisdom-James 1:5
- ◊ He will give us eternal life-John 3:16
- ◊ He will supply our needs-Philippians 4:19

Every promise is true, and God is trustworthy. All we have to do is just take Him at His word. Believe His promises because they are to each one of us!

NOVEMBER 28

Thankful for Nature

"Thou art worthy, O Lord, to receive glory and honour and power: for thou hast created all things, and for thy pleasure they are and were created."

Revelation 4:11

I have always been a lover of nature. God is the Creator of all things and I stand in awe of His creation. Even the sunrise and the sunset; some of them are just beyond description. I've tried to photograph them, but the pictures don't do them justice. They are so beautiful!

While it was still warm enough, my friends and I recently went on a boat ride. I looked at the trees, in all of their beauty, with the leaves changing colors. I saw sea gulls as some were sitting on the water, while others would fly off when we would get near them. I noticed the layout of the land where there were inlets and bays all along the way and marveled at God's design. I felt the warmth of the sun as it was shining on us while we made our way on our journey.

My husband, Rick, and I used to drive through a bison/elk range that is close to our home. There was once that a rather large buffalo walked right beside our car. Even though there was dried mud on its skin, I thought it was still a beautiful animal. And I saw several elk with very large antlers. I wondered how they could even hold their heads up with them on their heads.

And then I think about God's master design for everything. How every living thing is different yet has the same Creator. I am so thankful that God saw fit to allow us to enjoy life with all that He created. Thank You for such beauty in a midst of trying times in our world. You're a good, good God!

NOVEMBER 29

Thankful for the Still, Small Voice

"And after the earthquake a fire; but the Lord was not in the fire: and after the fire a still small voice."

I Kings 19:12

Our lives get so hectic sometimes that we cannot hear the voice of God speaking to us. And we get so busy that we don't take time to listen to Him.

We can read in 1 Kings 18 the account of Elijah's remarkable victory over the prophets of Baal. In the very next chapter, Elijah became afraid when Ahab's wife, Jezebel, send word that she would have him killed because of what he had done. (Take time to read these two chapters.)

So he ran and eventually hid in a cave. God asked Him why he was there and told him to go up on the mountain before Him. There came a strong wind, then an earthquake, and then a fire, but God's voice was not in any of those. The Bible tells us that the next thing to come was a still, small voice. After all that Elijah had been through and what he had just been shown, Elijah finally could hear God speak to him in the quietness of the moment.

There will be trials and hard times that come, and we will face some storms in our lives. He is with us during those difficult times, but we need to listen for His voice as we spend quiet times with Him. It is then that we can get away from distractions and hear what He has to say to us.

NOVEMBER 30

Always be Thankful

"In every thing give thanks:
for this is the will of God in Christ Jesus concerning you."
I Thessalonians 5:18

At the beginning of this month's devotions, I suggested that you make a list of things for which you are thankful. Now is the time to go back and read them all and ponder (as Mary did) on those things. There's just nothing like reminiscing about the goodness of God and looking forward to what He has in store for your future.

You may be asking, "How can I be thankful for having more "month" at the end of my "money?" How can I be thankful for this pain I constantly carry?" "How can I be thankful for the shape that our world is in?"

We must remember that God is with us no matter what situations we encounter, and He will take care of us. Here are a few scriptures verses to keep in mind:

◊ 1 Peter 5:7
◊ Psalm 145:18
◊ Isaiah 49:15
◊ Psalm 91:11
◊ Matthew 6:25-34
◊ Romans 8:31-32
◊ Exodus 15:26

There are many other scriptures letting us know that God will always meet whatever needs that we have, no matter if its financial, physical, spiritual, etc. If we just trust and believe in Him, He will always come through!

NOTES

DECEMBER 1

The Real Reason for the Season

"If ye then, being evil, know how to give good gifts unto your children, how much more shall your Father which is in heaven give good things to them that ask him?"

Matthew 7:11

December is a time of year that excites most people. You will see houses and stores brightly decorated for the Christmas season, although, many began their decorating in November, or some, even in October.

There was a time in our lives that I was very discouraged and did not even want to put up a Christmas tree. We had been called to pastor in Northern Texas and we had been there for four years. We met some wonderful people while we were there and considered them to be our family. But our time there came to an end, and we were called back home to Kentucky.

For a year, we lived with my parents, and we didn't seem to be able to find our place in any church. We had to learn to totally depend on God and humbly depend on my dad and mom. It was during that time that Christmas rolled around. As I said, I didn't even want to decorate for the holidays, which was a disappointment to our children. So, I eventually gave in and put up our tree.

I realized that I had lost the focus of what Christmas was all about. Sure we decorate and buy gifts but the main reason for this season is Jesus. No matter what circumstances we are facing, no matter if we have the money to buy gifts that we want to buy, we can still celebrate that God gave us His Son and that was the best gift ever given!

To me, all the decorating represents the star that shone brightly above the stable where Jesus was born. The gathering of family represents the shepherds and wise men that came to be with Jesus. The gift giving represents the gold, frankincense, and myrrh that the three wise men presented to Him.

So, go ahead and decorate, give gifts, and gather with family. But make sure you teach your kids the real purpose of this season, the birth of Jesus! Worship Him and keep Him at the forefront of your mind during this busy time.

DECEMBER 2

The Privilege of Giving

"Do not withhold good from those to whom it is due, when it is in your power to do it." ESV

Proverbs 3:27

Many years ago, I heard a minister say something that has stuck with me. He said, "If God can get it through you, He will get it to you." How many times has God given me things, money in particular, that I have not used in the way He intended?

The Bible tells us that He will supply our needs in Philippians 4:19, "But my God shall supply all your need according to his riches in glory by Christ Jesus." And again in Psalm 23:1, "The Lord is my shepherd; I shall not want."

But we are also told in Luke 6:38 to give and men will give to us in return. "Give, and it shall be given unto you; good measure, pressed down, and shaken together, and running over, shall men give into your bosom. For with the same measure that ye mete withal it shall be measured to you again. Philippians 2:4 tells us, "Look not every man on his own things, but every man also on the things of others."

Sure, we are to pay our own bills and provide for our own family, but God gives extra to us so that we may be a blessing to others as we give to them. It is a privilege to give as God directs us to; you will be greatly blessed (Luke 6:38) when you do!

DECEMBER 3

The Opportunity to Give

"Every man shall give as he is able, according to the blessing of the Lord thy God which he hath given thee."

Deuteronomy 16:17

God brings to our attention different times that we can give. It may be a financial need for those that have suffered due to a natural disaster or a person that is preparing to go on a mission trip. It may be giving to someone that is unable to work because of a serious illness. It may be to a family member or a complete stranger. God has just given you compassion for them during their time of need.

I want to tell you a story that happened to my husband, Rick, and me. We were in the midst of learning about the principle of giving and the obedience that comes with it. We went on a ministry trip and was trying to conserve our money so we would have enough to get home. We stopped at a restaurant advertising that two could eat for twenty dollars; so we stopped there.

When it was time to pay the bill and leave, God spoke to Rick to leave $50.00 under his plate. He questioned God about it, reminding him that we didn't have much money. Finally, he consented and told me about it. I agreed that he should leave the money there, just as God had instructed.

As we were in our car, our waitress followed us outside. While waving the money at us, she said, "Sir…sir! You left your money on the table!" To which Rick replied, "No, I left your money on the table." She said, "I just said to God this morning, 'If you are real, I need some money to buy my baby some Christmas gifts.' I guess He is real!" We were all in tears!

God allowed us to see how this woman was touched by us being obedient to what He told us to do. We may not always get to see the results; we just need to obey when He says to give. Thank you, God, for giving us the opportunity to bless her and for blessing us in return as we saw her reaction.

DECEMBER 4

Giving as a Lifestyle

"The generous will prosper; those who refresh others will themselves be refreshed." NLT

Proverbs 11:25

Our family has never been considered rich by the world's standards. We have seen some very lean times, especially in our early years. During those times, we were not able to buy our children things that we wanted them to have or take them to places we wanted them to go. But you know what? We gave them a home full of the love of God, as well as our love.

As the years went by, we became a little more financially stable and we began to learn the principle of giving. And we made it a practice to give to others when we saw a need and when God instructed us to give. I'm not saying that we never questioned God because we did! He proved faithful to us though and He continues to be.

My husband, Rick, was very sensitive to God when it came to giving. It was a lifestyle for him. Whether it was to give in an offering, to a certain individual, or to pay for the meal when we would go out to eat with others. He enjoyed excusing himself from the table to go to the restroom and while gone, he would slip to the counter and pay for everyone's meal. Or he may slip me his wallet under the table and have me to go pay for it. He just simply loved to give.

I have tried to continue that practice since he's been gone. We both have learned that God gives to you so that you can bless others. Make giving a lifestyle for yourself and see what God will do for you!

DECEMBER 5

The Gift of a Shepherd

"And I will give you pastors according to mine heart, which shall feed you with knowledge and understanding."

Jeremiah 3:15

Jesus is referred to as the Good Shepherd in John 10:11. In other verses in the Bible, He is called the Great Shepherd in Hebrews 13:20, the Chief Shepherd in 1 Peter 5:4.

But we have an "under-shepherd" that has been put in place in the church to watch over the people and that is the pastor. He has a heavy responsibility on his shoulders! A true pastor will realize that he cannot do this job on his own; he must rely on the power of the Holy Spirit to direct him as he guides the church over which he has been placed.

God has put your pastor in place to provide you with spiritual leadership, caring for you just a shepherd would for his sheep. Of course, you do have access to God yourself, but a shepherd will give you counseling when needed, explanation of the scriptures that you may not understand, be there for you during crisis times, and many other things that you can't do alone. And the good thing is that God will direct him in each of these situations.

Your shepherd, or pastor, is a gift from God to the church, and to you. Be a supporter of him and pray for him. And thank God for the gift of the shepherd. I love and respect mine, do you do the same for yours? If not, then you should!

DECEMBER 6

The Gift of Peace

"Let us therefore follow after the things which make for peace, and things wherewith one may edify another."

Romans 14:19

According to Profound-Answers.com, the word peace is mentioned in the King James Version of the Bible, 420 times. That is one for every day in a year, plus some extra! What a gift God has given us in the gift of peace.

You can have peace in your heart even if your life seems to be out of control. God gives the kind of peace that we just can't understand as we read about in Philippians 4:7, "And the peace of God, which passeth all understanding, shall keep your hearts and minds through Christ Jesus."

We are told to live in peace in 2 Corinthians 13:11, "Finally, brethren, farewell. Be perfect, be of good comfort, be of one mind, live in peace; and the God of love and peace shall be with you."

In Psalm 4:8, we learn that we can lie down and sleep in peace," I will both lay me down in peace, and sleep: for thou, Lord, only makest me dwell in safety."

From the words of Jesus Himself, found in John 14:27, we see where this peace comes from, "Peace I leave with you, my peace I give unto you: not as the world giveth, give I unto you. Let not your heart be troubled, neither let it be afraid."

This would make for a good study. Look for scriptures on peace and get them down deep in your heart. The peace of God is something that we all need. Allow Him to be your peace today!

DECEMBER 7

The Gift of Hope

"Happy is he that hath the God of Jacob for his help, whose hope is in the Lord his God:"

Psalm 146:5

Hope is such a powerful word! The definition from Merriam-Webster.com is "desire accompanied by expectation of or belief in fulfillment." The Biblical definition from Bible.org is "a strong and confident expectation."

You can read about hope all throughout scripture. David tells us in Psalm 71:5 that God is his hope, and then again in verse 14 that he will hope continually in Him. In Jeremiah 17:7, we are told that a man is blessed whose trust and hope are in the Lord. Titus 1:2 tells us that God promised the hope of eternal life. And in 1 Peter 3:15, we are told to be ready to give an answer to those asking about the hope that we have within us.

My hope, or my confidence, is in the Lord Jesus Christ. My hope, or my expectation, is to one day spend eternity with Him. My hope, or my belief in fulfillment, is in His promises to me.

Have you placed your hope in Jesus? Do you believe in His promises to you? Hebrews 6:19 says, "Which hope we have as an anchor of the soul, both sure and stedfast, and which entereth into that within the veil;" Make His hope the anchor of your soul today!

NOTES

DECEMBER 8

The Gift of Guidance

"I will instruct thee and teach thee in the way which thou shalt go: I will guide thee with mine eye."

Psalm 32:8

God has promised that He would lead and guide us in the way in which we should walk. We see this in Isaiah 30:21, "And thine ears shall hear a word behind thee, saying, This is the way, walk ye in it, when ye turn to the right hand, and when ye turn to the left."

There are times throughout our lives that we simply just don't know where to go or what to do. In times like these is when we can turn to God who gives us the guidance that we need. All that is required of us is to ask of Him and obey what He tells us to do.

Many times my husband, Rick, and I have ask God for His direction in decisions that we had to make, not knowing which way to turn. He never let us down and gave us the answer for which we were seeking.

Do you look for answers from God when you need guidance, or do you try to make those decisions on your own? I can tell you that following Him in the way that He guides you will bring His peace. There's nothing better than knowing God will guide you as you travel your life's journey!

DECEMBER 9

The Holy Spirit is a Giver

"Now there are diversities of gifts, but the same Spirit."

1 Corinthians 12:4

The Holy Spirit is real and not a myth, as is one popular belief. You can read about Him throughout the Bible. He was there when the world was formed. Genesis 1:2 tells us, "And the earth was without form, and void; and darkness was upon the face of the deep. And the **Spirit** of God moved upon the face of the waters." And in Revelation 22:17, we read of the Spirit and the bride still asking for sinners to come to Christ, "And the **Spirit** and the bride say, Come. And let him that heareth say, Come. And let him that is athirst come. And whosoever will, let him take the water of life freely."

Here are a few of the attributes of the Holy Spirit and where they are found in the Bible:

- ◊ He is omnipresent-Psalm 139:7-8
- ◊ He gives wisdom, understanding, knowledge, all manner of workmanship-Exodus 31:2-3
- ◊ He instructs-Nehemiah 9:20
- ◊ He dwells with us and in us-John 14:17
- ◊ He gives us power-Acts 1:8
- ◊ He guides-Romans 8:14

The Holy Spirit is all of this and so much more, including the giver of the gifts of the Spirit. We are encouraged by Paul to earnestly desire these gifts in 1 Corinthians 14:1. For the next few days, I want to delve more into them; you can find them listed in 1 Corinthians 12:8-10.

DECEMBER 10

The Nine Gifts of the Spirit

"But all these worketh that one and the self-same Spirit, dividing to every man severally as He will."

I Corinthians 12:11

We read in yesterday's devotion of the attributes of the Holy Spirit, and we are instructed to desire the gifts of the Spirit. These nine gifts are given to us by Him at His discretion.

When speaking of these gifts, we do not possess them, but rather they are contained within the Holy Spirit Himself. As we learn to yield to His leading, He will minister these gifts through our lives as He wills.

Everyone that is filled with the Holy Spirit has the potential to be used in all nine, if He chooses to use us in that fashion. These gifts are a part of the Holy Spirit Himself and He orchestrates the movement of the believers in their particular gifts, for the benefit of the body as a whole.

These gifts can be divided into three categories with three in each category. They are:

◊ Power: Faith, Healing, Miracles

◊ Revelation: Word of Wisdom, Word of Knowledge, Discerning of spirits

◊ Utterance: Tongues, Interpretation of tongues, Prophecy

Now, let's look at each one of these gifts of the Holy Spirit and learn about each one individually.

~ Rick Clendenen

DECEMBER 11

The Gift of Faith

"[4]Now there are diversities of gifts, but the same Spirit... [9a]To another faith by the same Spirit;"

I Corinthians 12:4, 9a

The simple definition of the gift of faith is having extraordinary belief in the power of God, believing that He will do what seems to be impossible or hopeless. No matter what circumstances occur, the person with the gift of faith stands strong in his belief and shows confidence in God's power and promises.

This gift is one of the power gifts as listed in yesterday's devotion. Those that the Holy Spirit uses in the gift of faith are not "super-Christians" but have just allowed Him to replace their fear with faith. And they have chosen to believe what God has said about a particular situation, having full confidence in Him that He will bring it to pass.

The gift of faith allows us to look beyond the obstacles that come across our path while we are holding onto God's promises. Even though difficulties may come, we can still cling to the word of God and believe that He will do what He said!

The Holy Spirit will give us the gift of faith as He sees fit. Let's all be available to be used in this gift when He desires to give it to us.

DECEMBER 12

The Gifts of Healing

"[4]Now there are diversities of gifts, but the same Spirit… [9b]to another the gifts of healing by the same Spirit;"

I Corinthians 12:4, 9b

This gift is the supernatural and miraculous physical healing without the intervention of medical science or human aid. It is the second of the gifts of power from the Holy Spirit.

You will notice that this one is listed as plural, "gifts of healing." One supposition is that there are many diseases, afflictions, illnesses, etc. that are considered incurable to the human person. But, in these instances, the Holy Spirit will use the believer to lay hands on and/or pray for the sick so that they can receive a supernatural touch from Him and be healed.

He can use any believer in the gifts of healing; it is the Holy Spirit that decides who will be used at any particular moment. It is nothing that we possess on our own that will make it happen. It is the power of the Holy Spirit, using a willing vessel with the gifts of healing. Be ready to be used in whatever gift that He desires to use you.

DECEMBER 13

The Gift of Working of Miracles

"[4]Now there are diversities of gifts, but the same Spirit... [10a]to another the working of miracles;"

I Corinthians 12:4, 10a

Working of miracles is a supernatural occurrence that cannot be explained by natural laws or thinking. This is the third power gift from the Holy Spirit. As with the other gifts, He gives this at His discretion and at whatever time He deems necessary.

Examples of working of miracles would be:

- ◊ A blind person can suddenly see.
- ◊ A person who has been lame for years can now walk.
- ◊ Cancer that was diagnosed and was proven by medical reports is no longer there.
- ◊ A large financial need is met without anyone else knowing that it existed.
- ◊ An unsaved child, who has left home, returns with a change of heart.
- ◊ Being saved from a natural disaster, such as a tornado, and watching it turn when it reaches your home.

I received a miracle in the early 1980's in my life. I was in the Intensive Care Unit, very sick with Toxic Shock Syndrome. At that time, it was an almost sure death sentence to be diagnosed with it. My doctor had even come to the hospital, fully expecting to sign my death certificate. People went to prayer for me, and I received my healing. It was a gradual healing but I began to improve every day as His miracle did its work throughout my body.

Has the working of a miracle happened to you? Or better yet, has the Holy Spirit used you to pray and you were able to see it occur for someone else? He can and He will use you if you are willing. He's a miracle working God and He wants you to be an extension of Himself as these miracles take place.

DECEMBER 14

The Gift of Word of Wisdom

"[4]Now there are diversities of gifts, but the same Spirit... [8a]For to one is given by the Spirit the word of wisdom;"

I Corinthians 12:4, 8a

Today we will begin to talk about the three revelation gifts. The first one is the gift of word of wisdom. This gift is closely related to the word of knowledge, and they are sometimes used in conjunction with each other. But they are different. This gift gives Godly direction, instruction, and insight to situations that we may be facing.

One does not learn to use this gift (word of wisdom) by going to school. Neither does a person use it because he is naturally wise. It is contained within the Holy Spirit; He is the one that decides who will use it and when it is to be used.

Be very careful when you feel you have a word of wisdom for someone. In my opinion, when you say, "Thus saith the Lord," you need to be absolutely sure that it is from God.

But on the other hand, the Holy Spirit will let you know in your heart if it is a word of wisdom from Him or a word from your own mind. Follow what the Holy Spirit says and allow this gift to flow through you.

NOTES

DECEMBER 15

The Gift of Word of Knowledge

"[4]Now there are diversities of gifts, but the same Spirit... [8b]to another the word of knowledge by the same Spirit;"

I Corinthians 12:4, 8b

As I shared in yesterday's devotion, the gifts of word of wisdom and word of knowledge are related but are still different gifts. The gift of the word of knowledge is specific knowledge given to you by the Holy Spirit of things that you would not have known otherwise. This is the second of the revelation gifts.

The Holy Spirit has used my husband, Rick, quite a few times with the word of knowledge. I want to relate to you one time in particular. He had been ministering at our local county jail. The jailer asked him to go into what was called "the bull pen" where the less dangerous offenders were held. It was a fairly large cell, and they had several there at the time.

There was one that the others thought was the toughest man there, and he played the part well. He would laugh and make fun of Rick as he ministered from the Word of God to them. At this point, the jailer allowed him to take them into another room one by one and talk to them individually. The "tough guy" was the first one and Rick knew nothing about him other than his name.

As they got into their conversation, the Holy Spirit used Rick with the word of knowledge. He began to tell this man about things that only the Holy Spirit could have known about him. He ended up giving his life to Jesus, to which many others followed. There was no more joking and laughing being done at that point!

That is one example of the word of knowledge. Rick didn't know anything about this man, but the Holy Spirit did. And the result was the salvation of many of those men. You, too, can allow the Holy Spirit to use you in the word of knowledge. You may just be the one that will lead that person to his/her salvation. Be open to Him using you!

DECEMBER 16

The Gift of Discerning of Spirits

"[4]Now there are diversities of gifts, but the same Spirit...
[10c]to another discerning of spirits;"

I Corinthians 12:4, 10c

This is the third gift of the revelation gifts. This gift is the ability to determine if a spirit is from God, from the devil or from over-zealous humans. The Holy Spirit will reveal this to you if you are in tune with Him.

There is certainly spirits in our world that is at work to draw us to them. Of course, we want to follow God, but we can be led astray by these other two spirits as well, sometimes without us even realizing it.

It is the will of the devil for you to choose him over the Holy Spirit's leading. But he knows that if you recognize him, then you will surely turn away. In other words, he won't show up in a red suit with horns, a long tail, and a pitchfork. He doesn't want you to recognize him so he will come disguised as something familiar to you or something that is pleasing to the eye. The Holy Spirit will help you to know just who the source of this spirit is.

He will also show you when some well-meaning people think they are giving words from God, but it is quite the opposite. They may not even know that they are being used by the devil, but it happens sometimes. That's just an opportunity for you to pray for them.

There is a different feeling when the Holy Spirit speaks. You can definitely discern when it is Him; even the atmosphere has changed. And when He speaks, there is a reverence that His Spirit brings as He speaks the Word.

The important thing to remember is to listen to the Holy Spirit. He will let us know if it is Him speaking or if it's from another source. Keep the Holy Spirit close to your heart. Then, when He does speak, you will know it is Him. As the song says, "The more you seek Him, the more you'll find Him."

DECEMBER 17

The Gift of Tongues

"[4]Now there are diversities of gifts, but the same Spirit… [10d]to another divers kinds of tongues;"

I Corinthians 12:4, 10d

We will focus on the last three of the nine gifts of the Holy Spirit and those are the gifts of utterance. The gift of tongues is the first of the gifts of utterance and is a controversial subject among many people. I believe it is only because they have not experienced this gift, so therefore, they do not believe that it is for today. But I want to let you know that it is a real thing.

I do not believe that the gifts of tongues is a supernatural ability to speak in other languages of which a person has not learned. It has also been called the language of angels but that is not my belief either. What I do believe is that it is a heavenly language or unknown tongue, given to us from the Holy Spirit, in which we can communicate with God. I also believe that it is used to give a message to the church as someone, whom the Holy Spirit chooses, will speak a word by using the gifts of tongues. Then, He will use someone else to interpret it. But keep in mind that the gift of tongues is different than simply speaking in tongues in worship and praise or in prayer. For lack of space, we will not get into the difference here.

We are told in 1 Corinthians 14:2, "For he that speaketh in an unknown tongue speaketh not unto men, but unto God: for no man understandeth him; howbeit in the spirit he speaketh mysteries." And again in Jude 1:20, "But ye, beloved, building up yourselves on your most holy faith, praying in the Holy Ghost," (The Holy Spirit and the Holy Ghost are interchangeable, so they are the same person.) As you can see, we are told to speak and to pray in the Holy Spirit.

Don't despise those that you hear speak in tongues. It is most certainly a gift from the Holy Spirit. Don't you want all that He has to offer?

DECEMBER 18

The Gift of Interpretation of Tongues

"[4]Now there are diversities of gifts, but the same Spirit... [10e]to another the interpretation of tongues:"

1 Corinthians 12:4, 10e

As I said in yesterday's devotion, I believe that the gift of tongues is used to give a message to the church. But, in order for that to happen, there must be an interpretation of those tongues. This is the second gift of the utterance gifts.

There are not many scriptures that speak about interpretation of tongues. Here are two of them:

◊ "[27]If any man speak in an unknown tongue, let it be by two, or at the most by three, and that by course; and let one interpret. [28]But if there be no interpreter, let him keep silence in the church; and let him speak to himself, and to God." 1 Corinthians 14:27-28

◊ "[13]Wherefore let him that speaketh in an unknown tongue pray that he may interpret. [14]For if I pray in an unknown tongue, my spirit prayeth, but my understanding is unfruitful." 1 Corinthians 14:13-14

The gift of interpretation works together with the gift of tongues. When someone gives a message in tongues, it is of no use to the church unless the interpretation is given as well. Be sensitive to the Holy Spirit if He speaks to you to give the interpretation when the gift of tongues is in use. It's up to Him who he chooses to speak His word!

DECEMBER 19

The Gift of Prophecy

"[4]Now there are diversities of gifts, but the same Spirit...
[10b]to another prophecy;"

I Corinthians 12:4, 10b

The gift of prophecy is the last of the nine gifts of the Spirit and the third of the utterance gifts. It can be compared to tongues and interpretation of tongues together. It is given as a word to the church or sometimes it is given to an individual.

We are told in 1 Corinthians 14:3, "But he that prophesieth speaketh unto men to edification, and exhortation, and comfort." In this verse, we are told that prophecy will edify, exhort, and comfort. Edify means to build up; Exhort is to advise or to embolden. And the definition of comfort is to relieve or encourage. It is my belief that the Holy Spirit, through the gift of prophecy, will not call anyone, for example, to a ministry, unless He has already spoken to them about it. Although, He will use this gift of prophecy to help confirm what has already been spoken.

But one thing to remember when you have been given a word of prophecy is to test it. In 1 Thessalonians 5:19-21, we read, "[19]Quench not the Spirit. **[20]**Despise not prophesyings. **[21]**Prove all things; hold fast that which is good." So, we see that it is okay to test or prove the prophesies; we are even encouraged to do it. Also, in verse 20, it says, "Despise not prophesyings." That means that we shouldn't deny that God speaks His word to men and women by using this gift.

Again, we should be open to being used by the Holy Spirit in any of the gifts that we have discussed the last few days. It is not a farce, or something that just happened in Bible times. The Holy Spirit is still moving in the world today. Do not despise any of the gifts but allow Him to use you as He sees fit.

DECEMBER 20

The Christmas Story-the Part Mary Played

"And, behold, thou shalt conceive in thy womb, and bring forth a son, and shalt call his name Jesus."

Luke 1:31

I have already talked about Mary earlier on May 16. But she is such a large part of the Christmas story that I didn't want to leave her out of this section.

The Bible doesn't tell us how old Mary was when Gabriel came to visit her. Theologians put her from thirteen to over twenty years of age. But no matter what her age, she accepted her calling to be the mother of Jesus.

While writing this devotion, I started thinking: What would have happened if Mary had decided to say no to Gabriel. She was betrothed, or engaged, to be married to Joseph and she may not have wanted him to face the embarrassment of her being pregnant. And would he even believe her incredible story of how this took place?

But she did say, "Yes!" And because of her obedience, she had the privilege to carry and to nurture the Son of God! She was willing to trust God and to trust Joseph, even down to riding the donkey all the way to Bethlehem with her being nine months pregnant! By the way, it is around 100 miles from Nazareth to Bethlehem!

Mary had found favor with God, as we read in Luke 1:30. She didn't understand how this seemingly impossible situation could happen but because she had a relationship with God, she agreed to be used by Him in this manner.

I wonder what thoughts were in Mary's mind the nine months that she carried Jesus. One thing is for sure, she did not doubt that Gabriel had been sent by God and she believed what he told her. What is your response when your called up to be used by God? All that He asks is a child-like trust in Him and you will see His will accomplished in your lives.

DECEMBER 21

The Christmas Story–the Part Gabriel Played

"And the angel answering said unto him,
I am Gabriel, that stand in the presence of God;
and am sent to speak unto thee,
and to shew thee these glad tidings."

Luke 1:19

Not only was Mary an integral part of the Christmas story, but so was Gabriel. It probably didn't happen this way in heaven, but I am going to take a little liberty with the part that Gabriel played.

I can just imagine that the angels in heaven were in expectations of the birth of the Messiah on the earth. Gabriel is called an angel of the Lord in Luke 1:11; many theologians call him a messenger angel since he was recorded as bringing messages from God to certain individuals.

But, on with my imagined story. I can see Gabriel asking God, "Is it time yet? Can I go tell Zacharias the news?" And God would say, "Not just yet." But the day finally came that He told Gabriel, "Today is the day; go tell him now."

And then, several months passed, and the excitement of the angels mounted. Because this time, Gabriel would tell Mary that she would give birth to the Son of God! What rejoicing was happening in Heaven as they watched the story unfold.

I have added a few extra details to this story and used my imagination to enhance it, but the truth is, Gabriel did play a very important role, both for Zacharias and Mary. What wonderful news he was able to deliver to these two people. And it happened just as he said it would!

We may not ever get a visit from Gabriel and receive a message from him, but God still communicates to His people today. We are able to talk with Him ourselves and the great thing is, He will talk to us! Wait on Him and listen to what He has to say!

NOTES

DECEMBER 22

The Christmas Story-the Part Elizabeth Played

"And she spake out with a loud voice, and said, Blessed art thou among women, and blessed is the fruit of thy womb."

Luke 1:42

I am pretty sure that Elizabeth spent years grieving that she and Zacharias could not have children. They were both well stricken in years, past child-bearing age. (Luke 1:7) But the Bible also says that they were both righteous before God, walking in all the commandments and ordinances of the Lord blameless. (Luke 1:6)

While Zacharias was doing his duty at the temple, Gabriel came to him and told him that they would have a son and were to name him John. We aren't told how Elizabeth responded when she heard the news, but since she was righteous before God, I'm sure she accepted it with joy.

After Gabriel visited Mary, she decided to go and visit her cousin. Elizabeth had hidden herself away from people because of her pregnancy so I don't know if Mary knew about it or not. But as soon as she greeted Elizabeth, John leaped in her womb and as we read in Luke 1:43, Mary would indeed be the mother of her Savior, Jesus.

Mary stayed there for three months and I'm sure the two women spent precious time together, relating to each other what Gabriel had told Zacharias and Mary. What a joy it is to have family that will rejoice with you. Can you say that you are that kind of person, one that will have joy for family and friends around you? We all need to be one that represents Jesus wherever we are!

DECEMBER 23

The Christmas Story-the Part Joseph Played

"Then Joseph being raised from sleep did as the angel of the Lord had bidden him, and took unto him his wife:"

Matthew 1:24

Joseph played a unique part in the Christmas story for sure. The Bible doesn't tell us much about him, but I would venture to say that he was a humble man and was one that obeyed the laws of God.

The story of Joseph, the earthly father of Jesus is found in the first chapter of Matthew. Can you just imagine how the meeting with Mary and Joseph went, as she told him of the visit from Gabriel? I am sure it was difficult for him to believe that Mary had not been with a man even though she was carrying a child. He must have loved her deeply because it was his plan to put her away quietly so she wouldn't have to face the ridicule from people around them.

But God had a different plan than did Joseph. He sent an angel (The Bible doesn't say it was Gabriel but one would assume that it was) to him in a dream, telling him, "...[20]Joseph, thou son of David, fear not to take unto thee Mary thy wife: for that which is conceived in her is of the Holy Ghost. [21]And she shall bring forth a son, and thou shalt call his name Jesus: for he shall save his people from their sins." (Matthew 1:20b-21)

He could have rejected that message and went ahead with his plan. But he was a just man, (Matthew 1:19) so he believed what the angel said and took Mary and raised Jesus as his very own earthly son, yet knowing that He was the Son of God.

God has a divine plan for all of us. It is up to us to accept it or reject it. My advice would be to fully embrace what He speaks and follow His plan. Because our plans will always fall apart if it doesn't agree with what God says!

DECEMBER 24

The Christmas Story-the Part the Innkeeper Played

"And she brought forth her firstborn son, and wrapped him in swaddling clothes, and laid him in a manger; because there was no room for them in the inn."

Luke 2:7

Do you know that the innkeeper is not mentioned in the Bible as we have heard about since we were small? The reference to there being no room in the inn is found in the above verse.

We don't even know if there was an innkeeper at all. But if there was, I wonder what kind of person he was. Was he a stubborn old man, with no thought of anything but making money during this busy time in the city of Bethlehem? (During this time, everyone was ordered to register in the town of their ancestors so there were many people there.) Perhaps he was compassionate, especially after seeing Mary's condition. I would like to think that he was the latter. He most likely offered the stable; at least it would be a place where she could lay down.

Another thought that crossed my mind was: What were his thoughts when he found out that the Son of God was born in his stable? Was he sincerely sorry that he hadn't made room in the inn for them?

We all need to ask ourselves these questions:

- ◊ Have we made room for Jesus in our heart?
- ◊ Have we openly welcomed Him to live there?
- ◊ Are we sorry for not having accepted Him earlier in our lives?

Ponder these as you think about your relationship with Jesus. Make it personal: Have you made room for Him in your life and is He welcome in your heart? Life with Jesus is the only thing that will last throughout eternity!

DECEMBER 25

Jesus: The Greatest Gift

"Thanks be unto God for his unspeakable gift."

2 Corinthians 9:15

I love this time of year! Everyone is in a festive mood and ready to enjoy spending time with family. But it is also the time that we celebrate the birth of our Lord and Savior, Jesus Christ. It has been debated as to why December 25 was the date chosen for this magnificent celebration.

According to OpenTheWord.org, "Tertullian (160 AD to 225 AD), a Christian apologist from Carthage, said March 25th was the date of Christ's death. An interesting theory began to develop shortly after this that Jesus' conception and death took place on the same day of the year — March 25th. Basically, Jesus arrived from heaven (His conception) and went back to heaven (His death) on the same day."

So, as this theory was discussed and began to be believed, it would only be the natural progression of pregnancy that Jesus would be born at the end of December. So the 25th was traditionally accepted as His birthday.

The truth is no one knows the actual day of the birth of Jesus, but this date is set aside so that we can celebrate the greatest gift ever given. Whatever the actual day, the settled fact is that Jesus came to earth, lived, suffered, died, and resurrected because of His great love for us. So in return, we should give Him our best and choose to live for Him.

DECEMBER 26

The Christmas Story-the Part the Shepherds Played

"And, lo, the angel of the Lord came upon them, and the glory of the Lord shone round about them: and they were sore afraid."

Luke 2:9

The story of the shepherds can be read in Luke 2:8-20. They were the first ones that were told about the birth of Jesus. What a glorious way they learned about Him.

It was at night, and it was naturally dark. But all of a sudden, a great light shown around them. Then, as we see in Luke 2:10-12, an angel appeared and told them, "[10]Fear not: for, behold, I bring you good tidings of great joy, which shall be to all people. [11]For unto you is born this day in the city of David a Saviour, which is Christ the Lord. [12]And this shall be a sign unto you; Ye shall find the babe wrapped in swaddling clothes, lying in a manger." They had to have been afraid and awestruck at the same time! After the angel's proclamation, there were a multitude of angels singing and praising God!

They believed the angel's news, and they hurried to find Jesus. They were overjoyed when they saw the baby lying in a manger, just as the angel had said. They had seen the Messiah!

Shepherds of that day would sit around the fire telling stories each night as they watched their sheep. When they returned to where they saw the angels, I am sure they had plenty to talk about.

We should all learn a lesson from them. Luke 2:17 tells us, "And when they had seen it, they made known abroad the saying which was told them concerning this child." After leaving the stable, they told what they had seen and heard to others. That's what we should be doing too, telling everyone about Jesus. It really is good news that all need to hear!

DECEMBER 27

The Christmas Story-the Part the Wise Men played

"Now when Jesus was born in Bethlehem of Judaea in the days of Herod the king, behold, there came wise men from the east to Jerusalem,"

Matthew 2:1

The Bible does not tell us how many wise men there were that came from the East in search of Jesus. It is just assumed that since there were three gifts brought by them, there were three wise men.

No matter how many there were, they had seen the star in the East and had come to see and worship Jesus. They entered Jerusalem and Herod asked them to go and find Him. Then come back and tell him so he could worship Him too. But we know that Herod only wanted to know where he was so he could kill Him.

So the wise men found Jesus and presented Him with gifts of gold, frankincense, and myrrh. God told them in a dream to not return to Herod, but to go home another way. These men did not know that Herod was not interested in worshipping Jesus as he had said. They didn't know that it was in his plan to have Jesus killed.

God uses the unsuspecting people to bring glory to His name. We don't always know why God wants us to do certain things; sometimes they don't even make sense. But He knows the future and He has a plan in mind. Rejoice in the fact that we are included in that plan!

DECEMBER 28

Giving of Yourself

"I beseech you therefore, brethren, by the mercies of God, that ye present your bodies a living sacrifice, holy, acceptable unto God, which is your reasonable service."

Romans 12:1

I want to draw a comparison in this devotion between the gifts brought by the wise men and what the shepherds brought.

We know that the wise men gave gold, frankincense, and myrrh. They must have believed that Jesus was a newborn King because these are gifts that one would give to royalty! Let's look at these.

◊ **Gold:** This was a precious metal back then, just as it is today. It was a measure of wealth. They most likely considered him as royalty.

◊ **Frankincense:** This is an aromatic gum resin, which can be used as incense. When burned, it has a strong and beautiful aroma.

◊ **Myrrh:** This is a fragrant spice obtained from the sap of a tree grown in the East. It can also be used as incense, as well as perfume, anointing oil or a medicinal tonic.

As described above, you can see that these would have been very expensive. But the shepherds did not have the means to give such extravagant gifts. All they brought was their awe, wonder, and worship for Jesus. Although the wise men also knelt before Him and worshipped Him, that is quite a contrast as they each brought what they had and offered it to Him.

This is all that Jesus expects of us: to bring Him what we have. The majority of us do not have gold, frankincense, and myrrh but we can give of ourselves to Him. We each have gifts and talents that He has given us. Let's see that we use them for His glory!

DECEMBER 29

The Gift that Keeps on Giving

"Know therefore that the Lord your God is God, the faithful God who keeps covenant and steadfast love with those who love him and keep his commandments, to a thousand generations," ESV

Deuteronomy 7:9

This slogan, used in the title, has been around for years, advertising many products. But there is only one gift that truly does keep on giving and that gift is Jesus Christ.

God gave His only begotten Son to give us a way of escape from our sins that would otherwise have sent us to Hell and away from Him forever. What love was shown to us because of that sacrifice!

We not only receive the gift of salvation when we accept Jesus as Lord and Savior, but we receive all the promises that He has made to us. He has promised to be with us and strengthen us-Isaiah 41:10. He has promised to never fail us nor forsake us-Deuteronomy 31:8. He has promised to uphold us with His hand-Psalm 37:23-24. He has promised rest to the weary-Matthew 11:28. He has promised to guard our hearts and minds-Philippians 4:7. He has promised healing for our bodies-1 Peter 2:24. He has promised to supply all our needs-Philippians 4:19. And much, much more!

I encourage you to read these verses and search out the scriptures for more of His great promises. God will never take back His promises. He will truly keep on giving; we can trust Him on that!

DECEMBER 30

The Gift that Jesus Honored

"And being in Bethany in the house of Simon the leper, as he sat at meat, there came a woman having an alabaster box of ointment of spikenard very precious; and she brake the box, and poured it on his head."

Mark 14:3

Giving is a part of our worship to God. It is generally related to money and that is certainly part of it. But we can give in other ways as well. Let's examine when a gift is really a gift as we look into the story of Mary found in Mark 14:3-9.

◊ Her gift was motivated by her love for Jesus. Love is the true gift we are giving; the gift itself only represents our love.

◊ Her gift reflected how Jesus was more valuable than the spikenard. When we love God as we should, all other things will lose their value.

◊ Her gift caused her to sacrifice. Your gift always means more when given out of sacrifice rather than out of abundance.

◊ Her gift was not understood by natural man. What appeared to be a waste to the natural man became a memorial to Mary.

Mary realized that Jesus was much more valuable than the costly spikenard, which was a valued and very precious perfume. And her gift was not understood by others, but Jesus said that it would be spoken of as a memorial to her. (Mark 14:9) By giving this expensive offering to Jesus, she was showing that nothing mattered more to her than Him.

If we keep these four things in our mind as we practice giving, then Jesus will honor and accept our gifts just as He did for Mary. As we give to others, we are giving to Him as well.

~ Rick Clendenen

DECEMBER 31

The Gift of God's Word

"Thy word have I hid in mine heart, that I might not sin against thee."
Psalm 119:11

How many times do you open the Bible and read God's Word? Do you have a daily, personal devotion time? I'm not asking these questions to condemn you. I just want you to think about them and consider making a change in your schedule each day, if you don't already have these things in your life.

I want to give you some reasons why you should spend time in God's Word.

◊ It is the Word of God; not just the parts in red (the words of Jesus) but all of it.
◊ We learn about who God is and how much He loves us.
◊ It will teach us how to pray.
◊ It will show us how to accept Jesus as Lord and Savior.
◊ It will teach us how to live a victorious life.
◊ It will show us how to trust God in all things.
◊ It is full of the promises of God.
◊ It teaches us how to love, forgive, and respect others.
◊ It tells us how to represent Jesus in all we do.
◊ It tells us about future events.

Reading and studying God's Word is so important in living a Christian life. The instructions contained within its pages will be a help to us in anything that we face.

As the new year approaches, make it a habit to read a portion of it every day. If there is something that you don't understand, seek out a seasoned Christian brother or sister and ask them questions about it. Just remember this: The more you know, the more you grow in your Christian walk.

NOTES

Made in the USA
Columbia, SC
29 November 2023

26815721R00246